Favorite
Activities
for the Teaching
of Psychology

Favorite Activities
for the Teaching of Psychology

Edited by Ludy T. Benjamin, Jr.

American Psychological Association • Washington, DC

Second Printing, September 2010

Published by
American Psychological Association
750 First Street, NE
Washington, DC 20002
www.apa.org

To order
APA Order Department
P.O. Box 92984
Washington, DC 20090-2984
Tel: (800) 374-2721; Direct: (202) 336-5510
Fax: (202) 336-5502; TDD/TTY: (202) 336-6123
Online: www.apa.org/books/
E-mail: order@apa.org

In the U.K., Europe, Africa, and the Middle East, copies may be ordered from
American Psychological Association
3 Henrietta Street
Covent Garden, London
WC2E 8LU England

Typeset in Trump Medieval by Circle Graphics, Columbia, MD

Printer: Cadmus Communications, Baltimore, MD
Cover Designer: Mercury Publishing Services, Rockville, MD
Technical/Production Editor: Kathryn Funk

The opinions and statements published are the responsibility of the authors, and such opinions and statements do not necessarily represent the policies of the American Psychological Association.

Library of Congress Cataloging-in-Publication Data

Favorite activities for the teaching of psychology / edited by Ludy T. Benjamin. — 1st ed.
     p. cm.
  Includes bibliographical references and index.
  ISBN-13: 978-1-4338-0349-9
  ISBN-10: 1-4338-0349-6
  1. Psychology—Study and teaching. I. Benjamin, Ludy T., 1945-

BF77.F38 2008
150.71—dc22
                                        2007044216

British Library Cataloguing-in-Publication Data
A CIP record is available from the British Library.

Printed in the United States of America

In memory of

Cliff Fawl,

Robert Goodale,

Mary Margaret Moffett,

and the countless other teachers who devoted their lives to sharing their

love of psychology with their students.

CONTENTS

PREFACE

In 1981, the American Psychological Association (APA) published the first volume of its series *Activities Handbook for the Teaching of Psychology* (Benjamin & Lowman, 1981). The book was not labeled Volume 1 because at the time it was not known whether there would be others. The rationale for the book was quite simple. In higher education, there was a growing recognition of the need for greater involvement of students in their own learning. In educational jargon the book was about *active learning*, that is, teaching exercises that ensured that students were active, hands-on participants in their education and not passive vessels, as in so many of their classrooms (see Mathie et al., 1993). The idea for that first volume grew out of discussions in APA's Committee on Psychology in the Secondary Schools. Such teaching activities had been a regular feature of the APA publication for high school teachers, initially a newsletter titled *Periodically* and later *High School Psychology Teacher*. Some of the activities published in that first volume had appeared originally in those publications. The rest were acquired from a call to teachers to submit their best active learning ideas for possible publication. The resulting book consisted of 88 activities covering the subjects typically found as chapter headings in an introductory psychology textbook and contained the favorite teaching activities of some of the best teachers in psychology. Kathleen Lowman and I, as staff in APA's Educational Affairs Office, had the privilege of editing that first volume.

The first printing sold out in a matter of months, testifying to the need that it was intended to meet. It was purchased by teachers in secondary schools and in colleges and universities. Over the next 18 years, three more volumes followed (Makosky, Whittemore, & Rogers, 1987; Makosky, Sileo, Whittemore, Landy, & Skutley, 1990; Benjamin, Nodine, Ernst, & Blair-Broeker, 1999), providing a total of 348 teaching activities ranging from taste and smell interactions to test reliability, from working memory capacity to substance abuse, from neural networking to research ethics, and from personality testing to attribution. Collectively, these activities proved to be an incredible boon to beginning teachers and a valuable addition to the arsenal of those with more experience.

Because my name is associated with two of these books, I have been privileged over almost a quarter century to hear numerous testimonials from teachers eager to tell me how much these books have helped them in their classrooms. These books have played an invaluable role for me as well, both in my own classes and in the workshops and courses I have taught on the teaching of psychology. Graduate student teachers have always welcomed active learning exercises as they build their teaching repertoire. Thus these volumes have been particularly helpful to them.

This book represents a departure in the Activities Handbook series. It is not Volume 5; none of its 67 activities are technically "new," although all have been revised for this volume. Rather, as the title suggests, these are the activities from the previous four volumes that were judged to represent the "favorites" from among the nearly 350 activities. For this book, we wanted to select the activities that users of the previous volumes judged to be exceptionally helpful. We were biased toward activities that required minimal preparation. From countless teaching workshops, I know that teachers are always stretched for time and that if you want an activity to be adopted in the classroom, it should be easy to use. We wanted activities that are nearly foolproof, that is, ones that will generate the expected outcome time after time. We cannot guarantee that that will be the case for you, but feedback on these activities suggests a very high rate of success. We wanted activities that cover some psychological topics that are often difficult to present as active learning exercises, such as psychotherapy or substance abuse or brain–behavior relationships. We wanted to emphasize activities that involve the entire class, not just a few students as demonstrators, and we wanted activities that could be used for all students regardless of class size. There are exceptions to these desires, but you will find that most activities in this book succeed in these ways. Finally, we wanted to select activities that covered the topics typically found in a course in introductory psychology. The earlier handbooks were not bound by that constraint; in each volume there was considerable breadth but the subject matter was always bound by the limits of the submissions. In this case we have been able to ensure a breadth of subject matter that matches the content of an introductory course. Although the majority of these activities are appropriate for a beginning course, all of them are suitable for other courses as well, including graduate courses.

My own teaching library includes all four previous volumes as well as other published collections of teaching activities. I enjoy having all that teaching wealth at my fingertips, and the dog-eared state of my activities handbooks testifies to their frequent use. But if your library space is small, then this is the book for you. If you teach a graduate course on the teaching of psychology, this is a book that your students should have. If you coordinate the teaching of introductory psychology at your university, supervising instructors or graduate students in your role, then this is a book your department should provide for each of those graduate student teachers. If you are a high school teacher teaching regular sections of psychology or advanced placement sections, this book will prove to be an invaluable resource for you. If you are a department head who regularly hires new assistant professors, some of whom will teach introductory psychology, this would be a good book to provide to them, saving them considerable time in their course preparation and, perhaps, improving their teaching evaluations. Again, although the greatest value of this book is for a beginning course, the activities are equally suitable in many advanced courses.

After the activities were selected for this book, authors were contacted about revisions. They were told that we wanted a revision that maintained the central concept of the original teaching activity but updated it in terms of changes in psychological knowledge and theory and with regard to changing teaching technologies. Remember that when the first volume was published, no one had heard of Bill Gates, the chalkboard was the principal visual aid in the classroom, and the library was a place where students went to browse the bookshelves in search of needed information. We also asked authors to reflect on their continued use of the activity and to modify the activity where needed on the basis of extra years of experience. Of course, references and sources for suggested reading have also been updated. In a few cases, authors are deceased. For those activities, I have made the revisions.

Similar to the earlier volumes, each activity in this book is presented in a cookbook format. Each begins with an *Abstract* that provides the following information: (a) what the activity is about, (b) the courses for which the activity is appropriate, (c) whether the activity is an in-class or out-of-class activity or both, (d) whether the activity involves all of the students, (e) the optimal and maximum class size for the activity, and (f) an estimate of the time required for the conduct of the activity. Thus the abstract should provide you with a quick assessment of the nature of the activity and its appropriateness for your class.

The abstract is followed by a section labeled *Concept,* which provides an expanded description of the psychological content of the activity. That section is followed by a *Materials Needed* section when appropriate. Like a recipe, it will tell you what is required for the activity. In the majority of activities the needs are minimal. If written materials are required—for example, a questionnaire—those materials are provided as part of the activity.

The next section is labeled *Instructions.* It describes, in sufficient detail, what you need to do to set up the activity, conduct it, and conclude it. A *Discussion* section follows that describes the expected outcome of the activity and offers suggestions for discussion, writing exercises, or other follow-up activities that can enhance the value of the active learning exercise. The final section is labeled *References and Suggested Reading,* and as the title indicates, it includes the full references of any resources mentioned in the activity as well as other sources that might prove useful to you or to students looking for additional information on the topic.

The 12 chapters parallel the organization of an introductory psychology textbook. For example, there are chapters on brain and sensory processes, perception, states of consciousness, learning and memory, and personality. The book closes with a chapter on race, gender, and multiculturalism.

The activities in this book are diverse in presentation style and in terms of the expectations for student participation. There are demonstrations, debates, discussions, experiments, observations, writing assignments, simulations, peer learning and peer teaching, and role-playing exercises. Throughout these activities there is an emphasis on critical thinking. Although that statement may be a cliché, critical thinking is a strong goal of virtually every activity in this book. Students take on different personas, experience seemingly paradoxical phenomena, have their common assumptions violated, learn what can and cannot be said of data, learn about multiple causation and about control, learn about the critical importance of appropriate sampling, have their perception altered both literally and figuratively, improve their discussion and listening skills, and write about these experiences to reflect their own learning. Ultimately, what is important is that students get involved in their own learning and that the instructor welcome them into the learning process through the inclusion that active learning demands.

The activities as presented here are as the authors use them in their own classes. In many cases the authors have included variations the instructor can choose to pursue. That said, you should remember that your class is yours. In reading about these activities you may decide that an activity may not work in your class as described. Still, if the activity catches your interest, consider modifying it to suit your needs. No one will worry if you make such modifications. As a teacher, those are your decisions to make. Of course, the activity may not work in such an altered form. Or it may work even better!

I want to thank my fellow editors on the previous *Activities Handbook* volumes: Kathy Lowman, Vivian Makosky, Linda Whittemore, Anne Poliakoff, Chi Chi Sileo, Christine Landy, Mary Lynn Skutley, Barbara Nodine, Randy Ernst, Charlie Blair-Broeker, and all staff members in APA's Educational Affairs Office. I owe a special debt of gratitude to the hundreds of great teachers who have shared their best teaching ideas with the rest of us through this series, and particularly to those who have revised their work for inclusion in this special volume.

Thanks are also extended to the staff of APA Books who initiated the idea for this book and guided it through production: Maureen Adams, Judy Nemes, and Katie Funk.

Those of us who teach psychology have the decided advantage of teaching one of the most interesting subjects in the curriculum. It is not a subject that needs "spicing up." And that is not the intent of this book or the earlier volumes. This book is about sharing the teaching of psychology in a very personal way, a way that draws students into the heart of our subject. Psychology has much to teach us about ourselves and the world of which we are a part. Our hope is that this book will help you in your task as a teacher, that you and your students may be changed in important ways through the insights and understandings provided by use of the activities described in this book.

Ludy T. Benjamin, Jr.

REFERENCES   Benjamin, L. T., Jr., & Lowman, K. D. (Eds.). (1981). *Activities handbook for the teaching of psychology* (Vol. 1). Washington, DC: American Psychological Association.

Benjamin, L. T., Jr., Nodine, B. F., Ernst, R. M., & Blair-Broeker, C. (Eds.). (1999). *Activities handbook for the teaching of psychology* (Vol. 4). Washington, DC: American Psychological Association.

Makosky, V. P., Sileo, C., Whittemore, L. G., Landy, C. P., & Skutley, M. L. (Eds.). (1990). *Activities handbook for the teaching of psychology* (Vol. 3). Washington, DC: American Psychological Association.

Makosky, V. P., Whittemore, L. G., & Rogers, A. M. (Eds.). (1987). *Activities handbook for the teaching of psychology* (Vol. 2). Washington, DC: American Psychological Association.

Mathie, V. A., Beins, B., Benjamin, L. T., Jr., Ewing, M. M., Hall, C. C. I., Henderson, B., McAdam, D. W., & Smith, R. A. (1993). Promoting active learning in psychology courses. In T. V. McGovern (Ed.), *Handbook for enhancing undergraduate education in psychology* (pp. 183–214). Washington, DC: American Psychological Association.

Favorite Activities

for the Teaching of Psychology

CHAPTER 1
HISTORY, STATISTICS,
AND RESEARCH METHODS

The eight activities in this chapter cover many of the topics typically included in introductory psychology textbooks: history of psychology and topics of statistics and research methods, including sampling error, central tendency measures, reliability and validity, correlation and causation, hypothesis testing, observational methods, independent and dependent variables, extraneous variables and control groups, and research ethics.

Mental chronometry—measuring the speed of mental processes—is the subject of Activity 1, offering students the opportunity to measure reaction times, recreating some of the earliest research in psychology, such as that conducted at Wilhelm Wundt's Leipzig laboratory.

Students like to eat, and Activity 2 offers them a chance to do that while learning about sampling distributions and especially the problems associated with small samples when trying to use those samples to estimate population parameters. This exercise uses small packages of M&M's as the individual samples. When the study is completed, students may consume their subjects.

Activity 3 asks the question, what is average? It focuses on the three measures of central tendency—mean, median, and mode—and allows students to see how those are differentially affected when distributions are skewed. The activity uses a linguistic analysis technique that historically has been used to determine authorship in disputed cases, thus showing the application of such statistical measures.

Activity 4 uses a standardized feminism survey to show students how to convert an attitude or trait into a scale score, and then how to use statistics to determine the reliability and validity of that score.

The differences between experimental and correlational research methods are the subject of Activity 5, which emphasize the subject of causation. Students will also learn the differences between negative and positive correlations.

Activity 6 uses three very clever demonstrations to create an impression that the instructor has psychic abilities. The demonstrations are used to engage students in critical thinking and to stimulate their thinking and talking about concepts of the experimental method, such as hypothesis testing, independent variables, dependent variables, control groups, and so forth.

The method of observation is the subject of Activity 7. Students are assigned to watch a common television program out of class and make various observations about what they see. This standardized observational experience can be used to demonstrate how differently students perceive the same experience and also to illustrate the difficulty and importance of developing agreed-upon observational strategies.

Activity 8 covers the important topic of ethics in human research. There are three separate activities, each designed to deal with different ethical issues in research. An overarching theme of the exercises is that ethics is always a part of research that is scientifically sound.

1 CHAIN REACTION TIME: MEASURING THE SPEED OF THOUGHT

Michael Wertheimer
University of Colorado

The experiments described here permit the in-class measurement of simple and choice reaction times using the entire class at once. They should work for classes as small as a dozen or so and as large as several hundred. Edwin G. Boring used them in his introductory psychology classes at Harvard University in the 1940s.

CONCEPT

Reaction time is one of the oldest behavioral measures in the history of psychology and was prominent in the first psychology laboratories. For example, studies of reaction time were used to measure the speed of mental processing in Wilhelm Wundt's psychology laboratory at the University of Leipzig. Wundt's first American psychology student, James McKeen Cattell, did research on that subject (Cattell, 1885). The technique used in this activity was first described in an 1868 article by a Dutch scientist, Franciscus Cornelis Donders (you can read an English translation of his article: Donders, 1969). The technique is still used today as part of the methodology of cognitive psychology under the label *mental chronometry*.

The first procedure in this demonstration deals with simple reaction time, the second with choice reaction time. In the first, a single stimulus is presented, calling for a single response; in the second, one of two different stimuli is presented, and one of two different responses is required. In both cases, the reaction time is the interval between the stimulus presentation and the response.

MATERIALS NEEDED

The only equipment needed for the experiments is a stopwatch or a watch with a stopwatch function. If you don't have such a watch, don't worry. Ask a student to bring one. It is virtually guaranteed that someone in your class will have one.

INSTRUCTIONS

Have all the students in the class line up in single file facing the same direction (in a large class, they can be lined up in an arc or in a circle or in a spiral). The right hand of each student should be placed on the right shoulder of the next student. The hand of the last student should be placed on the right shoulder of the last person in line, which should be the instructor who will be holding the stop watch. Tell the students that as soon as they are squeezed on the right shoulder, they are to squeeze the right shoulder of the next student in line. Note that the squeezes should be gentle but perceptible. Begin the experiment by saying "go," the stimulus for the first student in the chain to squeeze the shoulder of the individual in front of her/him. At the same moment that you say the word "go," start the stopwatch. Stop the watch when you feel the student behind you squeeze your shoulder. Record the elapsed time (usually to two decimal places) on a markerboard under the heading "simple reaction time." Repeat the exercise four more times to get a reasonably stable group reaction time. Record each of these times in the same column as the first. Then calculate the mean simple reaction time for the whole class and a mean simple reaction time for the average individual student; the mean reaction time for the entire class is obtained by dividing the sum of the column by five, and the mean for the average individual student is computed by dividing the class mean time by the number of students participating.

For a measurement of choice reaction time, have students place their right hands on the right shoulders of those in front of them and their left hands on these persons' left shoulders. Tell the students that when they feel their shoulder squeezed, they should squeeze the opposite shoulder of the person in front of them. Initiate the experiment by telling the first person in line that when you say "go," the student is to squeeze either the right or left shoulder of the person in front of her/him. That choice will be the student's and it is not announced. As before, begin each trial with the word "go" and the start of the stopwatch. (Of course, students should not look to see what is happening behind them.) Time the performance as before, and then repeat the exercise four more times. Some students may make an error and squeeze the wrong shoulder of the person in front of them, but even if this happens, other than leading to a bit of embarrassment, it should not seriously interfere with the success of the exercise. Record the times on the marker board in a column under "choice reaction time." As before, calculate means for the class and for the average individual student, and compare them with the values obtained in the first experiment. The mean reaction times in the second experiment will be much longer than those in the first.

DISCUSSION   The difference between the average simple and the average choice reaction times can lead into a discussion of some issues that psychologists were already dealing with more than a century ago, such as how much time the choice process takes. For, in effect, the difference between the average individual student means in the two experiments is the amount of time it took to make the decision about which shoulder to tap. That is, the afferent and efferent components of the two experiments were virtually identical. What was different between the two was the differences in the mental task required—a simple decision in the first, a more complicated choice in the second. Have students think about other situations in which choice reactions are required. What effect does the complexity of the situation have? What if there are multiple alternate stimuli or multiple alternate responses? What other factors besides complexity affect reaction time? Does research on reaction time have any potential practical consequences?

Simple and choice reaction times are discussed in many introductory psychology textbooks (check the index in the book you are using). Brief historical treatments can be found in Benjamin (2006, pp. 61–62), Leahey (2001, pp. 59–60), and Wertheimer (2002, p. 28); a slightly longer discussion is provided by Corsini and Auerbach (1996, pp. 770–772). Van Zandt (2002) presents a thorough, and quite advanced, analysis of the broader topic of response times. Luce (1986) provides a history of a century of work on mental chronometry beginning with Donders.

REFERENCES
AND
SUGGESTED
READING

Benjamin, L. T., Jr. (2006). *A history of psychology in letters* (2nd. ed.) Malden, MA: Blackwell.

Cattell, J. McK. (1885). The time it takes to see and name objects. *Mind, 11,* 63–65.

Corsini, R. J., & Auerbach, A. J. (1996). *Concise encyclopedia of psychology* (2nd ed.). New York: Wiley.

Donders, F. C. (1969). On the speed of psychological processes. *Acta Psychologica, 30,* 412–431. (Originally published in 1868)

Leahey, T. H. (2001). *A history of modern psychology* (3rd ed.). Upper Saddle River, NJ: Prentice Hall.

Luce, R. D. (1986). *Response times: Their role in inferring elementary mental organization.* New York: Oxford University Press.

Van Zandt, T. (2002). Analysis of response time distributions. In J. T. Wixted & H. Pashler (Eds.), *Stevens' handbook of experimental psychology* (3rd ed.): *Vol. 4. Methodology in experimental psychology* (pp. 461–516). New York: Wiley.

Wertheimer, M. (2002). *A brief history of psychology* (4th ed.). Fort Worth, TX: Harcourt College.

2 A Tasty Sample(r): Teaching About Sampling Using M&M's

Randolph A. Smith

Lamar University

This tasty demonstration exposes students to the concept of sampling and gives them a real-life sampling problem. Each student receives a small package of plain M&M's and quantifies the sample by color. Students use these data to hypothesize the population's color distribution. By pooling samples, students achieve closer approximations of the population distribution. This in-class activity is appropriate for classes in introductory psychology, statistics, and research methods. It requires about 15 to 30 minutes to complete, depending on discussion. Students (and faculty) find this demonstration compelling.

CONCEPT

One concept that causes psychology students some difficulty is sampling. Students do not always understand the need for sampling or the relation between a sample and its associated population. This knowledge is vital to understanding the research and inference process psychologists use.

MATERIALS NEEDED

Teachers will need a small package of plain M&M's for each student. You should also bring a napkin for each student. If students have calculators, the activity will be easier for them. Teachers can design a data sheet if they desire. (Note that students who are on special diets or who have food allergies may want to abstain from this activity.)

INSTRUCTIONS

This M&M sampling demonstration enlivens the presentation of sampling and makes it more relevant to students. Buy large sacks of fun-size packs of plain M&M's and allow each student to choose an "intact random sample" (one pack) from the population of samples. Students should sort their subjects by color, placing them on the napkin provided (much more sterile than the desk surface!). Note that it is important to use plain M&M's. The peanut variety raises the potential problem of peanut allergies, but worse, they have a habit of trying to escape by rolling off the desk.

Students should make a simple frequency distribution of the six M&M colors (blue, brown, green, orange, red, and yellow) on a data sheet you will provide (see Appendix 2.1); scratch paper will also suffice. Note that it is possible that some M&M packages will not contain all six colors. You should caution your students that they are to complete their frequency distribution before any premature subject mortality occurs!

Because sample sizes typically vary somewhat (you can raise quality control as another interesting concept *and* practical application) and because you will want the students to make some inferences about the population on the basis of their sample, have them convert their raw data into percentages.

Ask each student to generate a hypothesis about the distribution of M&M colors in the population on the basis of the student's sample. These estimates generally vary considerably. Students then form pairs to pool their data (not literally, of course) and generate a joint hypothesis. Finally, we pool the data for the entire class to generate an overall hypothesis.

Students learn some valuable lessons about sampling from this exercise. You can increase the sample size of M&M's (e.g., by using larger individual packages or 1-, 2-, or 3-lb bags) and demonstrate how larger samples typically yield better estimates of the population. Students gain an appreciation of statistics applied to real-life situations.

Because students individually generate hypotheses from small samples (usually about 24 M&M's in a fun-size pack), the hypothesized population parameters are usually low in accuracy. For example, it is not uncommon for one student to have eight of one color, say orange, whereas another student has only one orange M&M. Indeed, you will find that the bags, because the sample is so small, show considerable variability. However, as the students pair and combine their M&M's into larger samples, their estimates of the population proportions decrease in variability and more accurately approximate the population figures. When we combine the data for the entire class, variability decreases markedly, the samples become even better estimates of the population, and the hypotheses generally become more accurate.

Mars, Inc., is quite precise about the percentages of colors for the different M&M products, and the percentages are different for the various products. For plain M&M's, the current percentages are as follows: blue 24%, orange 20%, green 16%, yellow 14%, brown 13%, and red 13%. You can see those figures and the percentages for the other M&M products on the official M&M's Web site at http://www.m-ms.com. You should check percentages at the Web site before using the demonstration—when this activity was published less than 10 years ago, the percentage of brown M&M's was 30%, blue was 10%, and the other colors varied accordingly.

If you wish, you can compare the fit of your sample data to the population parameters using the chi-square statistic. I have collected large samples of data (more than 1,000 M&M's in each sample) on three different occasions. Interestingly enough, two of the three samples showed significant departure from the expected data ($p < .001$ in each case).

Students react quite favorably to this technique, especially in light of the fact that I teach statistics immediately before lunch. I can also report that this class session is probably the liveliest of the semester. Of course at the end of the activity you should tell your students that it is okay at that point to consume their subjects if they wish.

If you want to use a writing assignment with this activity, I suggest having the students write a letter to Mars, Inc., that describes the outcome of the class's findings. It is always challenging for students to attempt to communicate statistical findings in plain and easy-to-understand language. Such an assignment will help both the teacher and students discover whether they truly understand the concepts of sampling and of drawing inferences from samples. Students might also enjoy learning something about the history of M&M's from the company's Web site. Likely students and instructors will not know that the candies originated in 1941 and were sold to the military as a snack for American soldiers in World War II.

REFERENCES AND SUGGESTED READING

M&M/Mars. (1993). *A little illustrated encyclopedia of M&M/Mars.* Hackettstown, NJ: Author.

Proctor, R., & Capaldi, E. J. (2006). *Why science matters: Understanding the methods of psychological research.* Malden, MA: Blackwell Publishing.

Pryczak, F. (2006). Making sense of statistics: A conceptual overview (4th ed.). Los Angeles: Pryczak.

Smith, R. A., & Davis, S. F. (2007). *The psychologist as detective: An introduction to conducting research in psychology* (4th ed.). Upper Saddle River, NJ: Prentice Hall.

Appendix 2.1

Frequency Distribution Data Sheet

Record your sample data and make a prediction of what you think the population of M&M's looks like:

	Blue	Brown	Green	Orange	Red	Yellow
Observed f						
Predicted %						

3 ON THE AVERAGE . . .

Kurt Salzinger

Hofstra University

The object of this activity is to acquaint students with measures of central tendency and to show them in a concrete way the different conclusions that the different measures of central tendency lead them to. This activity is appropriate for classes in introductory psychology, statistics, and research methods, and it can be used with classes of virtually any size. The instructor will need to provide copies of the printed material to be analyzed. The students' tabulations can be done in or out of class. Students will need to have studied measures of central tendency.

CONCEPT

Benjamin Disraeli long ago divided lies into "lies, damned lies, and statistics." The point of this exercise is to show that we can find truth in average statistics if we understand what kind of average is used. Measures of central tendency are good sources for study because they do differ from one another, particularly for skewed distributions. In addition, samples of such distributions are often readily available to the student. What is more, it is constructive to have students see how we operationalize our concepts, that is, how we quantify them so that we can measure them, which in turn allows us to arrive at precise conclusions about our hypotheses.

The basic problem to be examined is whether different definitions of *average* result in the same conclusion. We will study verbal behavior. Suppose you wish to examine the hypothesis that one text is more difficult than another. You decide to measure difficulty by how many letters each word contains. This brings up the following problems: How can we select a representative sample? How large should the sample be? How can we summarize the average difficulty of each text using an adequate index of central tendency?

MATERIALS NEEDED

The basic materials are any English texts that differ from one another in manifest difficulty. Contrasting sources of word length can be found in novels versus textbooks or in such magazines as the *Reader's Digest* versus the *New York Review of Books*.

INSTRUCTIONS

Students should obtain their data from the same source so they can see how measures change as a function of the size and type of the sample. In this way, the class can divide the work of counting the length of words. The count can be performed by hand. Starting with a text sample of 200 words, each student can prepare a table listing word length (ranging from 1 letter to the length of the longest word) along the lefthand side of a sheet of paper. Next to each word-length, students will enter a tally mark for each same-size word that appears in the text. Computer graphics programs or any existing statistical package can be used to aggregate the data according to measure of central tendency, graphically display the distributions, and test for differences between various data sets.

Next, students can chart frequency distributions, with the number of letters displayed along the abscissa and the number of words corresponding to each word length displayed along the ordinate. The points should be connected so that students can clearly see that the distribution is skewed, that is, that the shorter words (three to four letters long) are the most frequent. Students should then compute the arithmetic *mean*, that is, the total number of letters divided by the total number of words. Next, students should compute the *median*, that is, the middlemost score, and finally, they should calculate the *mode*, the most frequently occurring word length.

Depending on how much time the teacher wishes to devote to this project, he or she can determine how many 200-word samples are to be collected by each student. In any case, the samples from each student can then be combined to produce a larger sample of word length, and each sample can be compared with every other sample to see how similar they are when they are of the same set (e.g., same book, same magazine, same topic) and how different they are when they are from different sets. The distributions of each set can then be combined into one large distribution, and the two distributions can be compared. For example, the combined distribution of all samples from the *Reader's Digest* could be compared with the combined distribution of all samples from the *New York Review of Books*.

DISCUSSION

Have the students compare the frequency distributions, means, medians, and modes first for the samples of the same text and then for the samples of the different texts. This should give students an intuitive idea of inferential statistics, which one uses to determine whether two sets of data differ from one another. Thus, students will be able to see (a) how one must establish that the difference between two sets of data exceeds the differences one finds among samples within a given set of data; (b) that some measures of central tendency differentiate the various samples better than others; and (c) that for word-length distributions the mean is the largest, the median is next in size, and the mode is the smallest. Finally, using inferential statistics, the students should be able to determine whether any two sets of data differ statistically in difficulty.

The word length measure was explored many years ago for cases of disputed authorship. Mendenhall (1887, 1901) examined the frequency distributions of the writings of Shakespeare and compared them with those of Bacon. He found, interestingly enough, that Shakespeare had a mode of four letters, whereas Bacon had a mode of three letters. Students might find a renewed interest in Shakespeare knowing that he prefers four-letter words. More recently, and in a more sophisticated way, Mosteller and Wallace (1964) returned to the problem of applying statistics to disputed authorship in a book. Today, efforts to determine literary authorship define the field of *stylometry*, the science of measuring literary style. This field uses the most modern of linguistic-analysis computer programs and artificial intelligence to identify authorship of disputed manuscripts (see Holmes & Kardos, 2003; Klarreich, 2003).

Finally, students might find of interest Darrell Huff's 1954 book, *How to Lie With Statistics*, in which the author describes how one can use different measures of central tendency to make different points. This easy-to-understand and very witty treatment of statistics is the number-one-selling statistics book of all time (Steele, 2005).

REFERENCES AND SUGGESTED READING

Holmes, D. J., & Kardos, J. (2003). Who was the author: An introduction to stylometry. *Chance, 16*(2), 5–8.

Huff, D. (1954). *How to lie with statistics*. New York: Norton.

Klarreich, E. (2003). Statistical tests are unraveling knotty literary mysteries. *Science News, 164*, 392.

Mendenhall, T. C. (1887). The characteristic curves of composition. *Science, 9*(Suppl.), 237–246.

Mendenhall, T. C. (1901). A mechanical solution of a literary problem. *Popular Science Monthly, 60,* 97–105.

Mosteller, F., & Wallace, D. L. (1964). *Inference and disputed authorship: The Federalist.* Reading, MA: Addison-Wesley.

Steele, J. M. (2005). Darrell Huff and fifty years of *How to Lie with Statistics. Statistical Science, 20,* 205–209.

4 CHECKING A TEST'S RELIABILITY AND VALIDITY

Harold Takooshian

Fordham University

This hands-on activity uses a standardized feminism survey to show students how to convert an attitude or trait into a scale score, then statistically check the reliability and validity of that score. This exercise assumes no prior knowledge and can be used in introductory psychology, psychological testing, as well as research methods classes of any size. It requires 40 minutes in Class 1, a homework assignment (to collect at least 10 surveys), then 20 minutes of Class 2 to review the outcome.

CONCEPT How do we determine the reliability of a test (its correlation with itself) and its validity (its correlation with behavior)? This simple activity spans two class meetings and is designed to give undergraduates some hands-on experience on how an attitude or a trait is converted into a score, and then statistically checked for reliability and validity. This exercise is suitable for any course in which students can learn to calculate a Pearson correlation.

MATERIALS NEEDED You will need the Feminism Survey, scoring grid, and reliability worksheet (see Appendixes 4.1, 4.2., and 4.3). If convenient, you might also use (a) the section on test validity/reliability from a textbook on testing (e.g., Anastasi & Urbina, 1997, pp. 95–97) or (b) some current article from *Psychology of Women Quarterly* on the wide diversity of views on women and gender (e.g., Rudman & Fairchild, 2007).

INSTRUCTIONS *During Class 1*

The students' first step in this activity is to self-score one test. Give students 10 min in class to complete the Feminism Survey (Takooshian & Stuart, 1983), which assesses one's belief in the equality of women and men (see Appendix 4.1). Once students have completed the survey, show them how to hand-score their own scales. To do this, give them 10 min to look over the five embedded items (10, 13, 16, 19, and 20), which actually measure authoritarianism, and score the remaining 15 items ("2" for every response on the far left, "1" for every N, and "0" for every response on the right). The total for these items will give them a feminist score ranging between 0 and 30. (The mean feminist score for a representative group of adult women in New York was 17.2 in 1983, 17.6 in 1997, and 17.6 in 2006.)

Next you will have students pair off into two-person teams and assign each team to distribute at least 10 Feminism Surveys by the next class. Five should go to expected feminists and five to expected antifeminists (e.g., high vs. low education, political liberals vs. conservatives, younger vs. older women)—to see if the scores turn out as expected. (Note: Students unable to pair up can work alone.) Give each student 10 Feminism Surveys plus the two assignment sheets—the scoring grid and the reliability worksheet (see Appendixes 4.2 and 4.3)—to be completed by the next class meeting. Take another 15 min to explain step by step (outlined in the following section) how to complete the grid, the reliability scatterplot, and Pearson *r*.

Before Class 2

Once students have collected their 10-plus completed surveys, the students should enter each response as a 2/1/0 score in the scoring grid. The Feminism Survey is structured so all responses on the left (regardless of D or A) are scored 2 points as profeminist, 1 point for neutral; all right-column responses are coded 0 as antifeminist. On the scoring grid, each respondent gets one column. Be sure to group the expected feminists in the first 5-plus columns to the left, then the antifeminists in 5-plus columns to the right.

After eliminating the filler items (10, 13, 16, 19, and 20), students should calculate an odd-score for each column by adding the odd-numbered items ($1 + 3 + 5 + 7 + 9 + 11 + 15 + 17$) and then an even-score by adding the even-numbered items ($2 + 4 + 6 + 8 + 12 + 14 + 18$). They can then arrive at a total feminist score by adding all 15 items. Write these O, E, T scores in the space below each column. (At 0–2 points per item, the odd scores must fall between 0 and 16, the even between 0 and 14, the total between 0 and 30.)

To check the validity of the scale, students should calculate the mean feminist scores of the expected high and low columns, to see if the expected high scorers did indeed score higher than the expected low scorers.

To determine if the scale is reliable, have students use the test reliability worksheet to answer items 1, 2, and 3 by scatterplotting all 10 pairs of odd–even scores. They can then calculate the Pearson correlation.

During Class 2

Review students' findings. Take 15 minutes to list each team's high versus low means and reliability *r* results on the chalkboard. With the class, try to discern a pattern across the teams' results.

Optional Additions

If time and interest permit, consider a few added exercises: (a) To complete the fifth item on the reliability worksheet, show students how to apply a Spearman–Brown correction to their obtained *r*, using the short formula

$$rsb = \frac{2r}{1+r}$$

found in many textbooks (e.g., Anastasi & Urbina, 1997, pp. 95–97). (b) Shuffle the assigned sheets, so each team double-checks another team's submission for the following class, particularly if one or more teams had findings that were highly discrepant from the others. (c) Pages 471 to 473 in Carole Beere's (1990) handbook on gender roles reviews psychometric data on the Feminism Survey; distribute this so students can compare their findings with published validity and reliability data. (d) The five-item authoritarianism scale (10, 13, 16, 19, and 20) by Janowitz and Marvick (1953) can also be scored with the same 2/1/0 method, to yield an authoritarianism score ranging from 0 (*low*) to 10 (*high*). Students who want extra practice computing a correlation can score their 10 authoritarian scales, then correlate this with the corresponding feminism scores—which normally correlate negatively, about $r = -.40$.

DISCUSSION

Several issues concerning validity and reliability make effective discussion topics. For example, ask students to consider whether the Feminism Survey is high in face validity. If students answer yes, ask them whether faking and the need for approval affect respondents' scores. Students might also be asked to think about how the reliability worksheet can be used to check the test–retest and alternate form reliability of the Feminism Survey.

Many students will notice that the As and Ds on the Feminism Survey are often reversed. This reversal is meant to reduce response set as well as simplify hand scoring. Students can be asked to consider whether the reversal is likely to affect the accuracy of one's scores. Last, the feminism scale dates from 1983, so certain terms such as *unisex* fashions (Item 4) and *women's liberationists* (Item 14) may be outdated. Students could be asked to consider whether a test's value is reduced when possibly dated terms are kept the same rather than updated.

REFERENCES AND SUGGESTED READING

Anastasi, A., & Urbina, S. P. (1997). *Psychological testing* (7th ed.). Upper Saddle River, NJ: Prentice-Hall.

Beere, C. A. (Ed.). (1990). *Gender roles: A handbook of tests and measures.* New York: Greenwood.

Janowitz, M., & Marvick, D. (1953). Authoritarianism and political behavior. *Public Opinion Quarterly, 17,* 185–200.

Rudman, L., & Fairchild, K. (2007). The F word: Is feminism compatible with beauty and romance? *Psychology of Women Quarterly, 31,* 125–136.

Takooshian, H., & Stuart, C. R. (1983). Ethnicity and feminism among American women: Opposing social trends? *International Journal of Group Tensions, 13,* 100–105.

Appendix 4.1

Opinion Survey

Americans seem to have very divided opinions about the feminist movement. We are researchers who would appreciate your frank opinions on the statements below. For each item, circle whether you Agree (**A**), Disagree (**D**), or have No opinion (**N**). This survey is anonymous. **Thank you.**

1. D N A   Women who do the same work as men should <u>not</u> necessarily get the same salary.
2. D N A   A woman should have more responsibility than a man in caring for a child.
3. D N A   Women should have more responsibility than men in doing household duties.
4. A N D   Unisex clothes are a good idea, so men and women can dress more alike.
5. D N A   By nature, women are more emotional than men.
6. D N A   By nature, women enjoy sex less than men.
7. D N A   When I meet a woman for the first time, I prefer to call her Miss or Mrs., rather than Ms.
8. D N A   I would prefer to call myself Miss or Mrs., rather than Ms.
9. D N A   A woman should adopt her husband's last name when they marry.
10. A N D   Human nature being what it is, there will always be war and conflict.
11. A N D   Married women with young children should work outside the home if they wish.
12. A N D   I'd say it's perfectly all right for a husband to stay at home while the wife supports the family.
13. A N D   People can <u>not</u> be trusted.
14. D N A   I'd say women's liberationists "rock the boat" too much.
15. D N A   Many women who deny their femininity are actually confused people.
16. A N D   A few leaders could make this country better than all the laws and talk.
17. D N A   The use of obscene language is more unbecoming for a woman than for a man.
18. D N A   The needs of a family should come before a woman's career.
19. A N D   Most people who don't get ahead just don't have enough willpower.
20. A N D   An insult to one's honor should not be forgotten.

21. What is your general feeling about the feminist movement? (More space on back)

22. Age: _____under 20   _____20–29   _____30–39   _____40–49
    _____50–59 _____60+.

23. Schoolwork: _____Grammar school   _____High school
    _____Some college _____College grad.   _____Grad school.

24. Marital status: _____Single _____Married _____Widowed
    _____Separated _____Divorced.

25. Are you now employed outside the home? _____No _____Yes, part-time
    _____Yes, full-time. If "yes," what occupation: _____

26. I am: _____female _____male.

27. (Optional:) Any comments to add here? (More space on back.)

Appendix 4.2

Psychological Test Scoring Sheet

Name:_____

Scale: _Feminism Scale_____

	(expected lower)	Respondent #	(expected higher)

Item 1

2

3

4

5

6

7

8

9

10*

11

12

13*

14

15

16*

17

18

19*

20*

Odd: ___ ___ ___ ___ ___ ___ ___ ___ ___ ___   ___ ___ ___ ___ ___ ___ ___ ___ ___ ___

Even: ___ ___ ___ ___ ___ ___ ___ ___ ___ ___   ___ ___ ___ ___ ___ ___ ___ ___ ___ ___

Total: ___ ___ ___ ___ ___ ___ ___ ___ ___ ___   ___ ___ ___ ___ ___ ___ ___ ___ ___ ___

* Note: Skip 5 items (#10, 13, 16, 19, 20), which actually assess "authoritarian personality."

Appendix 4.3

Test Reliability Worksheet

Name: _____/___/___

Scale: <u>Feminism Scale</u>

How reliable is the attitude scale our class
completed this month? Compute this here.

.

.

.

.

1. TYPE of reliability you

   are checking here is: _____.

   Explain.

.

.

.

.

.

2. SCATTERPLOT the two scores per person.

   Be sure to clearly mark the two axes.

.

.

.   .   .   .

_____

3. DIRECTION. Is the apparent

   relation of the two sets of scores

   negative / 0 / positive? Explain.

4. MAGNITUDE. What is the correlation of the two sets of scores above?

$$r = \frac{N\sum XY - (\sum X)(\sum Y)}{\sqrt{\left[N\sum X^2 - (\sum X)^2\right]\left[N\sum Y^2 - (\sum Y)^2\right]}}$$

5. SIGNIFICANCE. Is this a reliable scale, according to your data? Explain.

5 EXPERIMENTAL VERSUS CORRELATIONAL RESEARCH

Linda Leal

Eastern Illinois University

This activity is a vehicle for discussing the relations among experimental research, correlational research, and causal inferences at an introductory level. Students need a basic understanding of experimental and nonexperimental research methods, as well as positive and negative correlation coefficients. No advance preparation is needed, unless you wish to present the instructions for the research proposals as a handout or PowerPoint presentation. This is appropriate for any size of class and can be completed by students either in or outside of class. It can be used in classes in introductory psychology, critical thinking, or any class that deals with research methods.

CONCEPT Because research is so vital to what we know and what we do as psychologists, the ability to think critically about research is a skill we consistently nurture in our students. Initially, many students of psychology think all research is experimental. The following classroom activity illustrates the difference between experimental research and correlational research and may help students think more critically about research in general.

INSTRUCTIONS After you have discussed experimental and correlational research in class, have students work in groups of two to four. This has been accomplished successfully in sections of 90 or more students by having students work with those seated next to them.

Give students the following instructions:

"Suppose you are hired as a research psychologist by a dental products firm.

1. Outline an *experiment* in which you are trying to show that brushing with BEST toothpaste results in fewer cavities. Be sure to describe who your research participants will be and how you will assign them to different conditions or groups. Also identify your independent and dependent variables and list the benefits and limitations of your research design.

2. Outline a *correlational study* in which you are trying to determine whether there is a relation between brushing with BEST toothpaste and the number of cavities participants have. Suppose your correlational study resulted in a correlation coefficient of +.81. How would you interpret this result? How would you interpret a correlation coefficient of −.81? How would you interpret a correlation coefficient of +.08? Which correlation would the manufacturer of BEST toothpaste hope to find? What are the benefits and limitations of your research design?"

Variations

(1) You may wish to assign half of the class to work on Study 1 and half to work on Study 2. However, the difference between correlational and experimental research is appreciated better if students have experience planning both studies.

(2) This activity could also be presented to students as an out-of-class or homework assignment. On the date they are due, classroom discussion could focus on the reports of students who volunteer to describe their research studies to the class as a whole.

(3) As a follow-up exercise, you could ask students, on the basis of their knowledge of research, what is wrong with the following claim: "I know that BEST toothpaste prevents cavities because I've brushed with BEST toothpaste for the past year and have had no cavities."

(4) After students have participated in the in-class exercise, as an out-of-class assignment, they could be asked to locate an advertisement or commercial that makes the claim that one product is superior to another or that a product has been "proven effective." Students would then outline a research study that would test the claim that is made.

(5) Because of advances in technology, students are bombarded daily with new information that is often reported uncritically or in a sensational manner. Another possible follow-up exercise would be to have students bring in news articles from the Internet, newspapers, and magazines that summarize the results of recent research findings. Based on the information in each news article, classroom discussion could focus on determining the type of research (experimental or correlational) and related implications, as well as other possible limitations or criticisms of the information presented in the news article.

DISCUSSION   The major emphasis of the discussion should be on the following differences in interpretation between correlational research and experimental research: (a) How correlational studies allow us to make predictions but do not demonstrate causation, (b) why experimental research allows us to talk about causation, (c) why replication is important in determining causation, and (d) how both correlational and experimental designs are valuable research methods.

Inevitably, other topics for discussion also arise. For instance, students often question how to control for diet or the thoroughness of tooth brushing in their experimental design. This can lead to discussions about operational definitions, extraneous variables, random assignment, and difficulties with experimenter control groups for research that takes place outside of the traditional laboratory setting. Ethical concerns can be another topic for discussion when some students suggest a "no brushing" control group. This activity also provides an opportunity for conversations about experimenter and participant bias.

REFERENCES AND SUGGESTED READING

Dunn, D. S. (2007). *Best practices in teaching statistics and research methods in the behavioral sciences*. Hillsdale, NJ: Lawrence Erlbaum Associates.

Meltzoff, J. (1997). *Critical thinking about research: Psychology and related fields*. Washington, DC: American Psychological Association.

Proctor, R., & Capaldi, E. J. (2006). *Why science matters: Understanding the methods of psychological research*. Malden, MA: Blackwell Publishing.

Smith, R. A., & Davis, S. F. (2007). *The psychologist as detective: An introduction to conducting research in psychology* (4th ed.). Upper Saddle River, NJ: Prentice-Hall.

6 RESEARCH METHODS AND CRITICAL THINKING: EXPLAINING "PSYCHIC" PHENOMENA

Sandra Goss Lucas
University of Illinois

Douglas A. Bernstein
University of South Florida
University of Southampton

Rather than lecturing about research methods, we like to motivate students to learn about these methods as part of their efforts to generate scientific explanations for an apparent "psychic" phenomenon. After we present a set of easy-to-perform, but impressive, magic tricks as demonstrations of our "psychic power," students are challenged to explain how the tricks were done. This activity, which is appropriate for classes in introductory psychology or any class that covers research methods or critical thinking, takes minimum time to plan and set up and has been used successfully in classes of as many as 800 students. You should allocate at least 30 minutes to perform the demonstrations and engage the class in discussion of them.

CONCEPT
This classroom exercise introduces research methods by exploring a phenomenon of interest to students. Students are challenged to use critical thinking in explaining how the phenomenon occurred. Those who are skeptical about "paranormal" phenomena are eager to debunk these demonstrations, and those who are convinced of the reality of such phenomena are challenged to think scientifically about them, to prove they could not have been done through trickery.

MATERIALS NEEDED
For Demonstration 1 you will need an overhead projector, blank transparencies, and a marking pen. For Demonstration 2 you will need a cardboard box or a clean wastebasket, a pad of paper, and a pen. For Demonstration 3 you will need two identical telephone books (white pages), a large piece of poster board, a heavy black marking pen, and an accomplice. *Warning:* Be sure to practice these tricks with colleagues or students not in your current classes before you present them in class.

INSTRUCTIONS
Pose as a psychic or get a colleague to pose as one. We usually do one or more of our "psychic" demonstrations in the first class of the term, after lamenting the fact that the course schedule allows us time only to mention and quickly demonstrate one of the more important topics in psychology: extra sensory perception (ESP) and other paranormal phenomena.

Demonstration 1

This is basically a warm-up activity. Ask all of the students to (a) silently choose a number between 1 and 10, (b) a color, and (c) draw a picture. Then ask them to concentrate on their chosen number and try to "send" it to you telepathically. Research on proto-types suggests most people are likely to choose the number 5 or 7, choose the color red or blue; and draw either a tree or a house. As you begin to "receive" the students' messages, write the number 7 on the overhead, then mark it out and write 5 instead. Say something like, "I first thought it was a 7 but then I got a really strong perception of 5." Having received the choice of the majority of the audience will be moderately impressive. You can do the same feat with their chosen color or drawn object. As an alternative, you can send mental messages to the class, asking students to write the number, or color, or image they receive. Again, on base rates alone, most of your students will write down the stimulus you claim to have sent.

Demonstration 2

Stand at the front of the room with a pad of paper and a pen and ask your students to name some European cities. Paris will eventually be mentioned. It should appear that you are writing each city name on a separate sheet of paper, then wad it up, and throw it into the wastebasket. However, just write "Paris" on every sheet. Eventually, you will have a wastebasket full of crumpled papers, all of which say "Paris," but which your students assume are all different. (If Paris is named at the beginning of the demonstration, keep going until it appears that you have plenty of different cities in the basket.) Now ask a student to choose one of the crumpled balls from the basket (hold the basket high enough that the student cannot see into it) and after unfolding the paper, concentrate on the city name while you try to mentally "read" the student's mind. Many students will be amazed when you correctly state that the city named on the paper is Paris. (Requests from the same class for a repeat performance with a second wad of paper should be denied for obvious reasons, but suggest that it is because of time constraints).

Demonstration 3

Position your accomplice out of the students' sight (e.g., in the hallway or at the back of the classroom) with a telephone book, a black marker, and a piece of cardboard. Now choose a student at random and give him or her a copy of the same telephone book. It is best to choose a student who is sitting in a spot—such as the front of the room—where, when the rest of the class looks at him or her, they will be looking away from your accomplice's position. Ask this student to open the telephone book at random and announce the page number. Then ask another randomly selected student to say out loud which column on that page should be chosen, and ask yet another student to choose and announce a row in that column, counting down from the top (e.g., the 12th row). Ask the student holding the telephone book to locate and concentrate on the telephone number thus identified. Your hidden accomplice should locate the same number and, using a black marker, write it in large numerals on the cardboard, and hold the number up so you can see it. Be sure the accomplice is located so you can see the cardboard but your students cannot. Also be sure to clearly repeat the page, column, and line numbers as they are chosen by your students; this will help your accomplice write down the correct telephone number. (You can do so as if you are mentally focusing on this information: "Okay, we are on page 341, in the second column from the left, and the 14th number from the top.") The class will be stunned when you correctly "read your student's mind." (You can make the demonstration more dramatic if you are using an overhead projector, by turning off the projector, writing the "received" number on a transparency, and then turning the projector on so the class can see the number you wrote.)

<table>
<tr><td>DISCUSSION</td><td>Following these demonstrations, many of your students will be convinced that you really do have psychic abilities. This is the time to tell them that these were really nothing more than simple magic tricks and that their assignment for the next session is to try to figure out how they could have been performed without psychic power.</td></tr>
</table>

At the next class, students are usually eager to begin their research. Ask them for possible explanations of the trick that interests them the most. It is very easy at this point to include the proper experimental terminology, such as "Your hypothesis then is that I memorized the telephone book." As students attempt to explain how they might test their hypotheses, concepts such as independent variable, dependent variable, and other components of experimental design will arise, though the terms themselves may not be used. This makes it easy for you to label them ("OK, in scientific research terms, whether or not I am blindfolded would be the independent variable because . . ."). Students will challenge other students' designs and point out the need for control groups and double-blind designs, as well as the problems posed by confounding variables, sampling errors, and experimental bias. A lively discussion about experimental methods will probably occur, and the students will better appreciate their value in critical thinking.

Inevitably, your students will ask how you did each trick. If you ever want to use the trick again, you cannot tell them. Our solution to this problem is to say something like, "Some of your hypotheses were very close to the truth. However, scientists never know for sure when they have found the truth; they can only eliminate plausible alternative hypotheses and reach a conclusion with a statistically significant, but not absolutely certain, likelihood of being correct. Like scientists, you will have to be satisfied with this situation." If this does not satisfy them, just remind the students that magicians cannot reveal their tricks.

To further reinforce research methods and terminology, have students meet in small groups and submit a written explanation of how one of the demonstrations could have been performed without psychic abilities. Each group could generate a hypothesis and design an experiment for testing it (using research terminology). Small groups could then share their proposed experiment with the class.

REFERENCES AND SUGGESTED READING

Lilienfeld, S. O., Lohr, J. M., & Morier, D. (2001). The teaching of courses on the science and pseudoscience of psychology: Useful resources. *Teaching of Psychology, 28,* 182–191.

Morris, S. (1981). *Believing in ESP: Effects of dehoaxing.* In K. Frazier (Ed.), *Paranormal borderlands of science* (pp. 32–45). Buffalo, NY: Prometheus Books.

Randi, J. (1995). *An encyclopedia of claims, frauds, and hoaxes of the occult and supernatural.* New York: St. Martin's Press.

Shermer, M. (2002). *Why people believe weird things: Pseudoscience, superstition, and other confusions of our time.* New York: W. H. Freeman.

Smith, R. A. (2002). *Challenging your preconceptions: Thinking critically about psychology* (2nd ed.). Pacific Grove, CA: Brooks/Cole.

7 EXPERIMENTAL DESIGN: VARYING HEART RATE

Samuel Cameron, Jack Christiano, and Bernard Mausner
Arcadia University

This activity, involving pulse rate, can be used to illustrate the experimental method, the difference between an independent and a dependent variable, and the concept of a control group in experimentation. Simple descriptive statistics can be calculated from the data obtained. It is appropriate for classes in introductory psychology, requires approximately 20 to 25 minutes of class time, involves all of the students, and because of the time involved in the collection and analysis of data, works best with a class of 30 to 50 students.

CONCEPT
The activity illustrates the experimental method, the difference between an independent and a dependent variable, and the concept of a control group in experimentation. It also demonstrates that a measure of physiological arousal, pulse rate, can be affected by both thought processes and physical activity.

MATERIALS NEEDED
You will need a handout, one per experimenter that contains a short news story describing an act of violence—for example, a shooting. Select the story from an old or out-of-town paper so that the story will be novel and the persons involved will have no connection with the families or friends of your students. Each experimenter will also need an analog watch with a sweep second hand or a digital watch that displays seconds.

INSTRUCTIONS
Describe the following experiment to students and explain its purpose. Randomly designate students as experimenters or participants. Each experimenter will need a watch that displays seconds. Teach the experimenters the correct method of taking a pulse. (If you do not know the correct method, ask school health personnel.) To save time, have the experimenters count pulse beats over a 15-second interval and multiply that rate by four. Then provide each experimenter with a handout, and randomly pair him or her with a participant.

The experimenter's first task is to take the participant's pulse while the participant is at rest and comfortably seated. The pulse should be taken twice, with about 1 minute intervening between readings, and the rates should be recorded. Then the participant should read the handout aloud. Immediately after the reading, the experimenter should again take the participant's pulse and record the rate. The participant should then rest comfortably for 3 minutes, after which the experimenter should take the pulse twice again, with 1 minute intervening between readings. These rates should also be recorded. Finally, the experimenter should have the participant run in place for 30 seconds and should then take the participant's pulse and record the rate one last time.

On the chalkboard, collect the data for each participant under each condition: at rest #1, at rest #2, immediately after reading, 3 minutes after reading, 4 minutes after reading, and immediately after running. Total the rates under each condition for all participants and calculate the means.

DISCUSSION Focus on the following questions: What was the dependent variable? What were the independent variables? What other variables might have influenced the dependent variable? What was the purpose of the method of selecting experimenters and participants? Are there any improvements that could be made in this method?

The pulse rate of almost all participants will increase after running in place. However, there will be considerable variability in the increase in the participants' pulse rate following reading the news article. Some participants will show no increase in pulse rate; some will show a sizable increase. Students should be encouraged to explore what other factors—psychological, physiological, and social—could explain these differences in the participants' response to the reading.

REFERENCES AND SUGGESTED READING Pelham, B. W., & Blanton, H. (2007). *Conducting research in psychology: Measuring the weight of smoke* (3rd ed.). Belmont, CA: Wadsworth/Thompson Learning.

Pryczak, F. (2006). *Making sense of statistics: A conceptual overview* (4th ed.). Los Angeles: Pryczak.

8 THREE EXERCISES ON THE ETHICS OF RESEARCH ON HUMANS

Joan E. Sieber

California State University, East Bay

In this activity there are three exercises that can be done individually, in small groups, or in general class discussion. These exercises are appropriate for students at any level, in virtually any size class. Students will approach these activities somewhat differently, depending on the research focus or sophistication of the students; thus, it will serve students at their individual levels. No prior knowledge is required, and the only advance preparation for the teacher is copying material. The first exercise familiarizes students with the ethical principles that they will need to apply to proposed research plans in the other exercises. Exercise 1 can be a stand-alone discussion or used with Exercises 2, 3, or both.

CONCEPT At every stage in the planning and conduct of research, there are important decisions to be made. These decisions involve ethical as well as scientific elements. Unless the decisions are ethically sound, they will not be scientifically sound. Many students think *ethics* simply means being courteous or honest. As these exercises show, ethics means far more. Students are often surprised to realize that unethical research typically occurs because the scientist has been hurried, thoughtless, or too narrowly focused on gathering data, not because the scientist is a bad person. This activity and the exercises within it are designed to help the student overcome some of the kinds of thoughtlessness that naturally arise when one is intent on doing a research project.

MATERIALS NEEDED You will need to make copies of the three ethical principles, the sample letter, and the research project description.

INSTRUCTIONS *Exercise 1*

Have students study the handout listing the three main ethical principles for research on humans and the six scientific norms based on those principles. Ask them to explain how each norm relates to the principles designated. You may wish to divide the class into small groups, with each group then presenting its conclusions to the rest of the class (see handout for Exercise 1 in Appendix 8.1).

Exercise 2

This exercise is designed to test students' abilities to apply the above norms and principles. Describe to them each of the following research plans and have them discuss the ethical considerations of each. Compare their responses with the answers given here.

   A. You plan to study the effects of competition on ability to solve math problems. Half of the subjects will be told that you want to see what approach they take in solving math problems. The other half will be told that you want to see which person chooses the best approach.

Answer: This study requires withholding some information. Include in the informed consent statement that you cannot give subjects full information about the study ahead of time but that you will explain it all to them afterward. Those who do not like having information withheld may decline to participate. Those who participate should be debriefed immediately afterward if possible. The debriefing should have educational value and should not make the subjects feel foolish for having "fallen for" the deception. Rather, it might emphasize that stress can diminish problem-solving ability. Have the students brainstorm about how to reduce stress when confronted with a challenging problem.

B. You plan to compare the intellectual skills of retired people with those of sophomores. To recruit sophomores, you plan to arrange for volunteers to receive an *A* in their psychology course and for nonvolunteers to have their grade lowered. To recruit retired people, you plan to go to a retirement community each evening next week, knock at people's doors, and ask them to work some puzzles without explaining all of the details of the study because most would not understand.

Answer: For retired people to be meaningfully compared with sophomores, they must have equally good education, vision, test-taking skills, and so on— assumptions that are sure to be false. The proposed approach to recruitment of sophomores involves undue inducement and coercion. Elderly people are likely to be frightened and unwilling to let strangers in at night; besides, they deserve adequate informed consent. This is an example of a simple research idea that turns out to be very complex to operationalize. However, the example provides an opportunity for various kinds of brainstorming:

- It is unacceptable to approach elderly people in the way proposed. This is a good opportunity to challenge students to come up with creative ways to build trust and understanding in the way they arrange to recruit subjects. For example, they might solicit permission from the administration of the retirement community to give a presentation on their proposed project at lunch time at the retirement community, and begin the recruitment process there.
- It is unacceptable to assume that one need not give an adequate explanation just because subjects would not understand a technical explanation. This is a good opportunity for students to develop a correct explanation of their study, excluding all jargon and other detail that subjects wouldn't be interested in hearing about anyhow.

A next part of the assignment might be to enlist elderly persons, such as some of the students' grandparents or great-grandparents, to help them explain their study in a way that is likely to be understandable to that generation. This kind of consultation should be encouraged.

C. You plan to compare marijuana use in college freshmen and seniors. Because you may want to re-interview some subjects later, you plan to write their names and phone numbers on their data sheets. You plan to promise confidentiality so that subjects will trust you and to keep the data in your room in a locked file.

Answer: This is a study of criminal behavior. You should not promise confidentiality because you cannot assure it. Your data could be subpoenaed and you might have to choose between going to jail and handing over the data. If you hand over the data, subjects can sue you for breaking your promise of confidentiality. Research on criminal behavior is risky and should be left to professional scientists who are knowledgeable about the risks and about how to minimize them. Students who are curious about mechanisms for protecting confidentiality should be referred to the Web site of the American Statistical Association (http://www.amstat.org/comm/cmtepc).

D. You plan to study the effects of an educational (cable) TV curriculum on learning to read. You give access to the cable TV program to 100 homes with 5-year-olds whose parents want their child to watch the TV curriculum daily. You get permission to test those 100 children in 2 months, along with 100 matched control children who will not have access to the cable TV.

Answer: Because you do not know whether the curriculum will be effective, it is fair to "deprive" the control group for a while. Inform both sets of families and even things up later by giving the control families access to the cable TV after the study is over. (See Conner, 1982, for a description of the evaluation of "Sesame Street" and a discussion of the ethics of random assignment of subjects to conditions.)

E. To study self-esteem in children, you plan to have 8-year-olds draw pictures of themselves and their friends and to answer some questions, and provide their responses without their names or other unique identifiers. You plan to ask a teacher friend of yours to let you test some of her students.

Answer: This study involves special problems of consent having to do with children, coercion, and institutional responsibility. Children are easily coerced and cannot legally consent. Parents and persons in charge at institutions (e.g., schools, jails, hospitals, places of employment) may exert subtle pressures for conformity to their wishes, hence, autonomy and freedom from coercion may be difficult to ensure. Most schools probably would require that you get consent from the school board or the parents. You should also give each child an independent opportunity to decline to participate. Students who are interested in understanding federal law governing research on school children may wish to consult the *Family Educational Rights and Privacy Act (FERPA),* which can be accessed at http://www.ed.gov/policy/gen/reg/ferpa/index.html

F. To study how college students respond to the death of a parent, you plan to survey students in several classes to learn who has lost a parent in the last 10 years. You plan to recruit these students and interview them about what happened to their parent and how they coped with the death.

Answer: This is a very interesting and potentially important study because some college students do have to cope with the death of a parent. A properly conducted study in which the interviewer is objective and sensitive in approach can provide important closure to subjects who have experienced such trauma. It can also provide useful insights into college counselors who may be called on to help such students. However, it is important that a student researcher be properly trained and supervised to do such a study, and do some pilot research to ensure that their approach is indeed constructive and not harmful. For an introduction to the literature on ethical issues in trauma research and access to an instrument that assesses how subjects experience such a research experiment, please go to http://www.csueastbay.edu/JERHRE/notes/index.html, and see "Reactions to Sensitive Research."

Exercise 3

Students should be led through a discussion of the elements of informed consent before beginning this exercise. You should provide students a copy of the handout in Appendix 8.2.

Unfortunately, many investigators—scientists as well as students—fulfill the letter of these requirements but not their spirit. They make their explanations too technical, too long, and too uninteresting, with the result that subjects don't bother reading it, or read it and do not understand it. Because people hesitate to say that they don't understand, confusions are not clarified. Learning to make the description of one's research clear and interesting (free of jargon) actually requires a better understanding of the research methods than a jargon-filled description, hence is challenging to students who tend to emulate the confusing "scientese" that they read in journals. This is an excellent opportunity to foster both good writing and clear communication with research subjects.

Ask students to write a clear, friendly letter soliciting participation in the research project described in Appendix 8.3.

With the students, compare their letters with the sample letter in Appendix 8.4 and discuss what makes a letter engaging, clear, and a good basis for deciding whether one should participate in research. Be sure to discuss the significance of a letterhead that legitimizes the role of the researcher and research setting.

This is a particularly important lesson in writing because it has powerful implications for the student's ability to communicate with *any* audience. After this activity is completed, have students find particularly obscure descriptions of experimental procedures in the literature and practice writing consent letters to potential subjects.

DISCUSSION   Most students have, at one time or another, participated in research that annoyed them, which they considered foolish or objectionable. This might have been a telephone survey that was conducted in an amateurish way or at dinner time, or even a telephone survey that turned into a solicitation. Or it might have been academic research on their own campus that displeased them in some way. Often the negative attitude toward the research experience turns out to be because of poor communication, failure to respect the interests and needs of the student who was being recruited, and failure to explain the research in a way that was interesting and useful to the student. Sometimes it is because the research was truly foolish and will contribute nothing to a fund of knowledge. In any event, any of these circumstances can be related to the three ethical principles of human research.

It would be useful to begin by asking students to describe any kind of research in which they have participated that they considered foolish or objectionable. You will note that they probably do not think of this in terms of ethics, but only in terms of their being annoyed. As you launch into the ethical principles in Exercise 1, they will begin to reconceptualize what was wrong and why the research was objectionable. By the time they have completed Exercise 3, they will begin to understand the role of careful planning, mindfulness of ethical principles, and clear communication in fulfilling ethical requirements of social and behavioral research.

In one way or another, each case in Exercise 2 involves issues of communication. Students who wish to pursue skills of clear communication and informed consent further will benefit greatly from the work of Gordon Willis, who has written extensively about the use of cognitive interviewing as a method of learning how to communicate with subjects in language that is natural and understandable to them. Students may find a brief introduction to essentials of cognitive interviewing at http://www.csueastbay. edu/JERHRE/notes/index.html (Cognitive Interviewing). A more detailed discussion may be found at Willis (2006).

REFERENCES AND SUGGESTED READING

American Psychological Association. (2002). *Ethical principles of psychologists and code of conduct.* Retrieved from http://www.apa.org/ethics/code2002.html

American Statistical Association. (2003). American Statistical Association Committee on Privacy, Confidentiality and Data Security Web site. Retrieved from http://www. amstat.org/comm/cmtepc

Bersoff, D. (2003). *Ethical conflicts in psychology* (3rd ed.). Washington, DC: American Psychological Association.

Chastain, G., & Landrum, R. E. (1999). *Protecting human subjects: Departmental subject pools and institutional review boards.* Washington, DC: American Psychological Association.

Connor, R. F. (1982). Random assignment of clients in social experimentation. In J. E. Sieber (Ed.), *The ethics of social research: Surveys and experiments* (Vol. 1, pp. 57–77). New York: Springer-Verlag.

Newman, E., Risch, R., & Kassam-Adams, N. (2006). Ethical issues in trauma-related research: A review. *Journal of Empirical Research on Human Research Ethics, 1*(3), 29–46.

United States Department of Education. (2006). *Family Educational Rights and Privacy Act (FERPA).* Retrieved from http://www.ed.gov/policy/gen/reg/ferpa/index.html

Willis, G. (2006). Cognitive interviewing as a tool for improving the informed consent process. *Journal of Empirical Research on Human Research Ethics, 1*(1), 9–24.

Appendix 8.1

Handout for Exercise 1

The Three Basic Ethical Principles

The following three ethical principles should guide research on humans:

A. *Beneficence*—maximizing good outcomes and avoiding unnecessary risk.
B. *Respect*—concern for autonomy of persons and courtesy, including respect for the well-being of persons who lack autonomy, such as young children and others who have limited capacity to understand information and make decisions.
C. *Justice*—fair procedures and fair distribution of costs and benefits.

These three basic principles translate into six norms of scientific behavior:

1. *Valid research design.* Only valid research yields correct results. Valid design takes into account relevant theory, methods, and prior findings (Principles A and B).
2. *Competence of researcher.* Even well-designed research may yield invalid results or cause harm if the researcher is inadequately supervised or insufficiently qualified (Principles A and B).
3. *Identification of consequences.* Possible risks and benefits should be identified and considered before the research is conducted (Principles A, B, and C).
4. *Selection of subjects.* The population sampled should (a) be appropriate to the purposes of the study, (b) be the one that benefits from the research, and (c) not include persons having very limited power or autonomy (Principles A, B, and C).
5. *Voluntary informed consent.* Voluntary informed consent of subjects should be obtained beforehand. *Voluntary* means freely, without threat or undue inducement. *Informed* means that subjects know what reasonable persons in that situation would want to know before giving consent. *Consent* means explicit agreement to participate. Informed consent requires clear communication that subjects comprehend, not complex technical explanations or legal jargon (Principles A, B, and C).
6. *Compensation for injury.* The researcher is responsible for what happens to subjects and should compensate them for injury (Principles A, B, and C).

Appendix 8.2

Handout for Exercise 3

The Elements of Informed Consent

Federal law governing human research requires that informed consent statements do the following:

1. Explain the purpose of the research, the expected duration of subjects' participation, and a description of the procedures. Describe the procedure in terms subjects understand. Avoid jargon or explanations that are irrelevant to deciding whether to participate.
2. Describe any foreseeable risks or discomforts to subjects.
3. Describe any benefits reasonably to be expected from participation.
4. Describe alternatives to participation when appropriate.
5. Describe how confidentiality will be maintained.
6. For risky research, say whether compensation for harm is available.
7. Indicate whom to contact for answers to questions about the research and subjects' rights or in case of research-related injury.
8. Indicate that participation is voluntary, refusal to participate will involve no penalty or loss of benefits to which subjects are otherwise entitled, and subjects may discontinue participation at any time.

Appendix 8.3

Research Project Description

Eating disorders (e.g., cravings and aversions) have been observed among psychiatric patients receiving lithium treatment. You are a research psychologist at a Veterans Administration hospital and you propose that acuity for detecting and recognizing the four basic tastes (sweet, sour, salt, and bitter) be measured and preferences be determined among patients undergoing lithium therapy and matched control participants. You wish to test the hypothesis that lithium-medicated subjects have altered taste perception thresholds and taste preferences. The substances will consist of pure water and small concentrations of the following substances diluted in water: sucrose (sweet), salt, citric acid (sour), and quinine sulfate (bitter). These substances normally are used as food additives at higher levels of concentration. Three small samples will be presented simultaneously, two identical and one different, with the position varied so that odd and identical samples will be tried equally. Paired comparisons and a hedonic rating scale will be used to measure taste preference. Data acquired through taste testing will be analyzed in relation to age, sex, smoking history, duration of lithium administration, and current lithium concentration. Five 10–15 minute sessions per subject are required. Three threshold tests for each of the four test substances will be conducted on separate days. On the 5th day, preference testing will be conducted.

Appendix 8.4

Suggested Letter for Exercise 3

(Veterans Administration hospital letterhead)

Dear Patient,

We need your help in a new study on taste sensitivity and preference. The results of this study may help doctors and dietitians plant diets to improve health and may add to the understanding of taste perception.

In this study, we will find out how readily a person detects and identifies sweet, sour, salty, and bitter tastes, and what tastes they prefer. This information will be analyzed in relation to some information from patients' medical records. Persons participating in this study can expect to spend about 20 minutes on each of 5 different days. Participants will be asked to taste plain water and samples of water mixed with small amounts of some safe substances that normally are used to season food; they also will be asked to answer some questions about how the samples taste and which ones they prefer. There is no foreseeable risk or discomfort. Participants' identity and personal information will remain confidential.

Your participation is strictly voluntary. You may withdraw your participation at any time. Your decision as to whether to participate will have no effect on any benefits you may receive or wish to receive from any agency. For answers to questions pertaining to the research, research participants' rights, or in the event of a research-related injury, contact me at _____ (name, address, telephone number).

Sincerely yours,

John Doe, Research Scientist

Veterans Administration Clinic

CHAPTER 2
THE BRAIN AND SENSORY PROCESSES

The eight activities in this chapter cover topics of brain function and anatomy, such as the workings of the autonomic nervous system, cerebral lateralization, and the complex arrangement of neural networks. The functioning of the sensory systems are shown in activities demonstrating receptor adaptation in the eye, the distribution of rods and cones in the retina as they affect color perception in different parts of the visual field, genetic variations in taste that lead to some people experiencing a very different taste world, the interaction of taste and smell to produce the multitude of flavors we enjoy in eating, and the interdependent actions of our several sensory systems.

Activity 9 uses a writing activity to increase emotion and pulse rate as a dependent variable to teach students about the two components of the autonomic nervous system—the sympathetic and parasympathetic divisions. Students are also introduced to the concept of base-rate data and their importance in judging the impact of experimental interventions.

Asymmetry in the brain is the topic of Activity 10. Three demonstrations are described that illustrate cerebral lateralization. In addition, all of the demonstrations raise questions about gender differences in lateralization.

Activity 11 explores the concept of neural networking by asking students how well they know their toes and fingers. The authors write that "Most students have difficulty *not* thinking that the central nervous system constitutes a set of point-to-point wirings, believing that the brain is hardwired, functioning like a light switch—you turn on the switch and the light goes on. This belief impedes students' ability to grasp complex cortical functions such as perception, thought, and memory that result from neural pools and nodal probabilities." A set of clever demonstrations are intended to disabuse them of their point-to-point model.

Activity 12 uses a ganzfeld, a surface that produces a uniform distribution of light (via a half ping pong ball over one eye), to show how such homogenous visual fields lead to receptor adaptation and the disappearance of visual stimuli.

The distribution of rods and cones in the human retina is the principal determinant of accurate color perception in the color identification of objects. Activity 13 shows how color perception is impaired significantly when objects are presented in the periphery of the visual field.

Activity 14 draws on the research of Linda Bartoshuk on genetic variations in taste and the anatomical correlates of those variations. Students can learn whether they are supertasters, tasters, or nontasters and discover the correlation between their taste sensitivities and the anatomy of their tongue.

Continuing the theme of taste, Activity 15 shows the interaction of taste and smell. The expanding waistlines of Americans show that eating is the national pastime and taste is a critical part of the pleasure of eating. But how important is taste really? Might smell or other sensory factors be more important? The three activities described in this article seek to answer those questions.

Activity 16 consists of four demonstrations designed to illustrate how information obtained through one sensory modality shapes the experience of other sensory modalities. The article is entitled "Sensory Interdependencies," and a key message of the demonstrations is that the sensory systems work together, not independently.

9 THE AUTONOMIC NERVOUS SYSTEM

Allan L. LaVoie

The Lenfest Company, Elkins, West Virginia

This activity presents an illustration of the role the autonomic nervous system plays in emotional responding. No prior knowledge of psychology is necessary, and only minimal preparation is required. A stopwatch or timepiece with a second hand is needed. Several variations of the activity are suggested, in which the physiological response to contrasting emotional states can be examined. One demonstration and the following discussion consume one class period. This in-class activity is appropriate for classes in introductory psychology, biological psychology, and abnormal psychology. It involves all the students and works best in a class smaller than 60 students. It can, however, be used in larger classes.

CONCEPT

The autonomic nervous system (ANS) consists of two sets of nerves that have reciprocal or mutually inhibitory effects. One, the sympathetic nervous system (SNS), has variously been called the "fright, fight, or flight" system; the arousal system; or the stress system. It mobilizes resources for emergency responses such as self-defense, and its effects include increases in heart rate, blood pressure, and respiration, among others. The other set of nerves is called the parasympathetic nervous system (PNS). It works to preserve bodily resources by slowing down respiration and heart rate and reducing blood pressure. The PNS restores the body to a resting state and resumes the body's maintenance functions.

INSTRUCTIONS

A day or more before the demonstration, ask the students to write a very brief description of a situation that had made them feel very angry or fearful. These situations will not be revealed to the instructor or other students. Students should be cautioned not to choose an event that had been especially traumatic. A one-sentence description of a recent event will serve if it permits them to reexperience the event. The descriptions should be brought to class.

To begin the demonstration, have the students pair off and assign one of them to the subject role and one to the experimenter role. Show the experimenters how to take radial pulse rates on the inside of the wrist using just the fingertips to avoid a thumb echo, and give them a few minutes to practice. When all experimenters feel confident about taking the pulse, ask them to prepare a record sheet numbered 1 through 10, with two additional spaces marked 15 and 20. These correspond to the number of minutes that pass after beginning the exercise.

The first 3 minutes are called the *base rate period*; the next 3 are called the *arousal period*, during which the subjects will be writing; and the next 4 are called the *recovery period*. The last two time periods of 5 minutes each constitute the final base rate period. During each minute, the experimenter measures the subject's pulse rate for the first 30 seconds only, but he or she should write down the rate after multiplying it by 2 to create an estimate of beats per minute (BPM). Explain before beginning that you will be examining the ANS effects on heart rate. The subjects will attempt to arouse their SNS by writing a detailed essay on the event they chose earlier. They will begin writing immediately after the 3 minutes of the base rate period have elapsed. Encourage the students to write freely, assuring them that you will not be collecting the essays, and ask them to focus the essay on exactly what happened, how it made them feel, and what they did about it. At the end of the 6th minute, tell students to stop writing; some subjects get very involved and will have to be reminded. When all have stopped writing, tell them to sit quietly and relax for the next 4 minutes. The last two measures are taken 5 minutes and 10 minutes after the recovery period.

The procedure will take less time if you can coordinate everyone's activities. After explaining what the class will be doing, and the students have prepared the record sheets, begin timing. Announce when 30 seconds have expired (e.g., "Time, please multiply the pulse rate by 2 and write it down"), when 30 seconds of the 2nd minute expire ("Time, please write down the pulse rate for the second period"), and so on. When the 4th minute begins, ask subjects to begin writing. At the end of the 6th minute, have the subjects stop. The procedure for the last 4 minutes is the same as for the first 3; for the 15th and 20th minutes, you may want to set an alarm to remind the experimenters to begin recording again for 30 seconds. Make sure that all the experimenters have written down the BPM.

Next ask each pair of students to prepare a graph like the one shown at the end of this activity. The data I have plotted are the averages of a class of 25; your students will prepare individual data. Before finishing the exercise, assemble a graph based on class averages so that they will see results more closely approximating those theoretically expected. If the class is especially large you may need to collect the data sheets and provide the summary graph in a subsequent class period.

DISCUSSION   As the students examine their own graphs, I put data from a previous class on the board or display via a PowerPoint slide. I point out the drop in pulse rate during the first 3 minutes as evidence of the guinea pig effect, which is caused by the subjects' reaction to being measured. This effect always shows up. I next point out the relatively rapid rise in rate as the subjects began writing their essays. The class average is typically 4 to 6 BPM higher than the base rate, but some individuals will show rates more than 20 BPM higher. A discussion of such differences will reveal one or two subjects whose rate actually fell, an indication of an unusual response to fear or a failure to get involved with the writing task. The next period, recovery, shows a gradual decline in pulse rate as the PNS inhibits the SNS. You may note the PNS rebound, that is, the average heart rate may fall below the initial base rate as the system is returning to a resting state. Finally, the last base rate values should be very close to the values during the 3rd minute (i.e., after the guinea pig effect), showing that the system has been restored to normalcy.

This activity is very straightforward. It has been extremely reliable for me, is sensitive to the relatively slight changes produced by writing the essay, and clearly illustrates the role of the ANS in emotional response. If you are interested in doing more with this exercise, several variations are available. For example, instead of letting the subjects return to the base rate, you can attempt to force a faster return by having them write a relaxing essay (e.g., a picnic, a day at the beach) at the beginning of the 7th minute. Or you can examine the physiological response to emotions other than fear and anger by asking some subjects to write about Christmas, others about a depressing event, and so on. For more ideas, see Levinthal (1983) and McFarland (1981).

REFERENCES AND SUGGESTED READING

Bear, M. F., Connors, B., & Paradiso, M. (2006). *Neuroscience: Exploring the brain* (3rd ed.). Baltimore: Lippincott Williams & Wilkins.

Levinthal, C. F. (1983). *The physiological approach to psychology* (2nd ed.). Englewood Cliffs, NJ: Prentice-Hall.

McFarland, R. A. (1981). *Physiological psychology*. Palo Alto, CA: Mayfield.

Robertson, D. (Ed.). (2004). *Primer on the autonomic nervous system* (2nd ed.). San Diego, CA: Elsevier.

Rosenzweig, M. R., Breedlove, S. M., & Watson, N. V. (2005). *Biological psychology: An introduction to behavioral and cognitive neuroscience* (4th ed.). Sunderland, MA: Sinauer Associates.

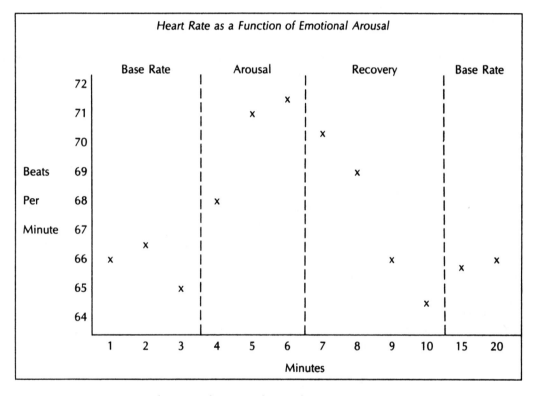

Figure 9.1.   Heart rate as a function of emotional arousal.

10 CEREBRAL LATERALIZATION

Ernest D. Kemble

University of Minnesota, Morris

This activity actually contains three separate exercises that examine different aspects of cerebral lateralization. All have been used in a course in research methods in psychology (enrollment = 35–45 students) but would be appropriate for introductory psychology courses as well. Exercise 1 uses the students as both experimental subjects/testers and would be appropriate for much higher enrollments (enrollment > 150 or more), whereas Exercises 2 and 3, appropriate for classes of 35 to 45, involve individual testing and require trained teaching assistants as experimenters. They all raise questions about gender differences in lateralization. Because the three activities might yield different conclusions about cerebral lateralization, this series would also be appropriate in a discussion of research methodology as well as biopsychology. No prior knowledge of psychology is necessary. Constructing the materials needed does not require a great deal of specialized skill or expertise. All three exercises are in-class activities.

CONCEPT

Articles describing research on commissurotomized ("split brain") patients and cerebral lateralization in normal subjects is an extremely popular subject among beginning students and is prominently featured in most introductory psychology texts. The following three exercises are all simple experiments requiring only inexpensive and readily available equipment and can be quickly completed in the classroom.

**EXERCISE 1:
VERBAL
INTERFERENCE
WITH A MANUAL
TASK**

Materials Needed

You will need one wooden dowel stick (approximately 1.25 cm in diameter and 92 cm long) for every two students, a stopwatch, and a list of 80 to 100 spelling problems (e.g., repeat the alphabet backwards, spell Mississippi backwards, and so on).

Instructions

The students are divided into pairs: one to serve as experimenter and the other as subject. The roles should be reversed on the second trial. The gender of each subject should be recorded. Allow the students to practice balancing the dowel stick vertically on the tip of the index finger for 5 minutes, alternating right and left hands. The students then receive eight test trials (right hand = 4, left hand = 4). On each trial the student positions the dowel stick on the tip of the right or left index finger using the other hand. On command the supporting hand is removed and the stopwatch started. The stopwatch is stopped when the dowel drops or touches any part of the student's body. On half of the trials with each hand, the trial is conducted in silence; on the remaining trials, the student is required to solve spelling tasks aloud. The order in which the right and left hands are tested and the order of the tasks should be systematically varied among students.

DISCUSSION

This activity is one example of a "competition task." When the student is solving a spelling problem a great deal of activity is required of the left hemisphere which also controls language in most people. Because the left hemisphere is also primarily responsible for control of the right hand, the spelling problem "competes" with the hemisphere's ability to balance the dowel and should decrease the time that a student can balance it. The right hemisphere, which controls the left hand, is thought to have only a minor role in language and should "compete" less with balancing. The data should be summarized separately for male and female students. Does the spelling task interfere more with right-hand balancing than with left-hand balancing, as expected? Is this effect found in both males and females? Because gender differences in this task are frequently found, this may also elicit discussion about possible gender differences in the organization of the human brain and how such differences might arise.

EXERCISE 2: TACTILE LETTER AND NUMBER IDENTIFICATION

Materials Needed

To conduct this exercise you will need a plywood or cardboard container (approximately $20 \times 45 \times 20$ cm) open at each end with a cloth curtain suspended over one end extending to the apparatus floor. A cue card depicting all stimuli should be placed on the apparatus at the curtained end facing the subject. Eighteen children's wooden alphabet blocks consisting of nine single letters and nine single digits are the stimuli. Choose blocks with sharp outlines of letters and digits or sharpen the outlines yourself with a small electric drill. Any raised borders on the blocks should be removed. Latencies are timed by a stopwatch.

Instructions

Subjects are seated at the curtained end of the apparatus with the experimenter opposite. Gender of each subject should be recorded. Each subject should be given at least eight practice trials alternating hands, letters, and digits. On each trial a single block is randomly selected and placed in the apparatus floor and the subjects told whether it is a letter or digit. The subject is then instructed to insert the right or left hand through the curtain, *lightly* trace the outlines of the stimulus and identify it (multiple guesses are permitted). The interval between touching and its correct identification is timed by stopwatch. The subject receives six letter and six digit trials with each hand. The order in which hands, letters, and digits are tested should be systematically varied across subjects. Mean identification latencies for digits and letters are calculated for each hand at the conclusion of testing.

DISCUSSION

Light touch projects predominantly (approximately 95%) to the contralateral hemisphere. If tactile information about letters must travel to hemisphere mechanisms for recognition and encoding as a verbal response, then the right hand should be superior in the identification of letters because it projects predominantly to the left hemisphere. In contrast, no hand difference would be expected in digit identification. When we conducted this experiment, we found that females were superior in letter identification with the right hand but showed no hand difference in identification of digits. Males, in contrast, showed no hand differences on either letters or digits. Because most behavioral measures (including Exercise 1) suggest that males are more lateralized than females, results such as these raise interesting questions about the of various measures of laterality in normal subjects. Which measure of laterality are we to believe? What cautions do such findings suggest about the study of cerebral lateralization in normal populations?

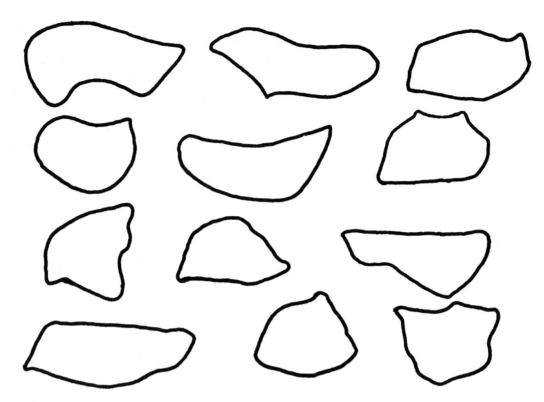

Figure 10.1.   Examples of sample stimuli.

EXERCISE 3:
DICHAPTIC
IDENTIFICATION
OF ABSTRACT
GEOMETRIC
SHAPES

Materials Needed

Tactile identification of abstract geometric shapes is carried out in a cardboard box (approximately 34 × 38 × 30 cm) divided into compartments for the right and left hands by a partition placed in the middle of the apparatus. The front wall of the apparatus contains two 10 × 10 cm openings covered by a hanging cloth curtain; the rear wall is open. The stimuli are 12 abstract geometric shapes cut from a Plexiglas sheet with a jigsaw. The sizes and shapes of sample stimuli are shown in Figure 10.1.

Instructions

Gender of each subject is recorded, and then they are instructed to insert the left and right hand through the openings in the box simultaneously. The experimenter randomly selects one of the 12 stimuli and places it in the subject's right hand (order of testing is reversed on each subsequent trial). The student feels the outlines of the stimuli for 10 seconds. The stimulus is removed, the student shown a key containing outlines of the 12 stimuli (e.g., a printed copy of Figure 10.1), the stopwatch started, and the subject is asked to identify the felt stimulus. The latency and correctness of the response are recorded. Each student receives four trials.

DISCUSSION

Because abstract geometric functions are thought to be mediated primarily by the right hemisphere, the left hand would be expected to be superior in the identification of abstract geometric forms. An early experiment by Witelson (1976) using right-handed children (ages 6–13) found the expected left-hand superiority in boys but no hand difference in girls. When we conducted this experiment, primarily with adult females, we found a significant right-hand superiority in females. These results contrast with Witelson's in two important ways: the right hand, not the left, was superior, and the laterality effect was found in females rather than males. Are the differences between the two studies a result of the age of the subjects? If so, does it suggest that functions can shift from one hemisphere to the other as a person grows older? In contrast, is it possible that the differences between children and adults on this task are a result of gender differences in previous tactile or manipulatory experience? Results such as those provided by these three exercises contradict any simplistic division of functions between the cerebral hemispheres and underscore the importance of methodological and experimental variables in understanding cerebral specialization of function.

REFERENCES AND SUGGESTED READING

Corballis, M. C., & Beale, I. L. (1983). *The ambivalent mind: The neuropsychology of left and right.* Chicago: Nelson-Hall.

Gazzaniga, M. S. (1970). *The bissected brain.* New York: Appleton-Century-Crofts.

Johnson, O., & Kozma, A. (1977). Effects of concurrent verbal and musical tasks on a unimanual skill. *Cortex, 13,* 11–16.

Kinsbourne, M., & Cook, J. (1971). Generalized and lateralized effects of concurrent verbalization on a unimanual skill. *Quarterly Journal of Experimental Psychology, 23,* 341–345.

Kolb, B., & Wishaw, I. Q. (2003). *Fundamentals of human neuropsychology* (5th ed.). New York: W. H. Freeman.

Springer, S., & Deutsch, G. (1998). *Left brain, right brain: Perspectives from cognitive neuroscience* (5th ed.). New York: W. H. Freeman.

Witelson, S. F. (1976). Sex and the single hemisphere: Specialization of the right hemisphere for spatial processing. *Science, 193,* 425–427.

11 Observing Neural Networking in Vivo

Philip Schatz
Saint Joseph's University

Anthony C. Ruocco

John Medaglia

Douglas L. Chute
Drexel University

This activity, which requires little preparation and materials, challenges students' belief that the central nervous system constitutes a set of point-to-point wirings. By touching a student's toes (while he or she is blindfolded), you can demonstrate that neural interactions are not hard-wired, and that perception is not directly mapped to sensation. This activity is appropriate for classes in introductory psychology, sensation and perception, cognitive psychology, and behavioral neuroscience, and is also suitable for distance learning classes. It can be demonstrated to a class of any size using a single student in class, and assigned to the rest of the students for an independent data collection exercise out of class. The activity requires 15 to 30 minutes, depending on discussion time.

CONCEPT
Most students have difficulty *not* thinking that the central nervous system constitutes a set of point-to-point wirings. In other words, they think that the brain has hard-wired functioning like a light switch—you turn on the switch and the light goes on. This belief impedes students' ability to grasp complex cortical functions such as perception, thought, and memory that result from neural pools and nodal probabilities.

Historically, Weir Mitchell first outlined this concept in an 1864 manuscript. Looking at the somatosensory ability to localize sensory stimuli applied to various parts of the body, he noted that some parts were better able to localize than others (such as the big toe as compared with the third or fourth toe). Mitchell wrote:

> In this connection, it is well to state a very singular instance of defective power to localize a touch—an instance so frequent, that its repetition on many occasions induced us to observe it with care; and finally to conclude that it was a normal defect, or at least that it exists in a considerable proportion of sound persons. . . . Let the observer, to test the matter, touch in succession the toes of a man whose eyes are covered. When he comes to the third and fourth toes, counting the great toe as the first, he will find in many cases that the man will mistake the third for the fourth, or the fourth for the third; or perhaps even the fourth for the fifth or little toe. (Mitchell, 1864; cited in Louis & York, 2006, p. 1242)

In fact, repeated direct electrical stimulation of the motor or sensory cortex yields *similar* but not *identical* antecedent movement or sensations. Neurons in the cortex participate in large probabilistic pools, and thus a single neuron does not always produce the same outcome—in other words the brain is not absolutely hard-wired. This probabilistic notion regarding cortical connections is the underpinning for many psychological studies in cognition and neuroscience, ranging from computer models of artificial intelligence to recovery of function following brain trauma. It is "human nature," however, to be quite certain of the truth of our sensation and the consistency of our thoughts. Thus, in the absence of simple experiential evidence, it is difficult to understand that neuronal interactions do not always lead to a predictable and certain outcome. For example, if someone were to touch your second, third, or fourth finger without your being able to see, you would normally tell with 100% certainty which was being touched. As the same is not true of your toes, the challenge for students is to think of reasons why.

MATERIALS NEEDED   You will need bare toes and a blindfold (or a trustworthy participant). A ballpoint pen makes a good stylus and allows the operationalization of a touch by leaving a mark on the pad of the toe. Use the same pen to keep score on a sheet of paper that has been set up according to various experimental parameters that can be investigated. A spreadsheet or data analysis program (e.g., Excel or SPSS) might be useful if you intend to use a complete research protocol beyond the simple demonstration level we typically use in introductory psychology teaching. May we suggest that the first time you try this, get a friend, colleague, or significant other to be a guinea pig before you do it in class.

INSTRUCTIONS   As a simple lecture demonstration, describe the experiment (this is a good time to mention informed consent and related ethical issues), ask for a volunteer, and seat him or her comfortably at the front of the class. The procedure allows many opportunities for a little light humor. (As a cautionary note, some Asian subcontinent cultures consider the foot an erogenous zone.) Have the participant take off his or her shoe and sock and put on the blindfold. Students in the front row can keep a record of which toe was touched and the accuracy of the report. Only touch the second, third, or fourth toes (counting from the big toe out). Touch them gently with the tip of a stylus or pen, not sufficient to move the toe but enough to make a mark or depress the skin. Pause briefly between each touch. (In the classroom demonstration we do not provide any immediate feedback as this leads to very rapid learning.) Participants will be surprised that their accuracy is typically only 80 to 90%. (For the purposes of demonstration you can decrease accuracy by touching slightly to the left or right of midline on each toe, deviating from random by perseverating on errors, touching medial aspects of the second and fourth toes, and so forth.

One might desire to decrease accuracy so that the demonstration is seen to work, but we think it is better for students to see acceptable scientific procedures. With practice and feedback over trials, accuracy will improve. If the first or fifth toe is touched, these references will greatly increase accuracy as well. This presumably happens because these toes experience discrete and regular tactile stimulation, even with shoes. An empirical question that can serve as a variation or assignment is to determine how much the touching the first or fifth can affect overall errors. However, for class demonstrations in introductory psychology we only touch the second, third, and fourth toes. At the end of the demonstration, so that the participant also believes what the rest of the class has clearly seen, we wait until the participant makes an error and, keeping the stylus in place, ask him or her to remove the blindfold and witness the result personally.

VARIATIONS   The experiment is most often performed by touching the middle three toes on each foot briefly with a pen tip or similar instrument. However, the toe-touching demonstration can easily be adapted and applied to experimental methodologies, with the percentage correct serving as the dependent measure, and assigned manipulations serving as the independent variable. Students can test effects of laterality, gender, age, adaptation over time, and sensitivity differences among sandal-wearing versus sneaker-wearing peers.

More pressure can be applied to each toe or the touch can be maintained longer. The first and fifth toe may also be included in trials. Verbal or visual feedback may also be given for responses to indicate to subjects whether they were correct or not in the previous trial.

Using a within-subjects design, students could plot learning and forgetting curves to further reinforce notions of neuroplastic phenomena. The big toe and the small toe have different enervation than the middle toes. Their performance is typically much better. A lengthy, carefully planned study can use errors to detect the dermatome boundaries. In the References and Suggested Reading section, we have included sample Web sites for enervation of the foot and dermatome regions.

DATA COLLECTION

As a take-home research experiment, all class members can collect data for group averages. We would typically deal with such data in a recitation or lab section, but this technique also can be used in lecture. By calculating a mean and standard deviation as a class norm, you can then determine a z score for any individual's percentage correct. This anticipates core concepts in psychometrics and individual differences and reinforces the key notion of probability in neural function. The basic phenomenon of localization of sign in toe touching can also be used in more advanced research protocols. Experiential data show that rate of learning is such that performance following feedback reaches asymptote at about 98% correct after as few as 10 trials.

In the event that you choose to turn this into a group exercise and have students run basic analyses on the data, it is best that students collect their own data on a spreadsheet, which can then be entered into a master database to be accessed by all students, perhaps posted online or sent via e-mail (see Table 11.1).

In our experience, it is generally easiest for students to singly touch each of the three middle toes in a predetermined order, once for each foot, and then repeat this procedure either three or six times, counterbalancing as appropriate. Students often will arrive at this design collectively when they are allowed to do so, though sometimes they may be distracted by hypotheses that stray from the intended purpose of the exercise. Data are often recorded simply as positives (hits) and anything other than a true positive (misses). The experiment can be counterbalanced over three or six trials. To demonstrate the effect of feedback, students may design the experiment to include more trials, and should make this distinction as they record data. Depending on the course level, you may want to include further data such as gender, handedness, age, and so on. We have found from time to time that students may be particularly ambitious in pursuing hypotheses about lateralization, so it may be advisable to guide them toward only a without/with feedback design for introductory purposes unless alternative hypotheses are acceptable.

Table 11.1. *A Model for Student Data Collection*

Trial	Right Foot			Left Foot		
Feedback: N Y	Second Toe	Third Toe	Fourth Toe	Second Toe	Third Toe	Fourth Toe
1(2,3,4)	X	X	X	O	O	X
2(3,2,4)	X	O	X	X	X	O
3(4,3,2)	O	O	O	O	X	X

Note. An "O" denotes an improper toe identification and an "X" denotes a proper toe identification. See Appendix 11.1 for data collection tables.

Analysis

Data can be collected and analyzed according to independent variables of interest (e.g., gender, handedness, shoes worn). Instructors should either set parameters for data analysis based on the purpose of the exercise or allow students to decide among themselves what analyses should be conducted.

Sample data collection forms and data tables are included in Appendix 11.1.

DISCUSSION   Students have a natural inclination to use metaphors for understanding the central nervous system and its organization that rely on the notions of electrical wiring between centers of function—a type of "conceptual phrenology" that is only partially informed by research data. Most students understand the implications of the toe-touching demonstration, and we solidify the discussion by referring to central concepts in the neurosciences, such as plasticity, neural networks, development, memory, motor action schemas, and rehabilitation. On occasion, you may have a student who denies the data and maintains a very concrete view. We normally recommend that such students conduct the experiment themselves with a friend or relative and report back (knowledge of the phenomenon does not effect results). If this empirical approach for a doubting student is not convenient, you might want to come prepared with a file card (where a dot and cross are marked) suitable for illustrating the blind spot or a visual presentation that creates an after-image (often an American flag). These demonstrations illustrate that we do not normally notice what is interpreted as perception in the absence of any neural wiring (blind spot) and that we can perceive information in the complete absence of visual stimulation (after-image).

Toe touching activates sensory neurons, but their integration and interpretation require experience and the support of higher cognitive functions. In fact, the process of identifying which toe is being touched selectively activates the brain's frontal lobes (Persinger, Webster, & Tiller, 1998), an area of the brain associated with complex cognitive functions. However, many areas of the brain are likely to be involved in toe identification. For example, Gerstmann syndrome is a neurological disorder for which a primary symptom is the complete inability to recognize which finger is being touched (known as *finger agnosia*). The syndrome is often associated with damage to a specific region of the brain (near the temporal and parietal lobe junction), and some people with this syndrome are also unable to recognize which toe is being touched (called *toe agnosia*). Further, the ability to recognize which toe is being touched is one of the strongest indicators of brain dysfunction in people with head trauma (Richards & Persinger, 1992). Thus, the toe-touching phenomenon shows that the nervous system does not come with sensory relationships prewired but that these relationships can be learned and forgotten, and sometimes (but not always) affected by damage to various regions of the brain. If nothing else, this phenomenon provides a justification for attempting rehabilitation following neurotrauma, an important field in which psychologists work.

Related Phenomena

A conceptually similar phenomenon that most students will spontaneously recall derives from two children's games. In the first, the individuals cross their arms in front of them, the palms clasped with fingers interlaced in either left-over-right or right-over-left order. Most people report one way of interlacing is more comfortable, and this can provide another potential variable for investigation.

The interlocked arms are then rotated in toward the body. The experimenter then indicates a finger to be moved by pointing to it (without touching it). Most subjects will report an increased latency to respond and sometimes make errors by moving the finger from the wrong hand. Requiring a rapid succession of movements for a number of fingers randomly across hands usually results in more errors. If the experimenter actually touches the individual's fingers, there are seldom errors in movement.

In the second "game" one individual closes their eyes and extends their arm (short sleeves or rolled-up sleeves to the biceps) and a second individual uses a stylus (pen, pencil, key) to move up and down the arm, slowly, from the wrist, until the first individual identifies the location at the exact bend of the elbow. As with the toe-touching experiment, afferent stimuli from a rather large portion of the inner elbow are "mapped" to the same spot, causing the perception that one's inner elbow is being stimulated when the stylus is, in fact, 1 inch away.

In these examples, the students should be thinking more about cognitive maps or body schema that are being disoriented in their visual-motor mode by the contortion, but not, of course, in their somatosensory-motor mode. Even persons experiencing mild concussions note that disturbances in such schema result in left-right confusion. For example, in a mental status examination (say on the bench of a football game), it is typical to ask a concussed athlete their name, the time, and where they are, as well as the individual's left and right orientation with regard to themselves and another person. Errors of perception and action seen in more serious neuropsychological situations (i.e., dementia) are conceptually similar to the sensory and motor phenomena illustrated.

This toe-touching phenomenon seems tangible to students, as it is possible at their level to make unique empirical observations, in this case derived from thinking about children's games.

REFERENCES AND SUGGESTED READING

Chute, D. L. (1968). *Localization of sign in toe touching.* Undergraduate paper presented in Sensation and Perception. University of Western Ontario.

Louis, E. D., & York, G. K. (2006). Weir Mitchell's observations on sensory localization and their influence on Jacksonian neurology. *Neurology, 66,* 1241–1244.

Mitchell, S. W., Morehouse, G. R., & Keen, W. W. (1864). *Gunshot wounds and other injuries of nerves.* Philadelphia: JB Lippincott.

Persinger, M. A., Webster, D., & Tiller, S. G. (1998). SPECT (HMPAO) support for activation of the medial prefrontal cortices during toe graphaesthesia. *Perceptual and Motor Skills, 87,* 59–63.

Richards, P., & Persinger, M. A. (1992). Toe graphaesthesia as a discriminator of brain impairment: The outstanding feet for neuropsychology. *Perceptual and Motor Skills, 74,* 1027–1030.

Tucha, O., Steup, A., Smely, C., & Lange, K. W. (1997). Toe agnosia in Gerstmann syndrome. *Journal of Neurology, Neurosurgery, and Psychiatry, 63,* 399–403.

Students may consult the following Web sites for more information:

Anatomy of the foot
http://www.foottrainer.com/foot/
Neuroanatomy of the foot
http://en.wikipedia.org/wiki/Plantar_nerve

Appendix 11.1

Instructions for using these tables: Students should circle "Y" (yes) or "N" (no) to indicate whether the trials were performed with feedback as to the correctness of the response. The numbers in parentheses indicate the order in which the toes are to be touched in each trial (i.e., the second toe is adjacent to the big toe, and so on). For example, the order for Trial 1 would be the second, third, and fourth toes.

Table 11.2.   *Use for three trials per toe*

Trial	Right Foot			Left Foot		
Feedback: Y N	Second Toe	Third Toe	Fourth Toe	Second Toe	Third Toe	Fourth Toe
1(2,3,4)						
2(3,2,4)						
3(4,3,2)						

Table 11.3.   *Use for six trials per toe*

Trial	Right Foot Test #			Left Foot Test #		
Feedback: Y N	Second Toe	Third Toe	Fourth Toe	Second Toe	Third Toe	Fourth Toe
1(2,3,4)						
2(3,2,4)						
3(4,3,2)						
4(2,4,3)						
5(3,4,2)						
6(4,2,3)						

Table 11.4.   *Actual data for over 10 trials for a class of 14 students*

Right			Left Foot		
Second Toe	Third Toe	Fourth Toe	Second Toe	Third Toe	Fourth Toe
79%	69%	70%	84%	75%	74%

On the basis of these data, there is overall approximately 75% accuracy when feedback was not provided. This performance rate remains stable over trials until feedback is given. These results may be higher or lower depending upon variations in experimentation (i.e., more/less pressure applied to each toe).

12 AND THEN THE LIGHTS WENT OUT: CONSTRUCTING A SIMPLE GANZFELD

Cathy A. Grover
Emporia State University

Stephen F. Davis
Morningside College

This in-class activity is appropriate for introductory psychology classes or classes in perception or cognition. Materials are readily available, but you will need to do some advance preparation. Student participation is limited by the number of red light-emitting diodes (LEDs) that are available and the number of ping-pong balls that you have. Each student experiences the phenomenon individually, requiring no more than 1 or 2 minutes for the demonstration.

CONCEPT

It is an easy matter to tell your students that their sensory systems require varied stimulation to maintain the figure–ground relation and to prevent receptor adaptation. However, the ability to make this point in a very convincing manner may prove to be more difficult. In this activity, we introduce the concept of the *Ganzfeld* (a surface that provides a uniform distribution of light energy) to demonstrate this phenomenon. Because the homogeneous viewing surface of the Ganzfeld prevents varied sensory stimulation, you can expect rapid receptor adaptation. To demonstrate this effect, we use the following activity that uses a modification of the procedure originally described by Hochberg, Triebel, and Seaman (1951).

MATERIALS NEEDED

You can construct a simple Ganzfeld with an ordinary ping-pong ball. Using a razor blade, cut the ping-pong ball in half along the seam. Discard the half that bears the manufacturer's stamp. To protect the student's eye, glue cotton around the outer rim of the remaining half. The construction of your homemade Ganzfeld is complete. To demonstrate receptor adaptation, you also will need access to a lighted *red* LED, such as you might find on items like a coffeemaker or cell phone, and so forth.

INSTRUCTIONS

Have your student(s) put the Ganzfeld over one eye. They should keep the covered eye open. Next they position the Ganzfeld so that it touches the red LED (i.e., the red glow should be visible through the ping-pong ball). Instruct the student to close the other eye, stare at the red light, and report anything that happens. Within a minute, the student should report that you have turned off the red light! Receptor adaptation, which causes the light to disappear as a result of the homogenous viewing surface of the Ganzfeld, has created this false impression. Have the student remove the Ganzfeld to see that this is not the case. To facilitate subsequent class discussion and understanding, have as many students as possible participate in the demonstration. You may wish to see additional references on the Ganzfeld (Cohen, 1957, 1958a, 1958b), which can help you create additional activities to use with your homemade Ganzfeld.

Although the Ganzfeld was first described in psychology as a way to create a contourless homogeneous visual field to study how vision was affected by such a cueless environment, the technique has been used in recent years in studies of extrasensory perception (ESP), especially mental telepathy. The research in this area is controversial, leading many psychologists to doubt that its use has produced convincing evidence of the existence of ESP. See Milton and Wiseman (1999), Milton and Wiseman (2001), and Storm and Ertel (2001).

REFERENCES AND SUGGESTED READING

Cohen, W. (1957). Spatial and textual characteristics of the Ganzfeld. *American Journal of Psychology, 70,* 403–410.

Cohen, W. (1958a). Apparent movement of figures in the Ganzfeld. *Perceptual and Motor Skills, 8,* 32.

Cohen, W. (1958b). Color perception in the chromatic Ganzfeld. *American Journal of Psychology, 71,* 390–394.

Hochberg, J. E., Triebel, W., & Seaman, G. (1951). Color adaptation under conditions of homogenous visual stimulation (Ganzfeld). *Journal of Experimental Psychology, 41,* 153–159.

Milton, J., & Wiseman, R. (1999). Does psi exist? Lack of replication of an anomalous process of information transfer. *Psychological Bulletin, 125,* 378–391.

Milton, J., & Wiseman, R. (2001). Does psi exist? Reply to Storm and Ertel (2001). *Psychological Bulletin, 127,* 434–438.

Storm, L., & Ertel, S. (2001). Does psi exist? Comments on Milton and Wiseman's (1999) meta-analysis of Ganzfeld research. *Psychological Bulletin, 127,* 424–433.

13 DISTRIBUTION OF RODS, CONES, AND COLOR VISION IN THE RETINA

Charles T. Blair-Broeker
Cedar Falls High School, Iowa

Douglas A. Bernstein
University of South Florida and University of Southampton

This simple activity illustrates the distribution of rods and cones in the retina, as well as the differing ability of these photoreceptors to detect color. It can be used in classes in introductory psychology, sensation/perception, or cognition. This in-class activity takes as little as 10 minutes and can be done in any size class. It is a demonstration involving a single student but could involve greater numbers with additional time and additional materials.

CONCEPT

The demonstration shows that stimuli in the center of the visual field are detected mainly by color-sensitive cones concentrated in the fovea, whereas stimuli at the edges of the visual field are detected mainly by non–color-sensitive rods in the periphery of the retina.

MATERIALS NEEDED

You will need a few pens, magic markers, or other objects of various colors (e.g., red, blue, green, yellow, and black) and a student volunteer with normal color vision.

INSTRUCTIONS

Ask your volunteer to sit or stand at the front of the room, facing the class, and at your signal, to stare fixedly ahead at a spot or object at the back of the room. If the participant's eyes stray from the fixation point, the demonstration will probably not work very well. Emphasize the need for concentrated fixation. Instruct the class not to provide any feedback to the volunteer regarding the accuracy of his or her answers.

Now stand at the volunteer's side. Hold one of the colored objects 3 or 4 feet away from the volunteer's ear, at about eye level. (Keep the object concealed prior to this time.) Ask the volunteer to identify the color of the object in your hand. The volunteer is not likely to be able to do this. If the volunteer answers, you can determine the level of confidence by asking how much he or she would be willing to bet on the correctness of the answer. Move a step toward the class and slightly more in front of the volunteer (imagine you are moving on an arcing track that would eventually place you directly in front of the volunteer), and ask the same question. Continue to move, one small step at a time, along the arc until the volunteer is certain of the object's color. You may want to pause before each step, briefly conceal the object, and give the volunteer a chance to relax the eyes. Make sure the volunteer is staring at the fixation point again before proceeding.

DISCUSSION

You will find that most participants have excellent peripheral vision, as reflected in their ability to recognize that the object is present even when it is far off to the side. However, for most people, it will take several small steps before they can recognize the object's color (most will first say it is black, because they are seeing it only with rods). The students will be surprised at how close to the center of the visual field the object must be before its color is clearly apparent. In real life, we perceive color in the periphery of the visual field because the brain remembers what color belongs there or makes an assumption about the likely color (e.g., the sky is usually blue). In this demonstration, however, there is no way for the brain to accurately guess the color of the object.

If the expected sequence of results does not occur, it is probably because the participant lost fixation or made a lucky guess about color. To confirm the distribution of rods and cones, and their color sensitivity, you can run more trials using different colors.

You can make this demonstration an active learning experience by asking students to predict the results of the procedure and to justify their predictions on the basis of material presented in class or in the textbook. Another option is to divide the class into teams of three and have them conduct the procedure, perhaps using objects of different sizes and colors, held at differing distances. Team members can take turns acting as volunteer, experimenter, and data recorder (whose job is to note the point on each trial where the object is first detected, correctly named, and its color identified). Afterward, teams can be asked to report their results to the class, including the effect of object size and distance and to suggest plausible explanations for discrepant data (e.g., individual differences in retinal anatomy, restricted peripheral vision, or loss of fixation during a trial).

REFERENCES AND SUGGESTED READING

Bernstein, D. A., Penner, L. A., Clarke-Stewart, A., & Roy, E. J. (2008). *Psychology* (8th ed.). Boston: Houghton Mifflin.

Goldstein, E. B. (2007). *Sensation and perception* (7th ed.). Belmont, CA: Thomson Wadsworth.

Mollon, J. D., Pokorny, J., & Knoblauch, K. (2003). *Normal and defective colour vision.* New York: Oxford University Press.

Wolfe, J. M., Kluender, K. R., Levi, D. M., Bartoshuk, L. M., Herz, R. S., Klatzky, R. L., & Lederman, S. J. (2006). *Sensation and perception.* Sunderland, MA: Sinauer Associates.

14 How Blue Are You? The World of Taste Variations

Margaret Davidson

L. V. Berkner High School, Richardson, Texas

The two parts of this activity are based on the work of Linda M. Bartoshuk and her colleagues. The purpose of these demonstrations is to identify individuals as supertasters, tasters, and nontasters and to illustrate an anatomical correlate of these genetic taste variations. The first part of the activity is a simple yet effective demonstration to visually identify and count the fungiform papillae on the tongue. Multiple participants provide the opportunity to view the variations in the distribution of these specialized structures. The second part of the activity is a dramatic follow-up demonstration to identify variations in taste experience through the presentation of a taste sample and the relation of those taste experiences to the density of the fungiform papillae on the tongue. Discussion leads students to an understanding of the differing worlds of taste. These activities are appropriate for the introductory psychology classroom of any size, as well as courses in perception or cognition. The in-class activities, both Part 1 and Part 2 can be completed in 15 minutes. The second part of the activity can be done in any size class; the first part can be done in larger classes but requires multiple sets of testing materials.

PART 1: CONCEPT

The purpose of this demonstration is to view the fungiform papillae, where taste buds are located, by painting the anterior tongue and observing the distribution of these papillae on individuals in the demonstration group. By using many volunteers in this demonstration, students can detect the variations in the density of taste receptors, which correlate with genetic differences in taste.

PART 1: MATERIALS NEEDED

Materials needed for this demonstration include a magnifying glass, flashlight, cotton swabs, blue food coloring, and wax paper (cut in a 1-in. square with a standard hole punch in the center of the paper) to be used as a viewing template. An alternate template for viewing would be a standard reinforcement (adhesive ring) used for notebook paper.

PART 1: INSTRUCTIONS

Initial observation will reveal varying bumps on the tongue. The most numerous of these are filiform papillae, which have no taste function. This demonstration is intended to make apparent the fungiform papillae that (under a microscope) look like tiny button mushrooms. These fungiform papillae contain the taste pores that are conduits to the taste buds that are themselves too small to be seen without a microscope. (Dr. Bartoshuk's analogy of size is that if the fungiform papillae are the size of a hamburger bun, the taste pore would be the size of a sesame seed.) To view the fungiform papillae, swab the tip of the tongue with a cotton swab dipped in a small quantity of blue food coloring. Inform participants that food coloring is not harmful to consume. The painting of the tongue should include the tip and about 1-inch back in the direction of the throat. Participants should close their mouths, then move their tongues around and swallow to distribute the blue dye. When the protruding tongue is inspected with a flashlight, magnifying glass, and viewing template, pink circles (small dots) will emerge from the blue background. These are the fungiform papillae, which appear pink because they do not stain as well as the more numerous filiform papillae (Bartoshuk, Duffy, & Miller, 1994). Students can view the painted tongue through the wax paper template placed at the tip of the tongue and directly to the right of the midline (see Figure 14.1). Using the standard size of viewing template to ensure that comparisons can be made, students can count and record the number of bumps on the tongue. The cotton swab and the wax paper template should be discarded after each participant has finished using them.

PART 2:
CONCEPT

This part of the activity is designed as a companion classroom demonstration to tongue painting as a means of classifying participants as supertasters, tasters, and nontasters. This demonstration is also modeled after the work of Linda M. Bartoshuk (Bartoshuk et al., 1994). Volunteer students will be asked to taste a piece of paper soaked in a solution of 6-n-propylthiouracil (PROP). Scaling of 6-n-propylthiouracil (bitterness) perception will lead to the identification of subsets of tasters who rate the taste from intensely bitter (supertasters), very strong to moderately bitter (tasters), to weak or barely detectable (nontasters).

PART 2:
MATERIALS
NEEDED

For this activity you will need PROP papers (see the following production directions) and copies of the modified Green scale for participant response notation and for classification of the taster (see Figures 14.2 and 14.3 in Appendix 14.1).

To produce PROP taste papers, use a pan to heat 500 ml water to near boiling. Dissolve 5 g PROP in heated water to make a saturated solution. Dip pieces of filter paper, such as coffee filters, in the PROP solution until they are completely soaked. The PROP crystallizes into the filter paper and allows a method of sanitary delivery of PROP crystals to the participant. Allow the sheets to dry on sheets of aluminum foil or by hanging sheets on a line in a previously prepared sanitary location. When dry, cut filter papers into 1-inch squares. Papers should be stored in a sanitary manner. (These instructions for PROP paper preparation were provided by Linda M. Bartoshuk, personal communication, October 1997.)

PROP is a medication used to treat Grave's disease (hyperthyroidism). An individual taking this medication for Grave's disease would be prescribed three to four tablets daily of 50 mg each. Those participating in this demonstration receive approximately 1.2 mg PROP (Linda M. Bartoshuk, personal communication, October 1997). A source of United States Pharmacopeia grade PROP is Spectrum, 14422 S. San Pedro Street, Gardena, CA 90248, phone (310) 516-8000. Their East Coast plant is located at 755 Jersey Ave., New Brunswick, NJ 08901, phone (732) 214-1300. Note that the warning labels accompanying this drug can be scary. For legal reasons the labels constitute "overwarning" (Linda Bartoshuk, personal communication, May 30, 2007). At the dosage levels used in this exercise, the concentration is so low that the drug is pharmacologically inactive.

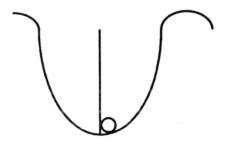

Figure 14.1. Template placement sketch.

Each participant should place a piece of PROP paper on her or his tongue. Participants may chew the paper if they wish. They should keep the paper in their mouths until the taste reaches maximum bitterness (for those who experience the bitter taste). After self-evaluation, participants should dispose of the PROP paper in an available receptacle. PROP papers should not be consumed (even though there is nothing harmful about the PROP papers).

Using the modified Green scale identified for participant use (see Figure 14.2), participants should rank their judgment of bitterness response on the vertical line at a defining point (Green, Shaffer, & Gilmore, 1993). The ratings can be converted to magnitude estimation on the scale identified for conversion to ratio properties (see Figure 14.3). Individuals can be identified as nontasters, tasters, and supertasters in terms of the ability to taste the PROP paper. This ability correlates with the number of fungiform papillae on the tongue as previously identified by tongue painting. Participants rating the PROP paper as less bitter ("What taste?") than moderate ("This is bitter.") are probably nontasters. Tasters indicate the bitterness perception as moderate to very strong ("This is bitter to very bitter."). Supertasters rate PROP paper as *extremely* bitter ("The worst possible taste!") (Bartoshuk et al., 1994). Note that this activity is for demonstration purposes only; scientifically accurate classification of nontaster, taster, and supertaster must take place in a laboratory setting.

DISCUSSION

"The number of taste buds on the human tongue correlates directly with tasting ability, and both vary according to a standard bell curve" (Levenson, 1995, p. 13). Sample area results for the right anterior tongue anatomy fungiform papillae density include a mean of 44 for the supertaster, 32 for the taster, and 24 for the nontaster.

Approximately 25% of the general population falls into the category of supertaster. Those in this category perceive stronger tastes from a variety of bitter and sweet substances, and they perceive more burn from oral irritants (alcohol and capsaicin; the latter is the ingredient in chili peppers that produces the burning sensation). It is interesting to note that a higher percentage of women fall into the category of supertaster (Bartoshuk et al., 1994). The world is built for regular tasters that experience food as not too sweet, bitter, salty, or sour. Fifty percent of the general population falls into the category of taster. The so-called nontaster has on average only half of the fungiform papillae of the supertaster. Approximately 25% of the general population falls into this classification. Nontasters simply do not experience the intensity of foods that others do. Nontasters tend to like very spicy foods, perhaps because they may be trying to experience some strong tastes. Nontasters do not taste the bitterness in heavily alcoholic drinks, for example. Bartoshuk has noted that nontasters live in a pastel taste world, whereas supertasters live in a neon taste world.

Research on the use of taste papers for identification of subsets of tasters began with Arthur L. Fox of the DuPont Company, who synthesized a chemical called *phylthiocarbamide* (PTC). Dr. Bartoshuk relates that after a PTC explosion in the laboratory, a colleague of Fox commented on the bitterness of the chemical. Fox was unable to taste the substance and was interested in researching taste differences. To test informally the notion of taster and nontaster, Fox handed out samples of PTC at the 1932 meeting of the American Association for the Advancement of Science. Passersby were asked to report on the taste (bitterness) of the substance. Approximately one fourth of the reports suggested that the individuals were nontasters. This established the notion of tasters and nontasters (Cartiere, 1997). Since this time, geneticists have discovered the presence of genes for the inherited quality of taste. Bartoshuk and her colleagues have extended the identification of tasters into a further subset of supertasters. Because of the health concerns with the use of PTC, research today uses the substance 6-n-propylthiouracil (PROP) in an infinitesimal amount. It has an intensely bitter taste to the supertaster and thus can discriminate between the types of tasters in the general population.

Following the demonstration of tongue painting, the students should analyze and categorize the individual variations of fungiform papillae among the demonstration sample. Following the taste test with the PROP taste papers, students' self-report perception of the sensation and semantic rankings can be transposed to magnitude estimations with ratio properties via the Green scale, a scaling system developed to rank bitterness of PROP paper, which has been adapted for demonstration purposes (Green et al., 1993). The general classification of tasters into the categories of supertaster, taster, and nontaster may encourage a discussion regarding the taste variations in the general population.

Students might interview the sample group in the nontaster and supertaster categories to determine individual food preferences. Following the interview, students can hypothesize the implications of these variations. You might ask, "Is it better to be a supertaster or nontaster? Are supertasters better informed about their environment?" Students should hypothesize about the possible effects of genetic taste perception on general health. Does one type of taster tend to prefer a particular type of food that becomes a health advantage? Is there perhaps a particular type of food that is conducive to general health that is lacking in the supertasters' diet because of the perceived unpleasant taste? Does the taster have a more balanced diet because prepared foods are produced for the taster's palate? Is it possible that the nontaster will eat possibly harmful, spoiled food as a result of her or his taste abilities? If one classification of taste is inherently better than another, why has natural selection created a population of equally represented supertasters and nontasters? Is there a cultural connection with the classification of taste? What might that be?

REFERENCES AND SUGGESTED READING

Bartoshuk, L. M. (2000). Comparing sensory experiences across individuals: Recent psychophysical advances illuminate genetic variation in taste perception. *Chemical Senses, 25,* 447–460.

Bartoshuk, L. M., Duffy, V. B., & Miller, I. J. (1994). PTC/PROP taste: Anatomy, psychophysics, and sex effects. *Physiology & Behavior, 56,* 1165–1171.

Bell, K. I., & Tepper, B. J. (2006). Short-term vegetable intake by young children classified by 6-n propylthoiuracil bitter-taste phenotype. *American Journal of Clinical Nutrition, 84,* 245–251.

Blakeslee, A. F. (1935). A dinner demonstration of threshold differences in taste and smell. *Science, 81,* 504–507.

Cartiere, R. (1997, April). Genetic clues to wine tasting? *Wine Business Monthly, 4,* 1–7.

Drewnowski, A., Henderson, S. A., Shore, A. B., & Barratt-Fornell, A. (1997). Nontasters, tasters and supertasters of 6-n-propythouracil (PROP) and hedonic response to sweet. *Physiology & Behavior, 62,* 649–655.

Getchell, T. V., Doty, R. L., Bartoshuk, L. M., & Snow, J. B. (Eds.). (1991). *Smell and taste in health and disease.* New York: Raven Press.

Goldstein, G. L., Daun, H., & Tepper, B. T. (2005). Adiposity in middle-aged women is associated with genetic taste blindness to 6-n-propythouracil. *Obesity, 13,* 1017–1023.

Green, B. G., Shaffer, G. S., & Gilmore, M. M. (1993). Derivation and evaluation of a semantic scale of oral sensation magnitude with apparent ratio properties. *Chemical Senses, 18,* 683–702.

Keller, K. L., & Tepper, B. J. (2004). Inherited taste sensitivity to 6-n-propythouracil and body weight in children. *Obesity, 12,* 904–912.

Levenson, T. (1995, January/February). Accounting for taste. *The Sciences, 35,* 13–15.

Tepper, B. J., & Nurse, R. J. (1998). PROP taster status is related to fat perception and preference. *Annals of the New York Academy of Sciences, 855,* 802–804.

Wolfe, J. M., Kluender, K. R., Levi, D. M., Bartoshuk, L. M., Herz, R. S., Klatzky, R. L., & Lederman, S. J. (2006). *Sensation and perception.* Sunderland, MA: Sinauer Associates.

Appendix 14.1

Green Scale Adaption

For Participant Use

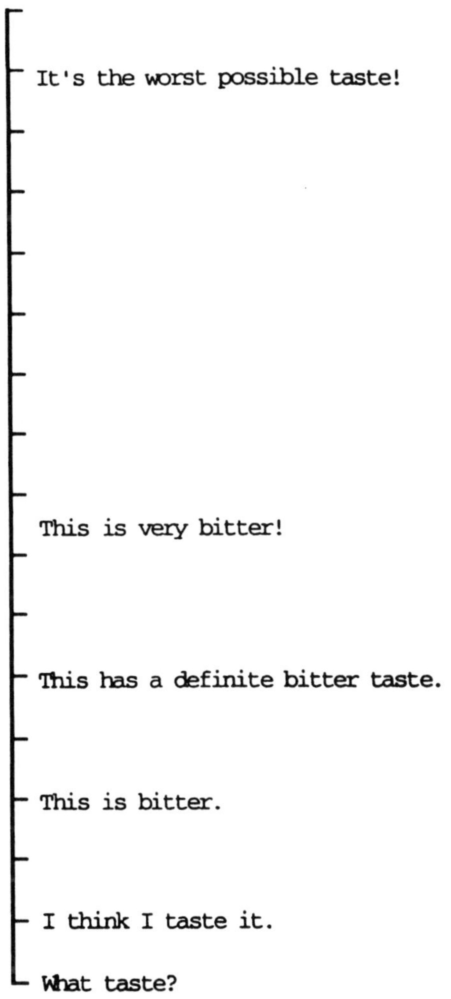

For Conversion to Ratio Properties

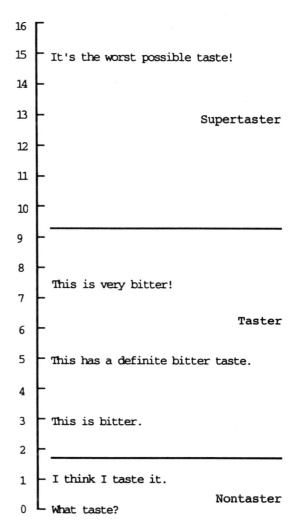

It's the worst possible taste!

This is very bitter!

This has a definite bitter taste.

This is bitter.

I think I taste it.

What taste?

Figure 14.2. Modified Green scale for participant use.

Figure 14.3. Modified Green scale for conversion to ratio properties.

15 THE INTERACTION OF TASTE AND SMELL TO CREATE FLAVOR

Bernard C. Beins

Ithaca College

This activity uses several different types of food to convey the importance of senses other than taste (gustation) in creating the overall perception of flavor. It can be used in introductory psychology as well as classes in sensation/perception and cognition. It is an in-class activity that can be used in any size of class. All students can be involved. This activity varies in time required, depending on how many parts of the activity are used. Some parts of the activity can be completed in 10 minutes or less.

CONCEPT

This demonstration shows students how important smell is to the sense of taste. Textbooks often say that taste and smell interact to generate flavor, but such a simple statement does not do justice to the role of smell and other senses when we eat. In this demonstration, students learn that if they cannot use olfactory cues to identify flavors, their sense of "taste" is quite impoverished. On the other hand, olfactory cues provide a rich experience that they normally associate only with taste. This activity allows students to experience and understand the profound relationship between smell, taste, and flavor.

MATERIALS NEEDED

Quite a few different foods will illustrate the importance of the different senses when people eat. Jelly beans work well because they come in a variety of flavors and colors. In selecting jelly beans, though, it is important to check that they come in different flavors; some brands are colored differently but all jelly beans have the same flavor. It is helpful to use some jelly beans whose color signals their flavor obviously and some that do not.

Beyond jelly beans, potato chips (e.g., regular and specialty types like sour cream and onion) and tortilla chips (e.g., Doritos Cool Ranch Tortilla Chips) provide an interesting demonstration of the generation of flavor. Students will be surprised that even standard potato chips show a significant olfactory component to their flavor. Any food flavored with vanilla also serves as a good smell stimulus for the demonstration.

Furthermore, one can demonstrate that taste has a tactile component. This aspect becomes apparent with the use of foods flavored with hot peppers or cinnamon.

INSTRUCTIONS

Before class, I place a few jelly beans in small plastic snack bags, one bag for each student. The students work in pairs; as one eats a jelly bean, the other records the reaction. They then reverse roles.

Activity 1

In this exercise, students take a jelly bean from the bag, hold their nose shut with their fingers, then put the jelly bean in their mouth and begin chewing (but do not swallow it). In one case, they keep their eyes closed; in the second, they keep them open. The task is to identify the flavor of the jelly bean while their nose is closed. (In the eyes-open condition, make sure the student sees the color of the jelly bean before placing it in her/his mouth.) Afterwards the recording student writes the guess about the jelly bean's flavor. The student, still chewing the jelly bean, then unplugs his or her nose and tries again to identify the flavor, and this second response is recorded as well. When students' noses are plugged, they will guess incorrectly most of the time; when they unplug their nose, full flavor emerges immediately and identification is easy. Opening the nose allows odors from the mouth to travel upwards into the nasal cavity by what is called *retronasal olfaction.*

Another sensory component of flavor involves vision. In this demonstration, students often use the color of the jelly bean as a guide to its flavor. For instance, in some cases, apple-flavored jelly beans are green; students who see the green color are sometimes inclined to label the jelly bean as lime when they initially taste it. If students close their eyes and plug their nose, they will have difficulty generating any meaningful guess. This fact shows that our response to food depends not only on taste and smell, but also on visual factors.

Activity 2

First, I ask the eaters to close their eyes as the recording student takes two jelly beans out of the bag. The recording student notes whether they are the same or different. Then the appropriate student plugs his or her nose and eats both jelly beans. The task is to determine whether the two jelly beans are the same or different flavors. After the student guesses, he or she unplugs the nose. In most cases, students cannot distinguish different types of jelly beans by taste alone, whereas differentiation is easy with olfactory cues. Depending on the instructor's desires, systematic trials involving same- and different-flavored pairs of jelly beans can expand the scope of the demonstration.

Activity 3

This part of the flavor demonstration moves beyond jelly beans to include a variety of different foods, which the tasters should not see before tasting them. In each case, students plug their nose and put the food in the mouth, as with the earlier versions. Then they try to identify the food before releasing the nose to let smell take over. Useful foods for this part of the demonstration include peanut butter cups, chocolate kisses, snack mixes made with Cajun spices, and cider vinegar.

With Cajun snack mix, the sensation on the tongue reveals the tactile component of taste, and, as with the other demonstrations, the flavor of the spices is entirely missing when the nose is plugged. It is clear when students eat the Cajun snack mix that part of the overall eating experience (i.e., flavor in its broadest sense) comes from the tingle caused by the peppery spices. Cinnamon-flavored jelly beans create the same effect of a tingle on the tongue, which is a separate aspect of perception from gustation or olfaction.

Chocolate is also a very aromatic food; in addition, the texture of peanut butter cups can be disconcerting if the eater is not aware that the food is supposed to be tasty; the peanut butter cups can have the texture of clay. Finally, if there is an adventuresome student in the class, it is possible to show that, sometimes, taste is better without smell. If one drinks a teaspoon of cider vinegar with the nose plugged, the sensation is of sweetness; when the nose is unplugged, the acrid flavor associated with vinegar becomes apparent. It would be a good idea to provide a food or drink for the students after they drink the vinegar to counter the taste of vinegar.

PLEASE NOTE—
IMPORTANT
CAUTION

It is important to note that some jelly beans are made with gelatin, which comes from animals. Strict vegetarians or people on sugar-free or reduced-sugar diets might not want to participate. Similarly, students who eat only kosher foods may abstain. Some students may simply not like jelly beans. It is prudent to know whether the jelly beans used in a particular demonstration are animal-based and to advise students accordingly.

This demonstration requires a degree of trust between the teacher and the students, particularly for demonstrations involving food like peanut butter cups. Students have to be willing to accept the teacher's assurance that all of the foods are common and that none are odious in a general sense.

Finally, if students have any allergies, problems could arise. An instructor can either make a general disclaimer that any student with any type of food allergy should refrain from participating. Or the instructor could prepare a list of foods that include peanuts, for example, and tell the students that if they are allergic to any of the items on the list, they should not participate. Most of the items on the list should be distracters whose presence will avoid alerting students to the foods they will actually encounter.

DISCUSSION

Typically, when their noses are plugged, students cannot identify the flavor of jelly beans unless they can see the jelly bean and guess the flavor from the color; nor can they distinguish different flavors until after they unplug their noses, when they experience an immediate burst of flavor. At this point, the students can distinguish the different flavors of jelly beans easily. Many introductory psychology textbooks provide a basic description of taste and smell and their development across the life span. Greater discussion of taste and smell appears in books on sensation and perception (e.g., Coren, Ward, & Enns, 2004).

After this demonstration, it is easy to make the point that flavor results from more than just the tongue. Remind students that the sense of taste recognizes four sensations and only four: saltiness, sweetness, sourness, and bitterness. All other "tastes," e.g., chocolate, lemon, peppermint, strawberry, come largely from the sense of smell. Thus the term flavor is used to represent the "taste" sensation generated by both taste and smell senses.

Students experience the fact that judgments of taste are influenced by smell and even by vision. Further, sometimes students can correctly identify cinnamon-flavored jelly beans because of the "bite" of the cinnamon on the tongue; such experience reveals that tactile stimulation also plays a role in flavor. Finally, one's expectations also affect flavor. The very strongly flavored popcorn Jelly Bellies may be perceived as disgusting until an individual knows what to expect.

Given what they have learned about the importance of smell in the perception of flavor, students can develop hypotheses about what components of the experience contributed to the overall experience. For instance, can a person identify the flavor of jelly beans simply by holding them under the nose and squeezing them to release the aroma? The students can easily test this hypothesis, talking (or writing) about their predictions and their findings.

Another activity might involve having a student place a jelly bean on the tongue and then squeezing another jelly bean under the nose to see whether the additional olfactory cues affect the sensation. In such a demonstration, students would taste and smell the jelly bean in their mouth, but smell something else as well. They can generate hypotheses and explain whether the results are consistent with that hypothesis.

A final hypothesis could address the purported decrease in olfactory capabilities of smokers and ex-smokers. Perkins et al. (1990) have shown that the sense of taste of smokers is equal to that of nonsmokers, although smokers experience less pleasure in the taste sensation. The sense of smell, however, differs in smokers and nonsmokers (Hepper, 1992). Students can generate hypotheses about the apparently equivalent taste responses but reduced overall flavor. One obvious speculation is that, although gustation may be normal in ex-smokers, olfaction may have deteriorated.

Two possible writing exercises that extend beyond the demonstration itself require students to comment on the experience of flavor more generally. First, students can identify different aspects of food that affect their enjoyment of different foods. For instance, soggy potato chips are not as enjoyable as those that crunch, suggesting the relevance of tactile and auditory cues. Also, students often react negatively to the notion of clam and tomato juice marketed as Clamato Juice or head cheese (made from boiling the head of a pig or a calf and then pressing the meat and fat into a cheese-like form) without ever having tasted it, reflecting the importance of culture on what is considered good food.

Second, in another writing exercise, I have asked my students to plan a meal for the elderly, who may have lost significant amounts of their olfactory capability while retaining the ability to taste (Bartoshuk, Rifkin, Marks, & Bars, 1986). The atmosphere of the meal, and the texture, color, and arrangement of the food may become more important elements in the meal. Further, students can suggest ways to adulterate food to make it "tastier."

REFERENCES AND SUGGESTED READING

Ackerman, D. (1990). *A natural history of the senses.* New York: Random House.

Bartoshuk, L. M. (1991). Sensory factors in eating behavior. *Bulletin of the Psychonomic Society, 29,* 350–355.

Bartoshuk, L. M., & Beauchamp, G. K. (1994). Chemical senses. *Annual Review of Psychology, 45,* 419–449.

Bartoshuk, L. M., Rifkin, B., Marks, L. E., & Bars, P. (1986). Taste and aging. *Journal of Gerontology, 41,* 51–57.

Coren, S., Ward, L. M., & Enns, J. T. (2004). *Sensation and perception* (6th ed.). Hoboken, NJ: Wiley.

Forsyth, A. (1985, November). Good scents and bad. *Natural History,* pp. 25–30.

Hepper, P. (1992). Smoking, passive smoking, and smell. *Medical Science Research, 30,* 205–206.

Labows, J. N., Jr. (1980, November). What the nose knows: Investigating the significance of human odors. *The Sciences,* pp. 10–13.

Murphy, C., & Cain, W. S. (1986). Odor identification: The blind are better. *Physiology and Behavior, 37,* 177–180.

Perkins, K. A., Epstein, L. H., Stiller, R. L., Fernstrom, M. H., Sexton, J. E., & Jacob, R. G. (1990). Perception and hedonics of sweet and fat taste in smokers and nonsmokers following nicotine intake. *Pharmacology, Biochemistry, and Behavior, 35,* 671–676.

Sherman, P. W., & Flaxman, S. M. (2001). Protecting ourselves from food. *American Scientist, 89,* 142–151.

Sokolov, R. (1989, September). Insects, worms, and other tidbits. *Natural History,* pp. 84–88.

Weiten, W. (2007). *Psychology: Themes and variations* (7th ed.). Belmont, CA: Wadsworth.

16 SENSORY INTERDEPENDENCIES

George M. Diekhoff

Midwestern State University

The four demonstrations described here show how information obtained through one sensory modality shapes our experience of other sensory modalities. The sensory systems work together, not independently. This activity is appropriate for classes of any size in introductory psychology or for upper-division perception/cognition classes. Each demonstration takes about 10 minutes. Demonstrations 1 through 3 involve small groups of volunteer participants or individual volunteers who are observed by the rest of the class. Demonstration 4 involves all of the students.

CONCEPT   With his doctrine of specific nerve energies, Johannes Müller formalized the observation that sensory experience depends less on the nature of the physical stimulus than on the cortical projection areas into which the sensory nerve terminates (Benjamin, 2007; Müller, 1842). Thus, for example, stimulation of the optic nerve with light, pressure, or electricity results in a visual experience. The existence of separate, highly specialized sensory projection areas suggests that sensory experiences would be equally separate and independent. In fact, however, the senses are less independent than one might expect. The following activities demonstrate some of the interdependencies that exist among the sensory modalities.

INSTRUCTIONS   *Demonstration 1: The influence of smell on taste.* Prepare bite-sized slices of apple and potato. Have volunteer participants close their eyes and hold their noses while they are fed slices of apple and potato in a random sequence. The participants' task is to identify what they are eating. The accuracy of their perceptions is given by the percentage of responses that are correct.

Next, repeat the procedure, but have participants breathe normally as they eat. Compare the accuracy of their taste perceptions with and without the contribution of the olfactory sense to show that the sense of smell is a major component of taste. (See Activity 15 for other demonstrations on the interaction of taste and smell.)

Demonstration 2: The influence of temperature on taste. Prepare four small glasses (8 oz) of water. To each add ¼ teaspoon of sugar and stir until dissolved. The water in the glasses should be ice cold, cool, lukewarm, and hot, respectively. Have a volunteer taste each sugar solution with instructions to rank its sweetness. (Obviously, the volunteer should not know in advance that the glasses contain equal amounts of sugar.) Reflecting the influence of temperature on taste, the cool and lukewarm solutions will be perceived as being sweeter than the ice cold or hot solutions.

Demonstration 3: The influence of size on perceived weight. For this activity you will need two coffee cans, one 1-lb can and one 3-lb can, filled with sand until they weigh the same. Tell a volunteer that you are testing his or her difference threshold for weight. Have the volunteer lift each container and select the one that feels heavier. Despite their equal weight, participants almost invariably identify the smaller container as weighing more, illustrating the size–weight illusion (see Activity 20). The influence of visual size on perceived weight is well established. Smaller objects of a given weight are judged to be heavier than larger objects of the same weight. That is, our perception of "weight" is, in part, the perception of density (i.e., weight/size).

Demonstration 4: Auditory–visual synesthesia. Read the list of vowel sounds shown below to your class with instructions to "Imagine that each sound has its own color. Your task is to match each sound to one of the following colors: red, yellow, white, black, blue."

Vowel sounds
ah, as in mama
eh, as in let
o, as in home
oo, as in boot

In a study of 400 nonsynesthetic subjects, Lawrence Marks (1975b) found evidence for a considerable degree of "cross-translation of the sensory modalities." Tabulate your students' most frequent responses to each of the vowel sounds and compare them with Marks' results:

Vowel sounds	Most frequent color response
ah	red or yellow
eh	white
o	red or black
oo	blue or black

Although the extent to which individuals display synesthesia varies widely, it is sufficiently salient in the experience of enough individuals to have led to the formation of the American Synesthetic Association, Inc. (http://www.synesthesia.info).

DISCUSSION   The sensory interdependencies demonstrated in this activity illustrate two fundamental principles of perception. First, the Gestalt part–whole attitude (i.e., the whole is different from the sum of its parts) applies not just to stimulus elements *within* sensory modalities, but *across* sensory modalities as well. Stimulus elements in one modality combine interactively with those in other modalities to determine the total sensory experience. Second, synesthetic experiences in particular suggest that incoming stimulation is translated into a database that is not modality specific but to which all sensory modalities have access. Thus, an auditory experience can give rise to a visual impression because both visual and auditory systems access the same modality–nonspecific sensory database. This notion also help explain some other interesting facts of perception, including cross-modal transfer of perceptual learning, people's ability to match intensities across sensory modalities, and nonverbal infants' ability to recognize visually objects that have only been experienced previously through touch. Through the sensory-nonspecific database, information presented in one sensory modality becomes available to the other modalities.

REFERENCES AND SUGGESTED READING   Benjamin, L. T. Jr. (2007). *A brief history of modern psychology*. Malden, MA: Blackwell Publishing.

Garfield, K. (2006). Are we all synesthetes? *Discover, 27*(12), 19.

Goldstein, E. B. (2007). *Sensation & perception* (7th ed.). Belmont, CA: Wadsworth.

Harrison, J. E., & Baron-Cohen, S. (Eds.) (1996). *Synesthesia: Classical and contemporary readings.* Cambridge, MA: Blackwell.

Marks, L. (1975a). On colored-hearing synesthesia: Cross-modal translation of sensory dimensions. *Psychological Bulletin, 82,* 303–330.

Marks, L. (1975b, January). Synesthesia: The lucky people with mixed up senses. *Psychology Today,* 48–52.

Müller, J. (1842). *Elements of physiology* (W. Baly, Trans.). London: Taylor & Walton.

CHAPTER 3
PERCEPTION

This chapter presents a fascinating and compelling set of activities on the subject of perception, mostly on visual perception. Topics covered include eye movements, illusory movement, perceptual adaptation, visual afterimages, the size–weight illusion, and the interplay of perceptual input and the brain.

Activity 17 is on the subject of eye movements. It illustrates the presence of saccadic eye movements and shows how their presence seriously compromises visual perception. Students will learn about the ways in which reading and reading speed are affected by fixations and visual saccades.

Reaching for and touching objects requires the cooperation of our visual system and motor responses, something that we have been successful at since infancy. But what happens when our visual field is displaced by a prism and objects are no longer where they appear to be? How long does it take to adapt to this change and what is the nature of the adaptation—a visual or motor change? Activity 18 allows students to experience a different visual world and to learn a new hand–eye coordination to function effectively in that new visual environment.

The subject of Activity 19 is the Pulfrich effect, an illusion of movement in which an object swinging in a straight line is actually perceived to be swinging in an elliptical or circular orbit. This activity illustrates the logic of perception as the brain creates a visual reality consistent with the differential feedback coming from the two eyes.

Which weighs more—a pound of feathers or a pound of lead? If you said they weigh the same you would be right in a physical sense but not a psychological one. The pound of lead would, in fact, be perceived by a human observer as much heavier than the pound of feathers. Activity 20 illustrates that point dramatically in a demonstration of what is called the *size–weight illusion*.

17 DECREASED VISUAL PERCEPTION DURING SACCADIC EYE MOVEMENTS

James W. Kalat

North Carolina State University

One person can see another person's eyes move, even over short distances, but cannot see his or her own eyes move in a mirror. During eye movements, visual perception is substantially impaired. This robust phenomenon can be used to illustrate any of several principles, including limitations on reading speed. This in-class activity is appropriate for introductory psychology classes as well as classes in perception and cognition. It can be used in small or very large classes and can involve all students, although perhaps not simultaneously.

CONCEPT

People have two kinds of eye movements: pursuit eye movements, in which the eyes follow a moving object, and saccadic (suh-KAH-dik) eye movements, in which the eyes alternate between *fixations* (periods of stationary focus) and *saccades* (ballistic jumps from one fixation point to another). Visual perception is greatly, though not entirely, suppressed during saccades. This suppression serves a useful function, as vision during a saccade would be blurry. People are not ordinarily aware of this suppression, any more than they are aware of the blind spot in each eye. A simple procedure demonstrates the great decrease in visual sensitivity during saccades.

MATERIALS NEEDED

Each student needs access to a small handheld mirror for a few seconds. Ask students to bring mirrors to class, if possible, on the day of this demonstration. You should bring additional mirrors, which you can buy inexpensively at a drug store. If you have even one mirror per row, students can pass a mirror down the row.

INSTRUCTIONS

First instruct students, "Look at your eyes in a mirror and focus on one eye. Then shift your focus to your other eye. Did you see your eyes move? Try it several times and then pass the mirror to the next person." They will agree that they did not see the eyes move. The simplest hypothesis is that the eye movement was too slight or too fast to be visible. You can discredit that hypothesis easily: "Now each person pick a partner. Look at your neighbor's eyes. One of you should focus on your partner's left eye, then move your focus to the right eye. Then reverse roles, so the person who previously watched is now moving his or her eyes. Did each of you see the other person's eyes move?" You might give an example by demonstrating with one student. Students consistently report that they could not see their own eyes move, but they do see the other person's eyes move. Therefore, the inability to see one's eye movement in the mirror is not a consequence of the high speed or short distance of the movement. Rather, it demonstrates saccadic suppression—decreased vision during a voluntary eye movement.

DISCUSSION

At least two mechanisms suppress visual perception during saccadic eye movements. First, certain brain areas monitor impending eye movements and send a message to the visual cortex to inhibit cortical activity during saccades. Even if someone is in total darkness, blood flow decreases to the visual cortex during a saccadic eye movement, especially in the magnocellular pathway, which is the primary pathway for movement detection (Burr, Morrone, & Ross, 1994; Paus, Marrett, Worsley, & Evans, 1995). Responsiveness of the visual cortex begins to decline for up to 75 milliseconds *before* the eye movement and continues for a similar time afterward (Vallines & Greenlee, 2006).

Second, one's perception at the end of a saccade produces backward masking that interferes with what one saw during the saccade. If a bright stimulus, such as an illuminated slit, flashes so that it starts and stops during a horizontal saccade, a viewer does perceive a blurry light, with its width proportional to the distance the eyes moved while the stimulus was present. However, if the stimulus persists at the end of the saccade, the viewer perceives the stimulus at the fixation and perceives the preceding blur either weakly or not at all (Matin, Clymer, & Matin, 1972). The longer the stimulus remains on during the fixation, the weaker the perception of the blur during the preceding saccade.

You can use the demonstration of saccadic suppression to illustrate any of several points. First, we read only during fixations, not during the saccades between them. Because most people see only about 11 characters per fixation (Just & Carpenter, 1987), maximum reading speed depends on the number of fixations per second. Most college students average about four fixations per second, with occasional backtracks and pauses, yielding an overall speed of about 200 words per minute. Readers can double or triple their reading speed by decreasing the duration of fixations (Just & Carpenter, 1987). However, each saccade lasts 25 to 50 milliseconds. Even if we unrealistically assumed fixation times of zero, and ignored the fact that saccadic suppression lasts longer than the saccades themselves, the theoretical maximum would be 20 to 40 fixations per second. When graduates of speed-reading courses claim to read 5,000 to 10,000 words per minute, we may safely infer that they are inferring most the words as opposed to actually reading them.

Second, you could use this demonstration to illustrate motion blindness. People with damage to part of the temporal lobe of the cortex lose the ability to perceive continuous movement (Marcar, Zihl, & Cowey, 1997; Zihl, von Cramon, & Mai, 1983). Although we can easily imagine what it is like to be colorblind, motion blindness is more baffling. The demonstration of saccadic suppression illustrates motion blindness on a very small scale, enough to give people a slight idea of what this experience might be.

Third, saccadic suppression makes a point about consciousness: We generally assume that we have a continuous stream of consciousness for all the stimuli that reach us. This demonstration shows that we have gaps in consciousness. During the 25 to 50 milliseconds that your eyes were moving and for a short time before and after, what was your conscious visual experience? The answer is, evidently nothing.

REFERENCES AND SUGGESTED READING

Burr, D. C., Morrone, M. C., & Ross, J. (1994). Selective suppression of the magnocellular visual pathway during saccadic eye movements. *Nature, 371,* 511–513.

Irwin, D. E., & Brockmole, J. R. (2004). Suppressing where but not what: The effect of saccades on dorsal- and ventral-stream visual processing. *Psychological Science, 15,* 467–473.

Just, M. A., & Carpenter, P. A. (1987). *The psychology of reading and language comprehension.* Boston: Allyn & Bacon.

Marcar, V. L., Zihl, J., & Cowey, A. (1997). Comparing the visual deficits of a motion blind patient with the visual deficits of monkeys with area MT removed. *Neuropsychologia, 35,* 1459–1465.

Matin, E., Clymer, A. B., & Matin, L. (1972). Metacontrast and saccadic suppression. *Science, 178,* 179–182.

Paus, T., Marrett, S., Worsley, K. J., & Evans, A. C. (1995). Extraretinal modulation of cerebral blood flow in the human visual cortex: Implications for saccadic suppression. *Journal of Neurophysiology, 74,* 2179–2183.

Vallines, I., & Greenlee, M. W. (2006). Saccadic suppression of retinotopically localized blood oxygen level-dependent responses in human primary visual area V1. *Journal of Neuroscience, 26,* 5965–5969.

Zihl, J., von Cramon, D., & Mai, N. (1983). Selective disturbance of movement vision after bilateral brain damage. *Brain, 106,* 313–340.

18 Using Prism Adaptation to Explore the Eye–Hand Control System

J. W. Kling
Brown University

This activity on perceptual adaptation can be done as a lecture demonstration or, for smaller classes or discussion groups, as an exercise in which all students may participate. It is appropriate for classes in introductory psychology, sensation/perception, and cognition. As a classroom demonstration, this may be done in 10 minutes. In sections or classes of 40 or fewer students, if you wish to collect data, leave about 20 minutes for each pair of students to complete the procedure. Suggestions for both individual and lecture demonstration are included.

CONCEPT

Reaching for and touching the objects at which we are looking requires so little conscious control of the movement that we are likely to consider the eye–hand coordination system to be an innate reflex. Instead, this activity demonstrates that it is a system that is constantly under modification. The demonstration is an example of the "displaced retinal image" experiments, studied in psychology for more than 100 years. George Stratton (1865–1957) and others (see Hochberg, 1971, p. 533) used lenses that inverted the retinal image and asked how long it might take to adapt behaviorally and whether the inverted visual world would ever look "normal." A minor version of such experiments is offered by displacing retinal images just a few degrees. Reaching for an object when first looking through a prism causes the hand and arm movements to be off target. Repeated reaching movements reduce the size of errors, and then removal of the prism results in overcompensation. The demonstration provides a useful supplement to discussions of sensory processes and adaptation, and can be relied on to stimulate discussions of nature and nurture.

MATERIALS NEEDED

The first method described assumes that students will work in pairs, and each student will in turn serve as subject and experimenter. If you have 10 prisms, 20 students can be working on this exercise, while others in the class work on some other demonstration, and then all can switch places.

You will need one ruled target for each pair of students. You can make these from adding machine tapes (available at office supply stores). Cut each piece 60 centimeters long, draw a midline from left to right, place a large X in the center, and make tic marks every centimeter for 15 centimeters to each side of the X. The size of the error that will occur depends largely on the prism, and with the ones described here, the typical errors are about 10 centimeters on the first prism trial. Tape the targets to the wall at approximately chest height.

You will also need one prism per pair of students. Prisms may be purchased from supply houses (e.g., Edmund Scientifics), but prisms adequate for experiments of this type can be made at relatively little cost. (A method for making prisms follows in Appendix 18.1.)

Students work in pairs. If you wish to gather data, each should have a data sheet like that shown (below). One student (S) *stands with the right shoulder directly in front of the **X*** and close enough to the wall so that his or her extended right arm just brings the index finger tip in contact with the ruled target. The other student (E) reads these instructions: "Put your left hand over your left eye. Drop your right arm to your side and relax. When I say 'UP,' bring your arm up with one smooth movement so that your index finger tip will touch the X in the center of the target strip. Leave your finger wherever it is when it reaches the target strip. That is, don't make any final adjustments. When I say 'DOWN,' drop your arm to your side. Okay? Ready? UP." E quickly writes down the value (the number of centimeters to the left or right of X) where the finger first strikes. After about 5 seconds, E says "DOWN." After a brief pause, S is then told "ready" and "UP," and the next trial is run. S should do five trials, with only 5- to 10-second intervals between trials (i.e., just long enough for E to record the deviation score for each trial). (Note: The ideal situation minimizes observation of the arm movement, but this demonstration works even though S can see some of the hand movement.)

Now S is given a prism to hold over the right eye with the left hand. The left hand helps keep the left eye closed. The prism is held with the thick part to the left and the paper square down, and it is kept in this position until five trials have been run. Again, S stands with his or her right hand by the side, and on the command "UP," executes one continuous, smooth motion to bring the index finger tip to the target strip. No correction of the finger position should be made. The deviation score is recorded, E says "DOWN," and the arm is dropped. As in the pretest series, five trials should be run, with approximately 5 to 10 seconds between trials for E to record the point where the finger hit the target strip. IT IS IMPORTANT THAT THE FINGER NOT BE MOVED AFTER IT HITS THE TARGET STRIP.

As soon as the arm is dropped after the fifth trial, S is told: "Close both eyes. Hand me the prism. Put your left hand over your left eye. Open your right eye, and again make the smooth movement of your finger to the X." As soon as the deviation score can be read, S is told: "DOWN." With 5 to 10 seconds between trials, a total of five trials are run.

Partners now change places and repeat the entire procedure. Group data then may be collected and average deviations computed.

Deviation Score

	Pretest	Adaptation	Posttest
Trial 1	_____	_____	_____
Trial 2	_____	_____	_____
Trial 3	_____	_____	_____
Trial 4	_____	_____	_____
Trial 5	_____	_____	_____

If the classroom is relatively small, a volunteer can run through the procedure outlined above and the class will be able to watch the prism effects. For a larger room, a volunteer may go through the above procedure while facing a blackboard and holding a piece of chalk in the right hand. Again, the right shoulder should be directly in front of the target. If the target is slightly above head height, the class can see where the chalk strikes the board.

If everyone holds the thick part of the prism to the left, all students will observe the same pattern of results: Pretest deviations will be essentially zero; adaptation trials will have fairly large deviations to the right of center on the first trials and decreasing deviations over the five trials; posttest trials will have deviations to the left that decrease over the five trials.

In discussing the results, the following points might be emphasized:

1. During the pretest trials, and on the first adaptation trial, the finger was moved to a point in space appropriate for the retinal location of the visual image. The data from the first six trials thus are consistent with the hypothesis that the arm moves to a point associated with the image being on a specific part of the retina.

2. The second, third, fourth, and fifth prism adaptation trials show decreasing deviations from X. Such observations disprove any hypothesis concerning a fixed and unchanging relation between retinal image and hand movement.

3. Most students will agree that their efforts to be more accurate seemed to have relatively little effect and that the improvement over the adaptation trials occurred essentially without deliberate efforts to counterbalance the error on the previous trial.

4. Improvement, for most students, is rapid, although it is common to have some error remaining after five trials. Thus it seems that the hand–eye system responds to the effects of experience in the familiar manner of other skill learning: a "learning curve" might be plotted and its implications discussed.

5. The posttest results show that hand–eye coordination has been modified rapidly by a relatively small amount of new experience. The results are consistent with the hypothesis that the felt position of the arm relative to the rest of the body is changed by the prism adaptation experience. The results also are consistent with explanations that assume a change in the relations of visual inputs to specific output signals. Redding and Wallace (2006) discuss contemporary interpretations of prism effects.

6. The results also show that the size of the posttest error is less than that which occurred during adaptation trials and that the rate of elimination of the error was more rapid than during adaptation. Both effects would be consistent with the hypothesis that the system weighs the effects of experience in proportion to the amount of experience. Again, point out the similarity to the negatively accelerated form of the learning curve.

This activity is based on experimental procedures borrowed from Harris (1965) and is similar to the well-known experiments of Stratton and others, who wore reversing lenses, and also to those of Roger Sperry, Eckhard Hess, and others, who modified the retinal image for salamanders, chicks, and other animals. Mammals adapt rather readily to displaced images; chicks and amphibians do not seem to adapt at all. You might ask students to compare this pattern of results with some of the other cross-species comparisons of nature–nurture interactions with which they are familiar.

Ask your students to consider the relationship of retinal image and hand position during infancy and early childhood when body size is increasing rapidly. Everyday situations that are similar to this demonstration might include the effects of wearing new eyeglasses, difficulties with new bifocals, and the errors made when parallel parking a car that has a distorting rearview mirror. Ask students whether changing from flat-soled shoes to high heels would produce similar effects. They might be reminded of Held and

Hein's (1963) conclusion that it is self-generated movement that is critical to adaptation, and they could be asked (with this in mind) to suggest ways of minimizing problems with new bifocals.

Supplementary exercise. If time permits, it is instructive to give each pair of students a tennis ball (relatively dead ones work best) and have them make a few underhand bounce passes with the ball. They should stand about 10 feet apart. Then, one student should place the prism over one eye and shut the other. Most students can catch the ball while viewing through the prism, but most will throw it off target when attempting the underhand bounce pass. Remind them of the differences between catching, where they can see their own catching hand and move it under the approaching ball, and throwing, where they cannot make the continuous adjustment. The latter is similar to bringing the right hand up to the target; the former is similar to moving the finger along the target until it hits the X. In the larger lecture room demonstration, variations on throwing and catching movements can be instructive (and sometimes entertaining).

You can find a good general account of displaced and distorted images in a chapter by Julian Hochberg (1971); the discussion of central versus peripheral explanations is especially helpful. Atkinson et al. (1999) have a brief summary of the role of experience in perception, including the Held and Hein experiment. Many of the classic papers can be found online at www.psychclassics.yorku.ca. The literature cited in Redding and Wallace (2006) includes many of the recent papers one might wish to examine.

REFERENCES AND SUGGESTED READING

Atkinson, R. L., Atkinson, R. C., Smith, E. E., Bem, D. J., & Nolen-Hoeksema, S. (1999). *Hilgard's introduction to psychology* (C. D. Smith, Ed.; 13th ed., pp. 184–185). New York: Harcourt Brace.

Harris, C. (1965). Perceptual adaptation to inverted, reversed, and displaced vision. *Psychological Review, 72,* 419–444.

Held, R., & Hein, A. (1963). Movement-produced stimulation in the development of visually guided behavior. *Journal of Comparative and Physiological Psychology, 56,* 872–876.

Hochberg, J. (1971). Perception II: Space and movement. In J. W. Kling & L. A. Riggs (Eds.), *Experimental psychology* (3rd ed., pp. 475–550). New York: Holt.

Redding, G. H., & Wallace, B. (2006). Generalization of prism adaptation. *Journal of Experimental Psychology: Human Perception and Performance, 32,* 1006–1022.

Appendix 18.1

Inexpensive Prisms You Can Make

(Note: this procedure appears complicated, but it is an easy and satisfying project that makes a nice break from grading student papers, or you might ask some of your students with such skills to create these prisms as a project for class.) Buy a piece of acrylic "window glass" (obtainable as 11- × 14-inch window panes at building supply stores for about $2.25) and cut it into 4 strips, each about 3.5 inches by 14 inches. (Note: the acrylic comes with a protective paper on both sides because it is relatively easy to scratch. Leave the paper on the sheet while cutting the long strips. Leave the paper on the outside of the strips until the project is finished.) Make two 14-inch-long wedge-shape molds by taping pairs of acrylic pieces together along one long edge and then opening the untaped sides about 1 inch. Use bricks or heavy books to hold the molds in place and in shape. Seal the open ends with duct tape. (Use duct tape. Masking tape adhesive dissolves in the resin.) One quart of resin (with the proper amount of hardener) sells for about $10 in marine or auto repair stores and is enough for this project. Pour about half of the resin into an old coffee can or other metal container and stir in about half of the hardener. Work in a well-ventilated space. Mix and pour slowly to avoid bubbles in the solution. Pour into one of your molds, then repeat the mix and pour for the second mold. This resin produces prisms that have a light brown tint, but they are perfectly satisfactory for these experiments. A quart of resin will fill the two forms to within about one-quarter of an inch (5 to 6 mm) of the top. Let the forms sit overnight. The resin bonds to the acrylic sheet. Slice the long wedges into pieces about 2 inches wide, making a total of 14 prisms. A band saw does this job nicely. Cut pieces of stiff paper (file folder paper works well) about 4 inches square and fasten one to the bottom of each prism with double-sided tape. The paper projecting forward works to keep the arm and hand out of sight during much of the movement.

19 THE PULFRICH PENDULUM EFFECT: WHEN TO AND FRO IS ROUNDABOUT

Ludy T. Benjamin, Jr.

Texas A&M University

This activity, which requires minimal preparation, demonstrates a dramatic illusion of movement and its underlying physiological cause. It is appropriate for classes in introductory psychology, sensation/perception, behavioral neuroscience, and cognition. It is an in-class activity that requires 10 to 15 minutes of class time, involves all of the students, and can be demonstrated in any size class.

CONCEPT

The *Pulfrich phenomenon*, or *Pulfrich pendulum* effect, is one of the most effective demonstrations in visual perception, producing some rather dramatic effects, and is one of the easiest demonstrations to prepare. This simple demonstration evokes a powerful illusion of movement or, more precisely, a perceived misdirection of movement. The observer views an object swinging back and forth at eye level in a plane perpendicular to the line of vision. Viewing is binocular, but one of the observer's eyes is covered with a sunglass lens or some other form of light filter. The swinging object will appear to be moving in an elliptical or circular orbit rather than in a straight line. When the lens is shifted from one eye to the other, the swinging object will be seen to reverse its direction of movement.

MATERIALS NEEDED

The simplest way to demonstrate the Pulfrich phenomenon is to attach a string to the ceiling with some kind of weight tied to the free end that will serve as the pendulum bob. A 9-volt transistor battery works quite well as the weight. A binder clip tied to the other end of the string permits the string to be attached easily to ceilings with lift-out tiles or to any kind of ceiling structure to which you can fasten the clip. The only problem with this technique (and it is not a drawback for demonstrational purposes) is that you will have to continually restart the pendulum action when the arc decreases substantially.

If motion of the object at a constant speed is important (e.g., for research purposes), then the pendulum should be attached to a motor. One solution is to find a motor designed for this kind of movement, that is, movement through an arc of 70 to 90 degrees. For example, many small motors used in window display advertising are often geared to moving an object back and forth in an appropriate arc. Typically these motors are not heavy duty, thus the shaft of the pendulum and the pendulum bob both must be lightweight. A thin aluminum rod and a ping pong ball (painted red for better visibility) work well with these small motors.

The only other materials needed are the light filters, one per student. Sunglasses work well for this purpose, but you cannot use the kind that darken only in sunlight (called *photochromic* or *photochromatic*). The darker the lenses, the greater will be the magnitude of the illusory movement. If you use this demonstration from year to year and announce to your classes that you welcome donations of broken sunglasses (where at least one of the lenses is still intact), you are likely, in a few years, to accumulate the needed number of these lenses. Any kind of light filter will work. For example, partly exposed film (if it isn't too dark) makes a great filter. If you don't have one filter per student it is still easy to do the demonstration for half the class and then have the students pass the lenses to students in the other half.

INSTRUCTIONS   Announce in advance that students should bring their sunglasses to class on the day of the demonstration. Position the students toward the center of the classroom if possible. Optimal viewing distance is 15 to 20 feet, although greater distances will work just fine. So, depending on the nature of the room, you might have to ask students in the first few rows to stand at the back of the room. If the room is especially wide, students at the periphery on either side will not have a good viewing angle for the demonstration. Again, you might have them move toward the back of the room. The string should be positioned at the front of the room so that the pendulum bob is roughly at eye level for seated students.

In demonstrating this phenomenon, the background is a critical variable. There should be ample distance (from 6 to 10 feet) between the path of the swinging object and any adjacent walls; otherwise the magnitude of the effect will be diminished as the perceived orbit of movement will flatten out against a wall.

Ask students to cover their right eyes with the sunglass lenses. In using an intact pair of sunglasses, the best procedure is to hold both legs of the sunglasses, one in each hand, with the sunglasses turned around and held in a vertical position. That is, the lenses are arranged up and down, with the student looking through the lower lens. This technique will allow rapid switching of the lens from one eye to the other.

When students have their lenses in place, remind them that they are to view the pendulum with *both eyes open.* Stand to one side or the other and start the bob swinging, asking students to observe the motion of the bob. After a few seconds ask students to describe what they are seeing. They will usually say that they see the bob moving in an ellipse or circle. When the right eye is covered, the movement of the front part of the orbit is seen as left to right. When the lens is shifted to the left eye, the perceived direction of movement changes. If you imagined an observer watching the movement from above, with the right eye covered the movement is counter clockwise, and with the left eye covered it is clockwise.

After the students have reported seeing the movement, have them quickly switch the lens to the left eye and describe the direction of movement. Once they see that it reverses, they can shift the lens from eye to eye to repeat the effect.

Ask the students to estimate the depth of the orbit (in feet) from front to back. Estimates range as high as 4 to 5 feet, indicating the dramatic nature of a perceived circular or elliptical path for an object that is, in fact, swinging in a straight line. You may note that students at the periphery of the room report a smaller magnitude of the depth of the orbit. Further, the perceived magnitude of this illusion is directly tied to the amount of light filtered out. Thus students using the darker lenses will perceive a greater effect of illusory movement in terms of the depth of the orbit.

Other interesting effects can also be observed. For example, if the instructor stands to the side of the arc and positions one hand so that it is in front of the bob near the end of the arc, the bob will appear to pass through the hand. Feel free to experiment with this effect, using objects (such as a book) or even your body. The bob will be seen to pass through some objects and around others.

DISCUSSION   You might start by asking the students how they think the perceived illusory movement is produced. My experience is that it is a rare student who can come up with an accurate

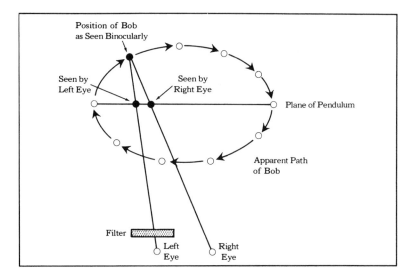

Figure 19.1. Pulfrich pendulum effect.

explanation for the phenomenon. The illusory movement that is the Pulfrich phenomenon is produced because of the disparity of information from the two eyes. The filtered eye sends information to the visual cortex at a slower rate than the unfiltered eye, meaning that the filtered eye always sees the bob in the past, that is, behind its actual location in the swing. The bob moves back and forth in mostly a horizontal plane. The greatest magnitude of the illusory movement comes in the middle of the swing where the bob reaches its maximal acceleration. At the end of the swing, the bob is stationary, which means there is no ocular disparity and thus no depth (Gregory, & Heard, 2003). To see how this is manifested visually, look at Figure 19.1. Here the left eye is covered, which means that because of the delayed transmission of information to the visual cortex, the bob is seen slightly behind its actual position. Combining the information on the bob's location for the two eyes results in the bob being seen to be moving in depth, that is, in an orbit rather than a straight line. With the left eye covered with the lens, the movement is clockwise, and when the right eye is covered, it is seen as counterclockwise. In essence, the brain makes sense of the disparate information coming from the two eyes by seeing the motion path of the object in three dimensions rather than two. It is interesting to note that the German scientist Carl Pulfrich (1858–1927), who, in 1922, discovered the phenomenon that bears his name, was unable to observe it. Pulfrich was blind in one eye (Christianson & Hofstetter, 1972).

Because of optical disorders that create differences in neural transmission latencies between the two eyes (for instance, optic neuritis), some individuals suffer from naturally occurring Pulfrich-like disorders. These perceptual problems can be particularly problematic, for example, preventing the individual from being able to drive a car. These problems usually can be corrected by a specially tinted contact lens (see Diaper, 1997).

The scientific and clinical literature on the Pulfrich phenomenon is richer than you might imagine and can add to your lecture on the effect. Many special populations have been studied, especially where visual skills, particularly depth and motion perception, are critical. See, for example, Hofeldt and Hoefle's (1993) study of professional baseball players that showed a correlation between players' batting averages and their susceptibility to the illusion, such that better hitters perceived lower magnitudes of the illusory movement.

REFERENCES AND SUGGESTED READING

Christianson, S., & Hofstetter, H. W. (1972). Some historical notes on Carl Pulfrich. *American Journal of Optometry and Archives of the American Academy of Optometry, 49,* 944–947.

Diaper, C. J. M. (1997). Pulfrich revisited. *Survey of Ophthalmology, 41,* 493–499.

Gregory, R., & Heard, P. (2003). Pulfrich on wheels. *Perception, 32,* 253–254.

Hofeldt, A. J., & Hoefle, F. B. (1993). Stereophotometric testing for Pulfrich's phenomenon in professional baseball players. *Perceptual and Motor Skills, 77,* 407–416.

20 SIZE–WEIGHT ILLUSION: A POUND IS A POUND THE WORLD AROUND?

Clifford L. Fawl

Late of Nebraska Wesleyan University

This activity illustrates the concept of perceptual relativity, that is, our judgment of objects in relation to the context of which they are a part. This activity is appropriate for introductory psychology as well as classes in perception, cognition, and even social psychology. It is an in-class activity, part of which can involve the entire class, part of which will involve only a few students. It can be used in a class of any size.

CONCEPT

Relativity is one of the fundamentals of psychology. Nowhere is this more evident than in the field of perception, where Gestalt psychologists, almost a century ago, demonstrated that it is difficult at best to perceive a part independent of the whole. For example, Circle A in Figure 20.1 may appear larger than Circle B, despite the fact that they are identical. And, in a (relative) sense it is: Circle A is larger relative to the context of which it is a part than Circle B is relative to its context. Circles A and B thus can be compared by absolute size, in which case they are identical, or by their size relative to context, in which case Circle A is larger. Perceptual judgments tend to be based on the relative aspects of an object even though the assumption is that one is attending to the absolute.

This fundamental principle can be demonstrated in many facets of perception: loudness, hue, motion, or even social perception (e.g., intelligence). Wallach (1959), in an easily read article published in *Scientific American*, presented an especially impressive case showing that the perception of the motion of a figure is dependent on the physical change in the relationship between the figure and its ground, even when it is the ground rather than the figure that is in actual motion. With effort, several classroom activities can be developed from this article.

Easier to exhibit, yet equally impressive in effect, is the size–weight illusion, originally described in 1891 by a French physician, Augustin Charpentier (1852–1916). (See Murray, Ellis, Bandomir, & Ross, 1999, for a translation of Charpentier's article.) It is easy to illustrate that the apparent weight of an object is profoundly affected by its context—in this case the context of its size. Below is an adaptation of a presentation found in a textbook by Krech, Crutchfield, and Livson (1974, p. 300).

MATERIALS NEEDED

A variety of materials may be used for this demonstration; however, the following are suggested: one large can (e.g., an empty, 46-oz. tomato juice can) filled with sufficient sand to weigh 200 grams (hereinafter referred to as *the standard*) and seven smaller cans of uniform size (e.g., empty, 6-oz. frozen orange juice cans) filled with sufficient sand to produce weights of 75, 100, 125, 150, 175, 200, and 225 grams (hereinafter to be called *the comparison cans*). Ideally, each can should have a cap to prevent visual inspection of the contents, and either a ring or knob by which it can be lifted; however, neither improvement is essential. The seven comparison cans should be coded in some way so that only the teacher will know the weight of each can. (Empty plastic 35 mm film can-

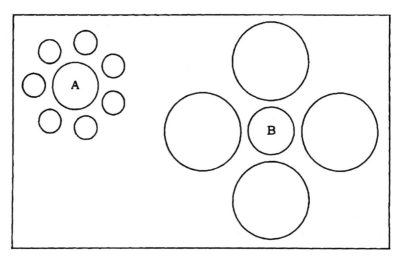

Figure 20.1. Adapted from D. Krech, R. S. Crutchfield, & N. Livson. (1974). Elements of psychology (3rd ed.). New York: Alfred Knopf.

isters will work as well for comparison weights and can be obtained from a film processing store—ask them to save some for you. A one-pound coffee can will serve well as the standard, complete with plastic lid.)

PREPARATION OF CLASS

Whereas a PowerPoint slide of the circles can be used to illustrate the principle of relativity in perception to the entire class, only one student at a time can be used for the size–weight demonstration. Nevertheless, because the procedure is brief it might be possible to allow many students to participate. If you create multiple sets of the weight stimuli, then many students can participate simultaneously. It is a fun activity, and most students will want to try it for themselves. Have the students record their responses privately so as not to influence other students who will serve as subjects later.

INSTRUCTIONS

Place the eight cans in a row on a table. The larger (standard) can should be first, followed in random order by the seven comparison cans. Inform the student that the larger can weighs exactly 200 grams. Have the student lift the can to get a notion of how heavy 200 grams feels. Next, with the large can as the standard, have the student lift each of the comparison cans in turn and record his or her estimate in grams of what each can weighs. The student may return to the standard can if desired, but not to a previous comparison can. If the student prefers, the standard can may be lifted in one hand while lifting the comparison can with the other hand. If asked, do not reveal whether any of the seven comparison cans is equal in weight to the standard can. The recorded weights should be handed to the teacher before the next student commences.

A second procedure may be used with either the same or a different group of students. Again, use only one student at a time. As before, arrange the seven comparison cans in a random order. This time, however, inform the student that one of the seven comparison cans weighs exactly the same (200 grams) as the standard. The student's task is to find which can it is. Once determined, he or she is to write down the code letter of the can on a piece of paper, which is then handed to the teacher. Because other students might be able to see which can was picked, rearrange the order of the comparison cans for the next student.

DISCUSSION

Results can be displayed easily to the class. For the first procedure, post either the mean or median weight assigned to each comparison can along with the actual weight of the can. The students most likely will have estimated the comparison cans to weigh considerably more than they actually do. Some students may report even the lightest comparison can (75 grams) to be heavier than the standard.

For the second procedure, the results can be reported in two ways. First, post the frequency with which each of the comparison weights was identified as being equal in weight to the standard. Second, determine the mean (or median) weight of the comparison can that was identified as equal to the standard. The findings are usually so surprising that students may question whether the eight cans have been weighed accurately. Have a balance scale available, accurate to the nearest gram, so that you can publicly weigh each can.

Is this an illusion to which one adapts quickly? Not really. Does the illusion evaporate once one knows the right answer? Again, not really. In fact, if time permits, have a few students repeat one or both procedures. Even though the magnitude of the illusion is lessened, most students will report that the smaller can of 200 grams still feels heavier than the standard.

Students often feel "stupid" or embarrassed when they find themselves vulnerable to an illusion, especially one involving judgment such as the present one. They may be relieved to learn that Crutchfield et al. (reported in Krech, Crutchfield, & Livson, 1974) found that a group of military officers also was highly susceptible to this illusion. The officers were given two boxes: Each weighed 300 grams, but one was eight times greater in volume than the other. The officers were told the weight of the larger box and asked to estimate the weight of the smaller one. Their average estimate was an incredible 750 grams, or two and one-half times the actual weight!

Perceptual judgments of weight are in part relative, not just absolute. As in the comparison of Circles A and B discussed at the beginning, there is a sense in which the comparison can of 200 grams *is* heavier than the standard can of 200 grams. The former is heavier relative to its size than is the latter. Obviously, one is being affected by the *density* of the cans, not just their absolute weights, and density, after all, is a *relative* measure (weight per unit of volume). Flanagan and Bandomir (2000) found that the illusion is maintained not only by weight differences but also by varying the grasp span of the tops of the cans.

The best way to demonstrate the influence of size on judgment of weight is to have the students lift the cans without seeing them, by using some lifting procedure that does not allow the student to touch the cans (e.g., a ring or string). Under such conditions they cannot know the size or volume and thus are more likely to respond purely on the basis of weight, with the result that the illusion disappears.

REFERENCES AND SUGGESTED READING

Flanagan, J. R., & Bandomir, C. A. (2000). Coming to grips with weight perception: Effects of grasp configuration on perceived heaviness. *Perception & Psychophysics, 62*, 1204–1219.

Horner, D. T., & Robinson, K. D. (1997). Demonstrations of the size–weight illusion. *Teaching of Psychology, 24*, 195–197.

Krech, D., Crutchfield, R. S., & Livson, N. (1974). *Elements of psychology* (3rd ed.). New York: Alfred Knopf.

Murray, D. J., Ellis, R. R., Bandomir, C. A., & Ross, H. E. (1999). Charpentier (1891) on the size–weight illusion. *Perception & Psychophysics, 61*, 1681–1685.

Wallach, H. (1959). The perception of motion. *Scientific American, 201*, 56–60.

CHAPTER 4
STATES OF
CONSCIOUSNESS

The activities in this chapter cover the principal areas that would be found in a chapter on states of consciousness in an introductory psychology textbook. The first two activities are on sleep and dreaming. The first uses a sleep and dreaming questionnaire to collect data from students, ideally for use in a class discussion. The second activity shows how different contexts can lead to radically different interpretations of the same dream content. The third activity involves students in a meditation exercise, emphasizing the stress-relief benefits of such a procedure. The final activity is a simulation exercise designed to allow students to experience some of the parameters of drug abuse in a safe setting.

Activity 21 uses an in-class questionnaire on sleep and dreaming with questions about sleep length, sleep quality, dream recall, and related topics. The information collected from the students can be used in a lecture or for an interesting class discussion. Dream interpretation is the subject of Activity 22, which demonstrates how prior knowledge, expectancies, and other top-down processes can radically alter the interpretation of dreams. The same dream is interpreted by different students who have been provided with differing contextual material, illustrating how this material influences the interpretations.

Activity 23 exposes students to meditation in an actual meditation exercise. It is intended to correct some of the misconceptions about meditation and demonstrate some of the potential benefits of such methods in altering states of consciousness.

Activity 24 is a simulation exercise intended to help students understand the psychological and physiological hold of addictive substances and what it means to be an addict. The activity uses aspects of the biological–psychological–social model of drug addiction. The out-of-class simulation is followed by an in-class discussion held in the form of a self-help recovery group meeting. This is a powerful exercise that immerses students in a safe but meaningful learning experience.

21 To Sleep, Perchance to Dream

Ludy T. Benjamin, Jr.
Texas A&M University

This activity uses a questionnaire to collect information on sleep and dreaming from the students as an adjunct to the instructor's lecture or as a vehicle for discussion. It is especially appropriate for the course in introductory psychology but can also be used in classes on sleep and dreaming, states of consciousness, and behavioral neuroscience. The questionnaire can be completed in class (on a single day) or used out of class for a longer and more reliable sample of behavior. All students participate, regardless of class size.

CONCEPT

There are probably more myths and misunderstandings about sleep and dreaming than about any other aspect of human behavior except sex. For most people, sleep and dreaming will occupy one third of their lives, yet few individuals are aware of even the most rudimentary information about this activity. The study of sleep and dreaming has progressed considerably since the discovery of REM sleep in 1953. The relationship of REM sleep to dreaming provided a particularly important window to study dreaming. For example, consider the following facts: There are at least five kinds of sleep as differentiated according to electroencephalographic criteria, and humans cycle in and out of these five stages throughout the sleep period. Apparently everyone dreams; that is, there may not be nondreamers, only nonrecallers. In an 8-hour night of sleep, most people will have from four to five dreams, usually on quite unrelated topics. The great majority of dreams are in color. There is little evidence that sleep learning occurs. Dreams are not always filled with easily interpretable psychological meanings, as popular literature would have one believe.

The specific purposes of this exercise are (a) to help students focus attention on their own sleep and dreaming patterns, (b) to generate data for class discussion, (c) to introduce students to the concept of data collection in sleep and dreaming, (d) to illustrate appropriate statistical measures for summarizing the data, and (e) to aid students in understanding the interpretation of data in general and these data in particular.

INSTRUCTION AND PREPARATION OF THE CLASS

Pass out the "Sleep and Dreaming Record" (Appendix 21.1) to each student, providing multiple copies—one for each day that records will be kept (14 consecutive nights provides a good sample). Tell the students why the data are being collected and indicate that participation is voluntary. Explain that they are to conceal their identity by marking their records with a number (six or seven digits in length) that they make up on their own. This procedure allows them to identify their statistics in reference to others in class when the summary data are provided later. Note that it takes a student only about 5 minutes each day to complete the record. Two weeks of records will provide a sample of sleep and dreaming behavior that is fairly reliable. But you can use a shorter time frame. You can even use the survey for a single day, asking students to answer the questions as descriptive of their usual sleep and dreaming behavior. Note, however, that reliability is compromised with this procedure; for example, students typically underestimate the amount of sleep they get.

Ask all students to begin their records on the same day and to keep their record sheets at their dorm, apartment, etc. Request that during the time the records are being kept, discussion among students regarding their sleep and dreaming patterns be minimal to avoid unintentional influences on the data. Give explicit instructions on record keeping. (It is a good idea to have one "practice run" to ensure that everyone understands the record-keeping system before continuing for 14 days.) The record provided is only a sample. Feel free to modify it as appropriate for your needs.

When the time period is completed and students have turned in all of their records, the tedious part begins for the teacher—the summarization of the data. An Excel file will handle the organization, but a calculator will be needed for some of the statistics. Each student's records should be summarized separately, and data should be analyzed for the group as a whole. A summary sheet for the students should then be prepared, which lists everyone who participated (by number) and provides the group analyses. For example, Student #107654 can examine that row of the summary sheet to find a mean sleep time of 7.3 hours (over 14 days), with a range of 5.6 to 9.7 hours. The student can then compare these figures with those of other students and with those for the class as a whole, on the basis of the group data.

There are many other questions you can add to your survey instrument. You can ask students about the period of the day when they are most or least alert, such as morning ("larks"), afternoon, evening, or late evening ("owls"). (See Coleman [1986] for a paper-and-pencil test you can give your students that determines whether they are owls or larks.) You can ask about their arousal from sleep—are they very easily awakened, average to awaken, or difficult to awaken? You can ask them about their sleep needs: Ask students to think about the amount of sleep they get, then ask them whether they wished they slept more? Less? About the same? You could ask questions about napping: Do they nap? For how long? When? Note that other than napping, answers to these questions should not differ from day to day. They are better for a one-time survey than for record keeping over an extended time. Again, construct the sleep questionnaire to fit your needs, especially in terms of the topics you want to cover in class, either in a lecture or discussion.

The data students generate will add considerable personal interest to the topic of sleep and dreaming. Further, the statistical treatments will help them understand how data are summarized and analyzed to make them more meaningful. You could even include questions on the basis of different measurement scales (i.e., nominal, ordinal, interval, ratio) as a way to help students understand the appropriateness or inappropriateness of various central tendency measures. It might be useful to save the summary statistics from classes for comparison with those of future classes.

Although it is not necessary, instructors may wish to examine statistically the relationship between some of the variables for which they have collected data. For example, is there a relationship between the number of hours people sleep and the number of dreams they recall? Or is there a relationship between the subjective sleep quality rating and the number of awakenings one experiences during the night? It is important to remember that correlation is a measure of the degree to which two variables are related and does not necessarily specify the *nature* of the relationship. That is, one *cannot* assume that if two variables are shown by correlation to be related, that the relationship is one of cause and effect.

REFERENCES AND SUGGESTED READING

Coleman, R. M. (1986). *Wide awake at 3:00 a.m.: By choice or by chance?* San Francisco: W. H. Freeman.

Dement, W. C., & Vaughan, C. (1999). *The promise of sleep.* New York: Delacorte Press.

Moorcroft, W. H. (2005). *Understanding sleep and dreaming.* New York: Springer Verlag.

Pace-Schott, E. F., Solms, M., Blagrove, M., & Harnad, S. (Eds.). (2003). *Sleep and dreaming: Scientific advances and reconsiderations.* New York: Cambridge University Press.

SUGGESTED WEB SITES

Stanford University, home of leading sleep researcher William Dement, provides an outstanding Web site of sources on sleep, dreaming, and sleep disorders medicine. See http://med.stanford.edu/school/psychiatry/coe

Appendix 21.1

Sleep and Dreaming Record

Student Number _____   Date _____

1. Total sleep time (in hours)_____. On the time line below, block out your sleep periods, including naps.

6:00	10:00	2:00	6:00	10:00	2:00	6:00
p.m.	p.m.	a.m.	a.m.	a.m.	p.m.	p.m.

2. Total number of awakenings during major sleep period _____ (Do not count the final morning awakening.)

3. On the scale below, rate the quality of your night's sleep (in your opinion). Circle one of the numbers from plus four to minus four.

   bad   –4   –3   –2   –10   +1   +2   +3   +4   good

4. In your judgment, how many separate dreams can you recall at least a fragment of? _____

5. It is possible that you will recall some of your dreams better than others. Using percentages, estimate the amount of each dream recalled.

   Dream 1 _____   Dream 2 _____   Dream 3 _____   Dream 4 _____

6. How many of these dreams could you relate to presleep experiences of the dream day? _____

7. Did you appear as a character in the dreams you recall? In how many? _____

8. How many of your dreams were in color?

9. Were there stimuli in your dreams of a nonvisual nature? Check the following if appropriate.

   sound _____   taste _____   touch _____   smell _____

22 THE ROLE OF PRIOR INFORMATION IN DREAM ANALYSIS

Douglas A. Bernstein

University of South Florida
University of Southampton

This activity is designed to help students understand that the interpretation of dreams, like the interpretation of other stimuli, can be influenced by prior knowledge, expectancies, motivation, emotion, and other top-down processes. It can be used in introductory psychology classes in the units on consciousness, personality assessment, psychotherapy, or even social cognition. This activity requires duplicating a handout for each student, takes 10 to 15 minutes of class time, involves all of the students, and can be demonstrated in any size class.

CONCEPT

Doris's dream (Ullman, 1986) illustrates how easily prior knowledge about a client can influence inferences about the meaning of dream content. Using it in this activity provides an easy way to show students the link between principles that guide the perception of objects and those that operate in social perception in general and in personality assessment and psychotherapy in particular.

MATERIALS NEEDED

You will need copies of each of the four dream handouts given in Appendixes 22.1, 22.2, 22.3, and 22.4. Before you hand them out, collate these four versions such that one fourth of the students will receive each version. Alternatively, you can divide the class into groups of 5 to 8 students and give each version to one fourth of the groups.

To aid class discussion of how varying dream interpretations were affected by differing kinds of prior information (including having no information), it is helpful to have each version of the dream handouts on PowerPoint slides or overhead transparencies, using a font large enough to be read from the back of the room.

INSTRUCTIONS

Give each student or small group a different version of the dream handout (or the dream-only handout in Appendix 22.1) and give them a few minutes to read it, along with the dream. Then ask the students to use the bottom, and perhaps the back, of the handouts to write their interpretations of the dream. If you choose to use the small group format, ask that one student from each group be assigned to record the group's interpretation. You can then collect all the interpretations and read some of them aloud, or you can ask for volunteer students or group recorders to read their interpretation for the class to hear.

DISCUSSION

As you read interpretations or as students present them, it will soon become obvious to the class that something is amiss, because some specific features of Doris's life will be unfamiliar to some individuals or groups. It would be ideal to begin by asking for interpretation from students or groups who were not exposed to any biasing information (the dream-only handout in Appendix 22.1), but this requires that you be aware of which students or groups these are. This is an ideal arrangement because these students often have little to offer in the way of interpretation, at least relative to that which will come from those who have been biased. These students' interpretations can be used as a sort of base-line against which to view the impact of having specific life history information about a dreamer.

Once it has become clear that individuals or groups have been exposed to different prior information, it is time to show all four handouts to the entire class and to point out the influence the differing handouts had on the interpretation of Doris's dream.

You can end this demonstration by pointing out that clinicians are aware of the role of prior knowledge in dream analysis (and other aspects of therapy). This is why, for example, they tend to base conclusions about clients on a series of dreams rather than on just one and why they seek to combine assessment information from various sources, such as tests and interviews. Lively class discussions often result from pointing out that clinicians are as vulnerable as the rest of us to the biasing effects of expectancy in dealing with clients.

As a follow-up, you might ask students to take 5 minutes after the demonstration or at the end of class to write a brief summary of the demonstration, its purpose, and what they learned from it. Reading these summaries can help you to determine whether the students understood the points that you were trying to make.

REFERENCES AND SUGGESTED READING

Domhoff, G. W. (2003). *The scientific study of dreams: Neural networks, cognitive development, and content analysis.* Washington, DC: American Psychological Association.

Schwartz, S. (2000). A historical loop of one hundred years: Similarities between 19th century and contemporary dream research. *Dreaming, 10,* 55–66.

Ullman, M. (1986). Access to dreams. In B. B. Wolman & M. Ullman (Eds.), *Handbook of states of consciousness* (pp. 524–552). New York: Van Nostrand Reinhold.

Appendix 22.1

Handout 1

Doris's Dream

"I am at my friend Betty's house. I call Ann up to make an appointment to get my hair highlighted. I speak to the receptionist at the beauty parlor. I speak in a Russian accent. She asks when I can come. I say in a couple of days. I think that might be Wednesday. She asks 'Are you sure because we are changing things around here,' implying that it won't be good if I change my mind and cancel the appointment. After speaking to her, I realize that I don't need to have my hair highlighted yet, because my hair hasn't grown out yet. But George and I go on the 'A' train to the beauty parlor. It goes through a neighborhood that I have never seen before. The train travels outside. George gets out at a stop as if he nonchalantly is doing something. The train leaves without him. I wave to him and feel bad that he is not on the train." From M. Ullman (1986). Access to dreams. In B. B. Wolman & M. Ullman (Eds.), *Handbook of states of consciousness.* New York: Van Nostrand Reinhold (p. 539).

Jot down notes about your interpretation of the dream in the space below:

Appendix 22.2

Handout 2

At the time of the following dream, Doris S. was a 65-year-old woman living in a Chicago suburb. She had four grown children, two boys and two girls. Her husband of 40 years died two years before she had the dream. Though in excellent health for decades, she had just been diagnosed as having breast cancer. Her prognosis was good, but she worried about her health. She also worried about one of her grandchildren, a boy, who was born autistic and retarded. Other than these rather unfortunate problems, Doris had lived a very normal life and never experienced serious psychological problems.

Doris's Dream

"I am at my friend Betty's house. I call Ann up to make an appointment to get my hair highlighted. I speak to the receptionist at the beauty parlor. I speak in a Russian accent. She asks when I can come. I say in a couple of days. I think that might be Wednesday. She asks 'Are you sure because we are changing things around here,' implying that it won't be good if I change my mind and cancel the appointment. After speaking to her, I realize that I don't need to have my hair highlighted yet, because my hair hasn't grown out yet. But George and I go on the 'A' train to the beauty parlor. It goes through a neighborhood that I have never seen before. The train travels outside. George gets out at a stop as if he nonchalantly is doing something. The train leaves without him. I wave to him and feel bad that he is not on the train." From M. Ullman (1986). Access to dreams. In B. B. Wolman & M. Ullman (Eds.), *Handbook of states of consciousness.* New York: Van Nostrand Reinhold (p. 539).

Jot down notes about your interpretation of the dream in the space below:

Appendix 22.3

Handout 3

At the time of the following dream, Doris S. was an 18-year-old woman living in a rural area. She was getting ready to graduate from high school and begin the long road toward a medical degree (she would have been the first child in her family to become a doctor) when she found out that she was pregnant. Her parents were not yet aware of the situation, and she and her boyfriend were in the midst of deciding whether to try to arrange an abortion or get married, though the latter option meant the end of her medical school aspirations. Beyond these rather unfortunate problems, Doris lived a very normal life and had never experienced serious psychological problems.

Doris's Dream

"I am at my friend Betty's house. I call Ann up to make an appointment to get my hair highlighted. I speak to the receptionist at the beauty parlor. I speak in a Russian accent. She asks when I can come. I say in a couple of days. I think that might be Wednesday. She asks 'Are you sure because we are changing things around here,' implying that it won't be good if I change my mind and cancel the appointment. After speaking to her, I realize that I don't need to have my hair highlighted yet, because my hair hasn't grown out yet. But George and I go on the 'A' train to the beauty parlor. It goes through a neighborhood that I have never seen before. The train travels outside. George gets out at a stop as if he nonchalantly is doing something. The train leaves without him. I wave to him and feel bad that he is not on the train." From M. Ullman (1986). Access to dreams. In B. B. Wolman & M. Ullman (Eds.), *Handbook of states of consciousness.* New York: Van Nostrand Reinhold (p. 539).

Jot down notes about your interpretation of the dream in the space below:

Appendix 22.4

Handout 4

At the time of the following dream, Doris S. was a happy and healthy 28-year-old woman living in a comfortable Chicago condominium with her husband of 5 years. Both she and her husband had high-paying jobs in advertising (they had met at work) and were generally enjoying life as "yuppies." They got along well together and, beyond the usual conflicts over small things, the only problems they had were her overbearing mother (who tried to run their lives) and a very stressful decision about whether to move to Los Angeles, where her husband, but not she, had the opportunity for an exciting new job at even higher pay. Beyond these rather routine problems, Doris lived a very normal life and had never experienced serious psychological problems.

Doris's Dream

"I am at my friend Betty's house. I call Ann up to make an appointment to get my hair highlighted. I speak to the receptionist at the beauty parlor. I speak in a Russian accent. She asks when I can come. I say in a couple of days. I think that might be Wednesday. She asks 'Are you sure because we are changing things around here,' implying that it won't be good if I change my mind and cancel the appointment. After speaking to her, I realize that I don't need to have my hair highlighted yet, because my hair hasn't grown out yet. But George and I go on the 'A' train to the beauty parlor. It goes through a neighborhood that I have never seen before. The train travels outside. George gets out at a stop as if he nonchalantly is doing something. The train leaves without him. I wave to him and feel bad that he is not on the train." From M. Ullman (1986). Access to dreams. In B. B. Wolman & M. Ullman (Eds.), *Handbook of states of consciousness.* New York: Van Nostrand Reinhold (p. 539).

Jot down notes about your interpretation of the dream in the space below:

23 An Introduction to Meditation

Antonio E. Puente

University of North Carolina Wilmington

■───■

This in-class activity presents both an introduction to meditation and a method of interfacing something often considered "mystical," subjective, and religious with the rigors of psychological science. One critical demand is that the location of the activity be free from distraction for 15 minutes continuously. The exercise could enable students to experience and understand through self-reflection and report. Additional information can be obtained with the recording of changes in simple physiological functions. This activity is appropriate for classes in introductory psychology, abnormal psychology, states of consciousness, stress and coping, or any class where meditation is a topic. It involves all students and requires about 30 to 45 minutes of class time, depending on the length of discussion allowed.

■───■

CONCEPT

In any introductory psychology course, students often arrive with preconceived notions about psychology. They often believe that the discipline involves the study of interesting phenomena, such as meditation. However, the integration of science with such topics often is considered a foreign concept. In many respects, this situation reflects the problem and the allure of psychology for the relatively naïve student.

Lectures on altered states of consciousness not only create a great deal of interest but also a significant degree of misunderstanding, especially when discussing more esoteric topics such as meditation. Students have heard about meditation and relaxation from numerous popular sources and thus may have formed some preconceived notions about the topic. This exercise is designed to help students develop a more accurate understanding of altered states of consciousness and of meditation in particular. In addition, it helps to bridge the gap between those things that the students consider curious and interesting and those things that psychologists consider measurable and scientific. Further, it introduces the student to the concept that a topic viable to psychology could have its roots in Eastern spirituality or religious tradition.

MATERIALS NEEDED

The basic requirement is a classroom or similar room, free from distraction. In addition, an easy-to-read time piece, preferably with a second hand, is necessary. Students will need paper and pencil.

INSTRUCTIONS

To begin you should explain basic meditation and relaxation strategies to the students. Several simple videos are available through the Web sites that are listed below. A clear understanding of the purposes of meditation is necessary to dispel myths, misconceptions, or fears that students may have. A few words about the potential benefits of these practices would also be helpful. This could focus especially on the use of meditation as a stress reliever and as an alternative health practice. In essence, the focus should be to remove the spiritual and mystical aspects of meditation and replace them with a pragmatic, scientific, and health perspective. At the same time, the experiential and personal perspective should also be considered.

Give students the option simply to sit quietly with their eyes closed if they do not wish to participate in the activity. After you have answered their questions, begin the exercise by asking students to write down three things:

1. Breathing rate (number of breaths in 60 seconds).
2. Heart rate (number of pulses in 60 seconds).
3. A brief paragraph of how they are feeling and thinking at that particular moment.

Explain that you will be providing a series of simple instructions that they must follow carefully. Turn off the room lights and make sure the room is free from distractions for the next 10 to 15 minutes. Instruct the students to sit erect in a comfortable posture, with their hands on the desk or lap, legs uncrossed, and feet on the ground. After students are in a relaxed position, ask them to take at least 30 seconds (if not longer) to slowly close their eyes. Once they have closed their eyes, they can slowly count to 10 before engaging in the meditation process. Encourage them to focus on whatever thoughts come into their minds, but to begin letting go of these thoughts; they should "entertain these thoughts briefly but let them go easily." At this point, tell students to clear their minds and to focus on their breathing. Say the following out loud: "Each breath should come from your abdomen; if possible, breathe through your nostrils. Inhale, let the air in, hold it, let it out slowly. Go ahead and continue this for the next 10 or so minutes. I will alert you once the time is up." After approximately 1 minute of breathing only, tell the students to try to experience a feeling of quietness.

As the students begin to breathe rhythmically, ask them to repeat the word *One (or OM, the more traditional word)* to themselves in an effortless and passive manner. Once they have initiated this pattern, encourage them to briefly entertain new thoughts or ideas that come into their minds, but to always return to breathing and repeating the word *One*. After 10 minutes of this exercise, ask them to stop repeating the word *One* and to focus only on their breathing. Allow up to one minute to slowly begin focusing just on the breathing itself. Give the students about 30 to 60 seconds of this reorientation period before asking them to slowly open their eyes and sit quietly for a moment. Then ask them to take their pulse and respiration rates again and to write a brief paragraph about how they feel now.

DISCUSSION

You should elicit general comments, positive and negative, about the exercise from the class. Next, have the students chart the pulse and respiration data to determine whether any physiological effects were noted. To ensure confidentiality, students can submit pre- and postmeditation data for both of the measures. Descriptive statistics, including a distribution graph, could be the basis of student discussion.

Discussion could involve focusing on both the interesting aspects of meditation as well as the scientific aspects. For the naïve students, psychological topics have been previously considered interesting but not scientific. The integration of what students consider interesting and what they consider scientific is one way to engage the student in appreciating the science of the mind.

REFERENCES AND SUGGESTED READING

Arias, A. J., Steinberg, K., Banga, A., & Trestman, R. L. (2006). Systematic review of the efficacy of meditation techniques as treatments for medical illness. *Journal of Alternative and Complementary Medicine, 12,* 817–832.

Benson, H. (1975). *The relaxation response.* New York: William Morrow.

Naranjo, C, & Ornstein, R. (1971). *On the psychology of meditation.* New York: Viking.

Shapiro, D. H., & Walsh, R. N. (1984). *Meditation: Classical and contemporary perspectives.* New York: Aldine.

Wallace, R. K., Orme-Johnson, D. W., & Dillbeck, M. C. (1990). *Scientific research on Maharishi's Transcendental Meditation and TM–Sidhi program.* Fairfield, IA: Maharishi University Press.

West, M. A. (1998). *Psychology of meditation.* New York: Oxford University Press.

SUGGESTED WEB SITES

http://www.mayoclinic.com/health/meditation/HQ01070 (Mayo Clinic's informative introduction with instructions)

http://www.nccam.nih/gov/health/meditation (National Center for Complementary and Alternative Medicine's overview of meditation)

http://www.noetic.org/research (Institute for Noetic Sciences' Research & Education page, featuring an extended electronic bibliography, arranged by author and topic)

http://www.smmr.de/en/journal (*Journal for Meditation and Meditation Research*)

http://www.tm.org (Transcendental Meditation Program's official Web site)

Appendix 23.1

Basic Meditation Instructions

Activity	Description
Preparation	Quiet room. Nonbinding clothing.
Posture	Comfortable posture (or more classical positions such as the lotus).
Breathing	Inhale and exhale slowly. If possible, breathe through the nose.
Thinking	Open attitude. Lack of specific focus.

24 ADDICTION SIMULATION EXERCISE: ICE CUBE ADDICTION

Todd C. Campbell

Marquette University

■───■

This activity presents a dynamic learning exercise aimed at exposing students—in a safe, involved, and effective manner—to the biological–psychological–social model of drug addiction. An outline of the exercise is presented, and student reactions to the exercise and recommendations for teachers are discussed. This activity is appropriate for classes in introductory psychology, abnormal psychology, substance abuse, or any course in which addiction is a topic. All of the students can participate in this activity, if they wish, regardless of class size. The activity takes place mostly as an out-of-class simulation, but an in-class discussion is involved as well.

■───■

CONCEPT

Drug addiction is one of the most pressing health problems facing the United States today (Substance Abuse and Mental Health Services Administration, 2006). The effects of drug addiction are studied in a wide array of disciplines including psychology, psychiatry, sociology, criminology, biology, political science, and economics. Considering the wide-ranging implications, it is important that students begin to grasp the dynamic processes that underlie drug addiction. These processes are biological, psychological, and sociological in nature (Goldstein, 2001), and collectively they form what is commonly referred to as the bio–psycho–social model of drug addiction.

Developing a safe, ethical, and effective active learning exercise on the subject of addiction carries many difficulties. The value of this simulation is that it allows students to experience and understand, through a safe, active learning exercise, the interaction of the biological, psychological, and sociological processes of drug addictions and the effects on the addicts themselves.

MATERIALS NEEDED

You will need a hospital patient identification bracelet for each participant (if you cannot obtain these bracelets, pieces of colorful yarn or dental floss can be used instead; do not tell the students *where* to wear the bracelets), and the Addiction Simulation Exercise: Ice Cube Addiction handout (see Appendix 24.1).

INSTRUCTIONS

Simply follow the guidelines put forth in the Addiction Simulation Exercise: Ice Cube Addiction handout. You should read Appendix 24.1 before proceeding with the rest of this article.

Because students tend to become very involved in this activity, it is important to stress to them that it is simply a *learning exercise.* Tell students not to engage in any behaviors that they deem to be immoral or illegal. Instruct them that although they will receive the most benefit from this exercise by participating in it fully, they can terminate their participation at anytime. Be aware that there is a methamphetamine drug known by the street name "ice." Make this known to the students and stress that this exercise involves frozen water and *frozen water only.* No other substances should be substituted for the ice. Some students have suggested that food or drink should be used, but with the prevalence of eating disorders, this would not be a wise decision.

The follow-up discussion is done in the format of a self-help recovery group (Alcoholics Anonymous, 2007; Narcotics Anonymous, 1991), even having the students introduce themselves as "Hi I'm _____ and I'm an ice cube addict." I suggest that instructors who plan to use this activity attend an open meeting of Alcoholics Anonymous (AA) or Narcotics Anonymous (NA) to familiarize themselves with the format. In keeping with the spirit of an open meeting, all students are encouraged to participate in the discussion, including those who did not begin or complete the first part of the exercise. In my experience, students readily fell into the role and seemed to enjoy this format for processing the exercise. During this time, students shared and processed their experiences with each other and the instructor. Though in an actual meeting of AA or NA, there is little cross-talk among the participants, open discussion is encouraged in this exercise. Particular attention should be paid to the emotional experiences, strategies used by the students, the insights gained from the exercise, and the process of change and recovery from a drug addiction. Students can use their logs and write-ups to aid in the discussion. I recommend that the follow-up discussion groups be no larger than 15 to 20 students. Thus in larger classes, you might have several groups meeting for this discussion at different times.

The range in level of participation of students can be a focus of discussion. Questions can be posed that use the different levels of participation to portray the abstinence–use–abuse–addiction continuum. Examples of such questions are as follows:

1. Why do some people develop addictions and others do not?
2. What kept you from even wanting to try this?
3. How did you just "dabble" for a day?
4. Were you surprised at the effort you expended?

DISCUSSION

In using this exercise, I have found that students were surprised at what little reaction their friends or family had to their bizarre behavior regarding their "addiction." Behavior that went unquestioned ranged from "knocking on dorm room doors at 11:00 p.m. asking for ice" to "putting ice in my coffee" to "using all of my roommate's ice and then turning the refrigerator on its side to fill it up with bags of ice" to "having a plastic bag of ice melt in my pocket." This allowed students to realize how easy it is to hide an addiction, even from those who should be aware.

Students were also surprised by some of their own actions, particularly some of the actions that, prior to the exercise, they had adamantly said that they would not do. These were actions such as putting ice in their coffee, carrying stashes of ice (in an insulated mug) at work, and avoiding roommates in the community bathroom so as not to show their "tracks." Several students stated that their obsession with planning manifested itself in learning where all the ice machines on campus were located.

This can be a very powerful active learning exercise that allows students to experience some of the biological, psychological, and sociological aspects of addiction. Processing the student's feelings and reactions about participating in this exercise is extremely important, because it may conjure up memories of significant others' true addictions, or possibly the students may even question their use or their friends' use of alcohol or other drugs. Instructors should be aware of resources that students can access to help with any difficulties that may arise from this exercise.

Student reaction to this exercise has been extremely positive. Most students participated fully, some students only participated for 1 day, and a few students chose not to do the exercise at all. Those students who did participate described gaining insight into the tremendous amount of planning it takes to maintain an addiction and some of the dynamics involved in maintaining an addiction. The ice cube addiction exercise brings out many psychological and sociological points and can be used as an effective and realistic simulation in helping students learn about the complexities of addiction.

REFERENCES AND SUGGESTED READING

Alcoholics Anonymous World Services. (2007). *Alcoholics Anonymous* (4th ed.). New York: Author.

DiClemente, C. C. (2003). *Addiction and change: How addictions develop and addicted people recover.* New York: Guilford.

Goldstein, A. (2001). *Addiction: From biology to drug policy* (2nd ed.). New York: Oxford University Press.

McNeece, C. A., & DiNitto, D. M. (2005). *Chemical dependency: A systems approach* (3rd ed.). Boston: Allyn & Bacon.

Miller, W. R., & Heather, N. (Eds.). (1998). *Treating addictive behaviors.* New York: Plenum Press.

Narcotics Anonymous World Service Office. (1991). *Narcotics Anonymous* (5th ed.). Van Nuys, CA: Author.

Substance Abuse and Mental Health Services Administration. (2006). *Results from the 2005 National Survey on Drug Use and Health* (Office of Applied Studies, NSDUH Series H–30, DHHS Publication No. SMA 06–4194). Rockville, MD.

Appendix 24.1

Addiction Simulation Exercise: Ice Cube Addiction (Handout)

RATIONALE

This exercise will allow you to experience, firsthand (though nowhere near to the same extent as an actual addiction), some of the physical (thirst being analogous to the cravings for drugs), social, cognitive, and emotional experiences of a person who is actually addicted to a drug. Participation in this exercise is voluntary. You may choose to end your participation at any time during the exercise, though you will achieve the full benefit of the exercise if you choose to follow through to the end.

PROTOCOL

You are to engage in this exercise for 48 consecutive hours sometime between now and the next class. The more strictly you adhere to the guidelines, the more effective the exercise will be for you.

1. *Drug.* Your drug of choice is ice cubes. You used to be able to "get off" simply on water, but your addiction has progressed way beyond this. You now need specially processed water—ice cubes. This is analogous to progressing from powder cocaine to crack cocaine.

2. *Craving.* Thirst is your craving for the drug ice cubes. Every time you take a drink of *any* liquid, you must have an ice cube in the liquid. Yes, this will be difficult and will require much planning. *Anticipate!* This applies to all drinking situations including coffee, water from drinking fountains, cans or bottles of beverages, and even late-night drinks of water after you have awakened from a deep sleep. (Make sure your ice trays are full before going to bed.)

3. *Legality.* Ice cubes are socially unacceptable and illegal. Do not let "regular people" see you or catch you using ice cubes. This applies to friends and family. The only people with whom it is acceptable to be open about your use of ice cubes are other "addicts" who are participating in this exercise. This will take some creative thinking at home, in restaurants, and other public places.

4. *Obsession.* To simulate the obsession aspect of drug addiction, you are to keep an hourly log (waking hours only). Please obtain a notebook in which you can answer the following questions hourly: 1. Are you thirsty now? 2. Where is your next ice cube coming from? 3. What is your plan to satisfy your cravings? Think ahead.

5. *Tracks.* You will be given a hospital patient identification bracelet to wear. Wear the bracelet at all times during the exercise. This bracelet is analogous to an addict's needle tracks, so it is socially unacceptable to wear the bracelet. Try your best to keep "regular people" from seeing the bracelet, because they might ask what it is about and this would put you in a difficult situation trying to explain it. Remember, you are trying to hide your addiction from "regular people." The bracelet will also serve as a reminder that you are participating in the exercise. It will be easy to forget for a few hours, so you will have to be diligent in your participation. Remember, addicts cannot turn off their cravings at will.

6. *Write-up.* At the end of the 48-hour period, please write one to two pages describing your thoughts, feelings, and reactions to the exercise. This paper is free form, so write in any manner that you feel is appropriate. Please bring your paper and log to the next class.

7. *Discussion.* This exercise will be discussed in the next class. We will use a simulation of a self-help recovery group to discuss your experiences.

CHAPTER 5
LEARNING AND MEMORY

The activities in this chapter illustrate many of the phenomena of classical and operant conditioning, such as acquisition, extinction, discrimination, and generalization. Concept learning, often called a higher form of learning, is also included, as is an exercise that exposes students to different levels of cognitive mastery of learned material, for example, understanding versus application versus evaluation. Activities on memory deal with working (short-term) and long-term memory and emphasize the importance of meaning. Concepts covered include context, chunking, memory capacity, levels of processing, and memory as a reconstructive process.

Activity 25 uses a toy watergun and a single student volunteer for a demonstration of a number of the phenomena associated with classical conditioning such as acquisition, generalization, discrimination, extinction, and spontaneous recovery.

The complete plans for an easy do-it-yourself Skinner box are provided in Activity 26. Cost of the box is approximately $25 to $30. The box can be used for nearly all of the standard exercises and demonstrations associated with operant conditioning such as magazine training, shaping, discrimination, and extinction.

Concept learning, sometimes called *category learning,* is the subject of Activity 27. Using Greek-letter trigrams, students attempt to learn what it is about these trigrams that makes some of them true and some of them false. The activity also allows for a discussion of how animals other than humans learn concepts.

Activity 28 engages students in writing multiple-choice questions that test different levels of cognitive mastery. Students write questions to measure retention, understanding, application, comparison, ability to contrast, and evaluation. This activity can aid students in their study skills and in their test-taking abilities.

Arguably nothing aids memory more than meaning. In Activity 29, students listen to the reading of a passage of 14 sentences and then try to recall, as exactly as possible, the wording of those sentences. The difficulty is that the sentences do not seem to make much sense. Some students do significantly better than others in their recall. Why? Because they were given a context that substantially added meaning to the seemingly meaningless collection of sentences.

Activity 30 is a demonstration of the capacity of working (or short-term) memory based on the work of George Miller and the magical number seven (plus or minus two). The activity also illustrates the issue of chunking and how it affects recall but not capacity.

The issue of meaning as it affects memory is the subject as well in Activity 31, an activity that demonstrates the effect of what is often called *levels of processing* or *depth of processing.* Students hear 20 nouns that they will later be asked to recall. In some cases they are asked to process the nouns in terms of their meaning. Those nouns are recalled far more frequently than the others for which meaning was not processed.

In Activity 32, students are shown that what is stored in long-term memory is the meaning of the message, and not a verbatim copy of the message. This activity also illustrates that retrieval of information from long-term memory is a reconstructive process that often involves confabulation, so that the recall is more a construction of what should have happened rather than what may actually have happened.

25 CLASSICAL CONDITIONING: AN ALL-PURPOSE DEMONSTRATION USING A TOY WATERGUN

Joel I. Shenker

University of Missouri—Columbia

In this popular in-class activity, students see human classical conditioning actively unfold in an entertaining, understandable, and memorable demonstration. This demonstration requires minimal preparation, is easy to execute, and reliably generates excellent student questions and observations. It is appropriate for classes in introductory psychology, learning and memory, and cognition. It involves one or two student volunteers, usually takes 10 to 20 minutes, and can be used in most any class size.

CONCEPT

Students may find classical conditioning an overly abstract concept and may have difficulty understanding how it applies to humans as well as nonhumans. This demonstration is an easy and entertaining way to give students a concrete example of classical conditioning in people, and it is sure to be one of the most memorable activities you will do in your course. It serves as a vehicle for discussion by giving easily identifiable and readily understood examples of classical conditioning phenomena. It is best used after students have studied classical conditioning. The basic idea is to read aloud a list of random words that intermittently contains a single "key" word and splash a student volunteer with a giant squirt gun each time the key word is read. The volunteer soon starts to show conditioned responses to the word alone.

MATERIALS NEEDED

You will need a large plastic garbage bag, scissors, a large capacity water gun or several water pistols, and a towel.

INSTRUCTIONS

Explain to the class that classical conditioning occurs in humans as well as nonhumans and is produced by a variety of different stimulus–response relationships. Ask for a volunteer, being careful to explain that participation will involve wearing a protective smock and being squirted in the face with water (it usually takes some good-natured coaxing to get a volunteer).

Cut a hole in one end of the bottom of the garbage bag so that the participant's head can just pass through. Turn the garbage bag upside-down and use it as a kind of poncho, sliding it over the volunteer to expose his or her head but cover the rest of his or her body. Place the volunteer sitting in a chair facing the class. It is important that the volunteer's eyes remain closed throughout the demonstration for safety reasons. As you proceed with the demonstration, tell the students to observe silently and carefully and to be ready to discuss what they have seen at the end.

After the student volunteer is in place, with his or her eyes closed, and everyone is ready, I usually say that I am going to be reading a list of words and ask everyone to watch the volunteer as I do so. Without any further explanation, I go to the word list below. I read each word aloud, in order, loudly enough so that the entire class can hear and at a rate of about one word every 2 seconds. You can have another student do this for you if you wish, but I have found that the whole thing works better if I do the reading. In the word list, note that the word *can* appears often, sometimes in uppercase bold letters (**CAN**) and sometimes in plain lowercase letters (can). Squirt the volunteer in the face only after you read the uppercase bold *can*, using a consistent delay of about ½ second or so. Do not squirt the volunteer when you see the plain lowercase *can*. These trials test the volunteer's conditioned responses to the target word. As I read the list, sometimes I pause, either strategically or to let laughter die down before proceeding with the rest of the list.

Here is the stimulus word list to be used for this demonstration:

cup, can, lime, **CAN,** dish, girl, chalk, can, dish, **CAN,** key, screen, ran, **CAN,** desk, **CAN,** knob, bag, tape, **CAN,** dish, clip, **CAN,** air, ban, cheese, **CAN,** door, can, box, dish, hair, **CAN,** ring, nail, **CAN,** boat, cap, dish, **CAN,** crane, wheel, fire, **CAN,** dish, king, cape, apple, **CAN,** dog, blue, can, dish, **CAN,** take, call, brick, pair, **CAN,** spin, chair, **CAN,** camp, **CAN,** dish, **CAN,** bridge, scale, can, fan, board, **CAN,** cool, three, horn, disk, **CAN,** can, cast, test, pen, dime, **CAN,** dish, van, can, card, stand, meat, pad, can, dish, set, can, tree, ice, plum, can, cost, bird, glass, can, light, can, sword, juice, can, dish, rock, smoke, grease, dish, keep, kid, tan, dice, hole, set, dish, eye, friend, wax, bill, bulb, dish, class, mine, mark, work, can, dish, can, bus, dish, phone, can, smart, first, can, crack, feet, can, tub, bowl, can, van, day, can, rake, dish, **CAN,** bluff, risk, **CAN,** salt, dish, **CAN,** ball, stack, **CAN,** rain, hat, food, can, van, disk, tree, can

After finishing the reading the volunteer can return to his or her seat. Be sure to give the volunteer a towel and a generous thank you. Ask your students to describe and discuss what they saw. On their own, they will probably bring up many of the important phenomena related to classical conditioning. You can name and expand on each of these as they arise in the discussion.

DISCUSSION | A number of topics that relate to classical conditioning can be tied to the demonstration:

1. The *unconditioned stimulus (UCS)* is the water squirted at the volunteer's face.
2. Examples of *unconditioned responses (UCR)* usually include the volunteer making a flinch, squint, or perhaps a distinct facial expression.
3. The *conditioned stimulus (CS)* is the sound of the word *can.*
4. A *conditioned response (CR)* is usually a flinch, squint, or facial expression. Note that the volunteer will also often develop some *operant conditioned responses* (e.g., turns head or ducks out of the way). If so, this can serve as an interesting contrast for comparison to a CR, giving another topic for discussion.
5. *Acquisition* is demonstrated. At first, the word *can* by itself causes no special response. After repeated pairings of the word *can* and the water, the word by itself gradually becomes more likely to cause a CR.
6. *Stimulus generalization* occurs when words that sound like *can* (e.g., ban, ran, cap, cast) lead to a CR.
7. *Stimulus discrimination* occurs when different stimulus words produce differences in the CRs. In the demonstration, CRs are strongest and most likely to occur after the word *can.* They are weakest and least likely to occur after stimulus words that do not sound at all like *can* (e.g., dish, board, smoke).
8. *Extinction* occurs when the CRs disappear or become less pronounced when the word *can* is uttered several times unaccompanied by a squirt.

9. *Spontaneous recovery* occurs if the word *can* again causes a CR after extinction and a long string of words where *can* is not included. Such a string occurs near the end of the demonstration.

10. *Reconditioning savings* is demonstrated at the end of the list, where the word *can* and a squirt are again paired. At this point, fewer trials are needed to achieve strong, reliable CRs compared with the original acquisition at the beginning of the list.

This demonstration serves several useful purposes. First, it provides vivid and concrete examples of classical conditioning phenomena. When confronted with new material relevant to classical conditioning, students can draw from their memory of the specifics of this demonstration to piece together again the components of classical conditioning. Having such concrete examples is particularly useful to students who may not grasp this material in an abstract form.

Second, this demonstration shows how classical conditioning can affect humans as well as nonhumans, a principle that students often fail to glean from many other classical conditioning examples they are otherwise likely to read or discuss.

Third, the volunteer probably developed more than one CR to the CS; he or she may have developed a flinch, an eye squint, a facial expression, an upper body movement, a particular breathing pattern, and so forth. Such observations are important because they highlight the extent to which classical conditioning in the real world (i.e., outside the controlled laboratory) allows for CSs to elicit a multitude of relevant CRs, not just some specific target response that an experimenter intended to create.

Fourth, and related to the last point, the demonstration illustrates the adaptive nature of classical conditioning. This viewpoint is especially useful to students who otherwise regard classical conditioning as trivial and unimportant when compared with operant conditioning. Thus, students discussing the demonstration may point to the utility of squinting just *before* water hits one's eyes, as opposed to waiting until after the moment of impact. It is easy to discuss why it makes sense for organisms to learn CRs to environmental events when such stimuli come to predict significant UCSs. Or students may observe the usefulness of extinction—why bother to continue to produce a squint response when the CS no longer predicts the water in the face? Students may see similar utility in spontaneous recovery or reconditioning savings.

REFERENCES AND SUGGESTED READING

Bitterman, M. E. (2006). Classical conditioning since Pavlov. *Review of General Psychology, 10,* 365–376.

Driscoll, M. P. (2003). *Psychology of learning for instruction* (3rd ed.). Boston: Allyn & Bacon.

Grant, L. K. (2002). Word diagrams in teaching classical conditioning. *Psychological Record, 52,* 129–138.

Kirsch, I., Lynn, S. J., Vigorito, M., & Miller, R. R. (2004). The role of cognition in classical and operant conditioning. *Journal of Clinical Psychology, 60,* 369–392.

Kohn, A., & Kalat, J. W. (1992). Preparing for an important event: Demonstrating the modern view of classical conditioning. *Teaching of Psychology, 19,* 100–102.

Pavlov, I. P. (1927). *Conditioned reflexes: An investigation of the physiological activity of the cerebral cortex* (G. V. Anrep, Trans.). London: Oxford University Press.

Sparrow, J., & Fernald, P. (1989). Teaching and demonstrating classical conditioning. *Teaching of Psychology, 16,* 204–206.

26 Operant Conditioning in the Classroom: An Inexpensive Student-Built Skinner Box

Kenneth D. Keith

University of San Diego

This activity shows how an inexpensive home-built Skinner box can provide opportunity for observation and shaping of rat behavior and can lead to meaningful exercises in writing and critical thinking. It is appropriate for classes in introductory psychology or psychology of learning. The apparatus, which students could build out of class or in laboratory time, allows for an in-class activity requiring 15 to 30 minutes of class time and involving any class size.

CONCEPT

Maintenance of animal laboratory facilities is financially and logistically prohibitive for many psychology programs. Nevertheless, students can gain a great deal from direct experience with animal activities and demonstrations. Psychology teachers have developed a variety of ingenious ways to demonstrate behavior principles in the absence of animal facilities (Abramson, 1990; Crisler, 1988; Owen & Scheuneman, 1993). However, alternatives may not be totally satisfying for the student and teacher who want to do more than simply imagine how animal behavior might have been shaped in Skinner's laboratory.

This activity involves construction and use of an inexpensive *Skinner box*—a term not favored by Skinner (1983) (who preferred the term *operant conditioning chamber*) but universally understood in reference to the standard operant conditioning apparatus. Students or faculty can easily build the apparatus, and its use offers many possibilities for demonstrations, behavioral observation, critical thinking, and writing.

MATERIALS NEEDED

To assemble the Skinner box you will need a small plastic or Plexiglas animal cage (readily available in pet stores), a few feet of lightweight electrical wire, and the following standard Radio Shack items: plastic battery holder 2-C, #270-385; 1.5 v DC Minibuzzer, #273-053; E10 lamp base, #272-357; PK16 wire nuts, #64-3057; C Enercell alkaline batteries, #23-871; SMini SPDT lever, #275-016; and SQ NO push switch, #275-618.

In addition to these parts, you will require sufficient aluminum foil and duct tape to fashion a food hopper on the outside surface of the box and (on the inside) a small plastic receptacle to serve as a feeder. It will also be helpful to lengthen the lever by gluing a short length of wood (e.g., a piece of tongue depressor) to it. Assemble these items on a simple plywood base as shown in Figure 26.1.

The faculty member could build this device for classroom demonstration purposes, it could be built by an individual student or, for a large class, small groups of students could collaborate to build it. The resulting apparatus is a chamber equipped with a lever that can be easily depressed by a laboratory rat, a receptacle into which food pellets can be dropped via the hopper, and visual and auditory stimulus sources that are activated by the lever and a handheld switch. The total cost is approximately $25 to $30.

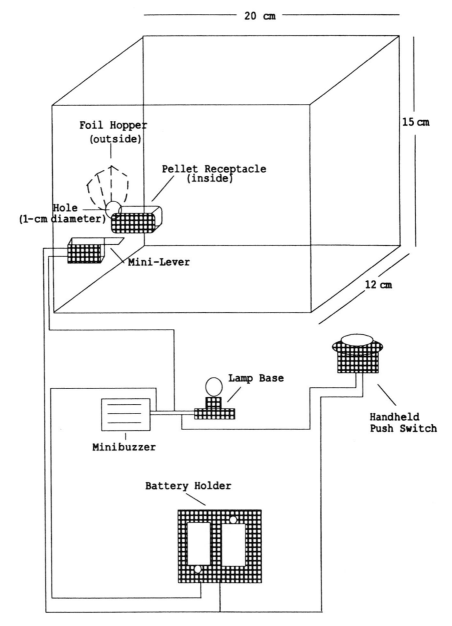

20 cm

15 cm

Foil Hopper
(outside)

Pellet Receptacle
(inside)

Hole
(1-cm diameter)

Mini-Lever

12 cm

Lamp Base

Handheld
Push Switch

Minibuzzer

Battery Holder

Figure 26.1.   Diagram of the home-built Skinner box showing wiring connections to light, buzzer, lever, hand switch, and battery holder. The design of this apparatus is provided compliments of Sean Heard, who, with the assistance of his father and with consultation from our laboratory, built the prototype for a public school science fair in Lincoln, Nebraska.

INSTRUCTIONS   The student-built Skinner box can be used for nearly all the standard exercises and demonstrations that have long distinguished laboratory work in operant conditioning. These include magazine training, behavior shaping, discrimination, and extinction, among others (Michael, 1963). The apparatus is appropriate for teacher-conducted demonstrations or for active engagement by students, individually or in small groups— each with their own Skinner box.

You can readily magazine train a hungry rat through repeated presentation of the light and buzzer along with food pellets dropped into the feeder. Precision food pellets

(45 mg) are available from Bio-Serv of Frenchtown, New Jersey (http://www.bio-serv.com), or from Purina TestDiet of Richmond, Indiana (http://www.testdiet.com). Small bits of ordinary rat chow will also work, and Skinner (1956) reported using uncooked pearl barley. After a few trials the rat will go to the feeder when the light and buzzer are presented. You can then shape the rat to press the lever by reinforcing successive approximations in the manner commonly described in introductory psychology textbooks (e.g., Davis & Palladino, 2007; Myers, 2007), and you can easily add more exercises (e.g., extinction, discrimination, intermittent schedules of reinforcement).

DISCUSSION   Animal research has a long and significant history in American psychology. Our field would clearly not be the same without such names as E. L. Thorndike, Margaret Washburn, John B. Watson, E. C. Tolman, B. F. Skinner, Martin Seligman, and John Garcia. As Davis (1993) argued, if our students are to understand the science of the discipline, we must expose them to animal research and to methods and facilities appropriate to that research.

Although the majority of the top undergraduate colleges maintain animal facilities in psychology (Benedict & Stoloff, 1991; Cunningham, 2003), the fact remains that laboratory equipment can be extremely expensive and that maintenance of an animal colony is impossible for many (perhaps most) colleges and high schools. In my own department, animal laboratory costs are the single largest item in the operating budget.

The apparatus I have described allows a low-cost, hands-on activity that can provide students with a meaningful animal laboratory experience. The fact that its components require manual operation is an advantage for introductory teaching purposes, to the extent this ensures that students will examine the importance of immediacy of reinforcement, the role of discriminative stimuli, the significance of careful observation, and other key behavioral processes.

Computer-based programs are available to simulate animal behavior laboratory exercises (Alloway, Graham, Wilson, & Krames, 2000; Venneman & Knowles, 2005). Nevertheless, I am not convinced that these virtual experiences engender the same enthusiasm that Skinner (1956) felt when he realized, while tinkering with his own apparatus, his kinship with Pavlov. That excitement *is* possible, however, when students have direct experience observing and shaping animal behavior.

Further, activities using the Skinner box lend themselves to a variety of critical-thinking and writing opportunities. One useful strategy is to ask students to prepare and discuss written answers to questions that might arise during observation of the behavior of the rat in the apparatus. Some examples would include the following:

1. Suppose that, instead of delivering a food pellet after each lever press, you simply dropped in a pellet every 30 seconds. What form might the rat's behavior take? Why?
2. When the rat presses the lever you can control how quickly a pellet is delivered. What would happen if you waited 20 seconds before dropping a pellet?
3. In natural environments many behaviors are maintained on intermittent reinforcement schedules. Identify and discuss some examples.
4. You have paired the light and buzzer with food as you have shaped the rat's lever pressing. What role might they play in controlling the rat's behavior? How could you determine this?

Finally, activities using the Skinner box provide opportunity for meaningful discussion of animal rights, research ethics, and humane standards of animal care (e.g., Akins, Panicker, & Cunningham, 2005; Herzog, 1990).

REFERENCES AND SUGGESTED READING

Abramson, C. I. (1990). *Invertebrate learning: A laboratory manual and source book.* Washington, DC: American Psychological Association.

Akins, C. K., Panicker, S., & Cunningham, C. L. (Eds.). (2005). *Laboratory animals in research and teaching: Ethics, care, and methods.* Washington, DC: American Psychological Association.

Alloway, T. M., Graham, J., Wilson, G., & Krames, L. (2000). *Sniffy the virtual rat, pro version.* Pacific Grove, CA: Wadsworth Publishing.

Bare, J. K. (1987). Human operant conditioning. In V. P. Makosky, L. G. Whittemore, & A. M. Rogers (Eds.), *Activities handbook for the teaching of psychology: Volume 2* (pp. 67–68). Washington, DC: American Psychological Association.

Benedict, J., & Stoloff, M. (1991). Animal laboratory facilities at "America's best" undergraduate colleges. *American Psychologist, 46,* 535–536.

Corey, J. R. (1990). The use of goldfish in operant conditioning. In V. P. Makosky, C. C. Sileo, L. G. Whittemore, C. P. Landry, & M. L. Skutley (Eds.), *Activities handbook for the teaching of psychology* (Vol. 3, pp. 106–108). Washington, DC: American Psychological Association.

Crisler, J. C. (1988). Conditioning the instructor's behavior: A class project in psychology of learning. *Teaching of Psychology, 15,* 135–137.

Cunningham, P. F. (2003). Animal use, student choice, and nonanimal alternatives at "America's best" undergraduate colleges. *Teaching of Psychology, 30,* 288–296.

Davis, S. F. (1993). Animals in the classroom. *Psychological Science Agenda, 6*(5), 8.

Davis, S. F., & Palladino, J. J. (2007). *Psychology* (5th ed.). Upper Saddle River, NJ: Prentice-Hall.

Domjan, M. (2003). *The principles of learning and behavior* (5th ed.). Belmont, CA: Thomson/Wadsworth.

Herzog, H. A. (1990). Discussing animal rights and animal research in the classroom. *Teaching of Psychology, 17,* 90–94.

Michael, J. (1963). *Laboratory studies in operant behavior.* New York: McGraw-Hill.

Myers, D. G. (2007). *Psychology* (8th ed.). New York: Worth.

National Research Council. (1996). *Guide for the care and use of laboratory animals.* Washington, DC: National Academy Press.

Owen, M. J., & Scheuneman, D. L. (1993). An inexpensive habituation and sensitization learning laboratory exercise using planarians. *Teaching of Psychology, 20,* 226–228.

Sharp, P. E., & LaRegina, M. C. (1998). *The laboratory rat.* Boca Raton, FL: CRC Press.

Skinner, B. F. (1956). A case history in scientific method. *American Psychologist, 11,* 221–233.

Skinner, B. F. (1983). *A matter of consequences.* New York: Knopf.

Venneman, S. S., & Knowles, L. R. (2005). Sniffing out efficacy: Sniffy Lite, a virtual animal lab. *Teaching of Psychology, 32,* 66–68.

27 CONCEPT LEARNING

Ludy T. Benjamin, Jr.

Texas A&M University

■──■

This demonstration illustrates an important form of human learning known as concept learning. *It is appropriate especially for introductory psychology classes as well as classes in learning and cognition. The demonstration takes place in class, involves all students, and can be used in a class of any size. It usually requires 30 to 40 minutes to complete, including discussion.*

■──■

CONCEPT

In our everyday lives we deal with a great variety of concepts acquired in previous learning—from simple concepts such as "cat" and "apple" to more complex concepts such as "animal," "fruit," "generosity," "intelligence," and "a good night's sleep." We learn concepts because they are extremely useful as a shorthand form of learning. Concept learning (also called *concept formation* or *learning by examples*) allows us to apply the same label to a number of objects or events on the basis of the recognition of a property common to those objects and events. It allows us to make sense of novel stimuli that we might encounter in our environment. This activity describes a concept-learning task that can be performed easily in the classroom with any number of students. The demonstration is usually more effective if students have read the section on concept learning in their textbooks prior to participating in this task.

MATERIALS NEEDED

You will need a set of stimulus slides (PowerPoint is superb for this) and multiple copies of a scoring sheet for student use. Greek-letter trigrams such as ΔΘΓ or ΣΦΔ are excellent stimuli for this demonstration because they are likely to be devoid of meaning because they are low in association value (as long as you don't select trigrams that signify fraternities, sororities, honorary societies, and so forth). Further, students are generally poorly acquainted with the symbols, meaning that they are not easily pronounced. Both of those factors reduce the memorization of the trigrams used in this task.

The slides are easy to make by importing the Greek-letter trigrams from almost any word processing program. Prepare your slides so that the letter theta (Θ) appears in half of the trigrams and the letter phi (Φ) in the other half. But those two letters should *never* appear in the same slide together. The position of those two letters should vary across slides, appearing sometimes as the first letter, sometimes in the middle, and sometimes as the last letter. Use other Greek letters to fill out the trigrams. The concept that students will be learning in this demonstration is that of truth and falsity. The trigrams that contain theta will always be true, whereas the phi trigrams will always be false. In selecting the other Greek letters, it is important that each of them appears sometimes in true slides and sometimes in false slides.

In constructing your slides, arrange them in trial blocks of 12 trigrams. For Trial Block 1, the first slide will be a trigram followed by the answer slide ("true" or "false"). Then another trigram followed by the answer slide. You should construct slides for about six to eight trial blocks, or you can repeat some of them if you wish.

The score sheet that the students use is made up of eight columns of 12 rows. Thus Trial Block 1 uses the first column, and students write their answers in each of the 12 rows below.

INSTRUCTIONS   Provide the following instructions for the class:

> You are going to participate in a concept-learning task. In a moment I will show you some slides that contain three Greek letters forming a trigram. Some of these trigrams are true, whereas others are false. Your task is to learn which ones are true and which ones are false, by learning what characteristic of the trigrams determines their truth or falseness. That is the concept you are to learn. I will present the trigrams in trial blocks of 12, showing them to you one at a time. Each trigram will be followed by an answer slide indicating whether the previous slide was true or false. Look at the answer sheet I have given you. Begin with Column 1, marking your answers down the column. The task will proceed as follows: A Greek-letter trigram will appear on the screen very briefly, for approximately 5 seconds. As soon as you see it, you are to decide whether it is true or false and then mark either the letter T or F in the first box under Column 1. The next slide is an answer slide and will tell you if you were correct. If the answer slide indicates you were not correct, circle that box on your answer sheet and be ready for the next trigram. Note that the task will proceed very rapidly. All slides, both trigrams and answers, will appear on the screen for approximately 5 seconds each. Thus you must work very rapidly.
>
> When you have learned the concept, you should keep that knowledge to yourself. Let your neighbors learn on their own. I will define learning in this task as two successive trial blocks without an error (i.e., 24 correct responses in a row). When you reach that criterion you should sit quietly at your desk until the completion of this demonstration. We are ready to begin.

At this point many students will have a puzzled look on their faces, feeling that you have forgotten to tell them something. Some may even ask, "How do we tell whether the trigrams are true or false?" Simply indicate that you have given them all of the information necessary for the task. Say to them again that this is a learning task, that there is something about each of the trigrams that determines whether they are true or false and that their job is to discover what that something is.

Show the first trial block of 24 slides (trigrams and answers), which will require approximately 2 minutes. At the end of that block ask for a show of hands from those who got them all right. Rarely does anyone get them all right at this point, but there will be some students who have learned the concept in this first trial block. Begin the second trial block and at the end call for a show of hands. Usually there are several people who have mastered the task by this time. Run through seven or eight complete trial blocks (or less if you have less time). I have found that after seven trial blocks, approximately 60% to 75% of the students have met the learning criterion of 24 correct responses in a row.

When you finish the last trial block, caution the students not to talk, because the demonstration is not concluded. Show a slide containing a 20-digit number (e.g., 42,685,791,004,434,201,559). Tell the students that you are reasonably confident that none of them has ever seen that number before. Then ask them if the number is odd or even. They will, of course, easily be able to answer that question. But how do they know that when they have never seen that particular number before? They will tell you that they learned the rule for what makes numbers odd or even, that is, they have learned the concept for oddness and evenness as it relates to numbers.

This illustration provides a lead-in to a discussion of the concept-learning task just demonstrated. Now show a slide with the following trigram: ΔΘΦ. Tell the students that this is a trigram they have not seen and that you want those who reached the learning criterion in the concept-learning task to vote on this new trigram. Is it true? Is it false? Or is it ambiguous? Ask for a show of hands on each question and record the number on the board beside the labels True, False, and Ambiguous. Usually there will be students who raise their hands for each category.

Tell the students that they have actually participated in a double concept-learning task. That is, there were two concepts—theta means true, phi means false. Those students who learned both concepts voted that the new trigram was thus ambiguous. Yet students who learned only one of the concepts were able to perform perfectly in the concept-learning task. For example, students who answered "true" to the new trigram learned that trigrams which contained a theta were true and that trigrams without theta were false. Those who answered "false" learned the opposite concept—trigrams with phi are false, trigrams without a phi are true.

DISCUSSION

Discuss the shape of the learning curve one obtains in a concept-learning task. The curve would initially show performance around the chance level (50%), but once the concept was discovered, performance would be at the 100% success level. Is this an example of gradual learning or is it indicative of one-trial learning? Get the students to talk about the strategies they used in attempting to learn the concept. What false hypotheses did they test before arriving at the correct one?

Talk about concept learning as an aid to human functioning. Get the students to give examples of this facilitative process. Discuss concepts that are learned that hinder us in our perceptions, judgments, and so forth. For example, stereotypes are a type of concept learning in which we learn to label a number of people on the basis of our belief that they share common qualities or attributes.

The overwhelming focus in most psychology textbooks is on classical and operant conditioning. But there are other forms of learning as illustrated by this demonstration. Concept learning is an especially important kind of learning for humans. But is it limited to humans? It clearly is not, as shown by recent animal research, including a long line of studies looking at animal language.

REFERENCES AND SUGGESTED READING

Brainerd, C. J. (1979). Cognitive development and concept learning: An interpretive review. *Psychological Bulletin, 77,* 919–939.

Cofer, C. N. (1961). Experimental studies of verbal processes in concept formation and problem solving. *Annals of the New York Academy of Sciences, 92,* 94–107.

Mitchell, T. (1997). *Machine learning.* New York: McGraw-Hill.

Rosch, E., & Lloyd, B. (1978). *Cognition and categorization.* Hillsdale, NJ: Lawrence Erlbaum.

Sternberg, R. J. (2006). *Cognitive psychology* (4th ed.). Belmont, CA: Thomson-Wadsworth Publishing.

28 A Cognitive Taxonomy of Multiple-Choice Questions

Drew C. Appleby

Indiana University Purdue University Indianapolis

This activity helps students understand that multiple-choice questions (MCQs) can be written to test different levels of cognitive mastery of a single psychological concept. It is ideally suited to the introductory class because many students at this level have not been exposed to MCQs that test higher-level critical-thinking skills. This situation often causes them to perform poorly and to react negatively to their poor performance, because they perceive the questions they answer incorrectly to be unfair, ambiguous, or tricky. This in-class activity requires approximately 20 minutes, can be used in any size of class, and involves all the students in a class.

CONCEPT

This activity describes a cognitive taxonomy (Anderson & Krathwohl, 2001; Bloom, Englehart, Furst, & Krathwohl, 1956) of MCQs that demonstrates how this type of question can measure different levels of cognitive mastery of the same concept. Although the ability of MCQs to measure higher-order thinking skills has been challenged, testing experts such as Haladyna (1994) have come to their defense with statements such as, "Under most circumstances, the multiple-choice format is more effective than the essay format for measuring knowledge. In some instances, the multiple-choice format might be as effective or even more effective for measuring some mental skills, such as problem solving or clinical judgment" (p. 34). Although high-quality MCQs are often more difficult to create than essay questions, there are many advantages to using this format in the introductory course where MCQs are abundantly available in test banks that accompany introductory texts. Ease and objectivity of scoring, computerized item analysis, higher reliability, and equal or higher validity are advantages that Haladyna identifies. The purpose of this activity is to demonstrate to students that MCQs can be written to measure the mastery of psychological concepts far beyond the mere memorization of definitions. The use of the handout contained in this activity can increase mastery of course content, guide study techniques, decrease student criticism of test questions, lower test anxiety levels, and negate the old myth that MCQs can measure only rote-learned material.

MATERIALS NEEDED

The only materials needed are copies of the three-page handout that appears in Appendix 28.1. Although the taxonomy can be reproduced verbatim, it is best used as a model for the construction of an original taxonomy. Constructing their own taxonomies will encourage teachers to take a hard look at the quality and type of MCQs they create or select from test banks. Some teachers may discover that many of their test items measure only memorization or surface understanding of the concepts they present to their students. Others may find their questions measure relations so complex that they would be more appropriate for upper-level classes. The process of creating a taxonomy will also help teachers to develop an accurate set of student learning outcomes for their class syllabus (e.g., to retain, understand, apply, compare, contrast, and evaluate psychological terms, concepts, and methods). If a teacher decides to create an original taxonomy, it will be beneficial to choose a question topic that is complex enough so that a number of sample MCQs can be written about it at several levels of cognitive complexity.

INSTRUCTIONS

After the three-page taxonomy handout has been distributed, students should be told that its purpose is to help them understand and give them some practice with the different types of MCQs they will encounter on their first test. The teacher should instruct the students to study the first page of the handout as if it were part of the assigned readings for their first test (i.e., read it carefully, underline important information, take notes in the margins). After studying the first page for approximately 5 minutes, instruct students to turn the page and answer the six questions, without referring back to the first page. After approximately 5 minutes, the teacher should read each question aloud, ask the class to answer it, read the explanation following it on the taxonomy, and then solicit questions regarding the nature of the thought processes required to answer the question correctly. During this process, students begin to realize they must not only memorize the material presented in class or in their textbook, but they must also understand, apply, compare, contrast, and evaluate this material to perform well on tests. They should be urged to develop study techniques that will enable them to answer any type of MCQ on the taxonomy that is written about any of the material presented to them in the class. The third page of the handout provides a set of suggestions for studying for MCQ tests, and teachers should be prepared to offer some helpful strategies to students who suddenly realize that their lack of study techniques may limit their ability to perform up to their levels of expectation. A discussion of Craik and Lockhart's (1972) levels of processing theory can be very beneficial at this point. Students seem to be particularly receptive to this theory when they realize how relevant it is to their academic performance.

DISCUSSION

There are several reasons why most teachers of the introductory class use MCQs to test their students. First, MCQs can be scored easily, quickly, and accurately. Second, MCQs can produce high levels of content validity in subject areas involving large quantities of widely divergent material. Third, MCQs are provided in abundance by the publishers of introductory psychology textbooks. Unfortunately, students do not always share their instructors' enthusiasm for this type of test item and often feel there is something inherently unfair or tricky about MCQs, especially those they answer incorrectly. This results in one of the least pleasant aspects of teaching the introductory class, the necessity of defending the validity of individual questions challenged by students when their tests are returned. These posttest interchanges can provide valuable feedback to both students and teachers, but this beneficial effect is often overshadowed by the negative emotions produced when students believe they are being tested unfairly and teachers feel their authority is being questioned. Providing students with examples of the questions they can expect on their tests decreases the frequency of their criticisms. It places the responsibility for missed questions on students who have failed to learn concepts on a variety of levels instead of on the teacher whose questions are labeled as tricky, ambiguous, or unfair by the students who miss them.

Perry (1970) described freshman-level students as dualistic in their thinking; that is, they believe that knowledge is either right or wrong in a very absolute and concrete way. Students at this level firmly believe that a teacher's primary purpose is to provide them with the facts and then ask them to simply recognize or recall these facts—in the original form in which they were presented—on tests. Students operating in this stage feel most comfortable with, study for, and perform best on test items that are fact oriented (i.e., items that test retention of terms and their definitions as they are presented in textbooks and lectures). Their level of discomfort rises dramatically as they are required to demonstrate increasingly more complex mastery of terms, principles, and theories with questions that require them to comprehend, apply, compare, contrast, or evaluate this information.

Consider these comments. "You never told us you were going to ask this type of question!" "If I had known you were going to ask these types of question, I would have studied differently and gotten a better grade!" "I can't figure out what your questions mean, let alone answer them!" If a teacher has ever heard any of these comments after a test, this taxonomy will be very beneficial. It can help students to progress in a more informed—and therefore less painful—manner to more sophisticated stages of cognitive development by introducing them to questions that require a deeper understanding and mastery of psychological concepts in a nonthreatening atmosphere (i.e., during a classroom demonstration instead of a test). Many students have previously experienced only MCQs that measure the ability to memorize facts, and it is disconcerting for them when they encounter questions that require more complex cognitive skills without advance warning. Students appreciate being exposed to the types of questions they will encounter on their first test and report a correspondingly lower level of test anxiety. For many, it will be the first time a teacher has cared enough to take the time to show them exactly the types of questions they will encounter on their first test and how to prepare for them.

REFERENCES AND SUGGESTED READING

Anderson, L. W., & Krathwohl, D. R. (Eds.). (2001). *A taxonomy for learning, teaching, and assessing: A revision of Bloom's taxonomy of educational objectives.* New York: Allyn & Bacon.

Bloom, B. S., Englehart, M. D., Furst, E. J., & Krathwohl, D. R. (1956). *Taxonomy of educational objectives: Cognitive domain.* New York: McKay.

Craik, F. I. M., & Lockhart, R. S. (1972). Levels of processing: A framework for memory research. *Journal of Verbal Learning and Verbal Behavior, 11,* 671–684.

Haladyna, T. M. (1994). *Developing and validating multiple-choice test items.* Hillsdale, NJ: Erlbaum.

Perry, W. G. (1970). *Forms of intellectual and ethical development in college.* New York: Holt, Rinehart & Winston.

Appendix 28.1

The Human Memory System

Human memory is composed of three interconnected memory stores. Information from our senses is initially stored in **sensory memory (SM)** in the same way it is processed by our senses (e.g., as images or sounds). Although information is retained in SM for less than 2 seconds, this is long enough for us to interpret it and to decide which parts of it are important enough to pay attention to and transfer to **working memory (WM)**, where we can continue to "work" on it. Information in WM is stored primarily in terms of how it sounds (i.e., acoustically), and only about 7 pieces of information (e.g., numbers, letters, or words) can be held in WM for only about 30 seconds unless we continue to maintain them by repeating them to ourselves. Forgetting occurs in WM when we transfer more information from SM into WM—and therefore exceed our 7-item capacity—or if we stop repeating the information currently stored in WM. This repetition process, known as rehearsal, serves two purposes. First, it allows us to maintain information in WM as long as we continue to repeat it to ourselves. Second, rehearsal enables us to transfer information we wish to remember more permanently to our third and final memory store, known as **long-term memory (LTM).** Information in LTM is stored predominantly in terms of its meaning (i.e., semantically), and this memory store is often compared with a library whose contents are organized in a number of different meaningful ways (e.g., by subject matter, title, or author's name). We are not always able to retrieve information from LTM when we want to—in the same way that a book in a library may be sometimes hard to find—but once it is stored there, it is stored permanently. We do not actually forget information once it is stored in LTM; it simply becomes unavailable to us because we cannot retrieve it successfully.

1. Which of the following types of memory stores information for approximately 30 seconds?
   a. SM   b. WM   c. LTM   d. none of the above

   This question tests your ability to recognize a single, defining characteristic of a specific concept (e.g., information in WM lasts for only about 30 seconds). This requires you merely to *memorize a term and its definition.*

2. Which of the following is *true* about WM?
   a. It can hold only about 7 pieces of information.
   b. Information stored in it is mainly encoded acoustically.
   c. Information stored in it lasts only about 30 second unless it is rehearsed.
   d. all of the above

   This question measures your ability to *learn a set of characteristics* common to a particular concept (e.g., WM can hold only a certain amount of information in a certain form for only a certain period of time). It requires a more thorough knowledge of a concept than does Question 1, but is still based primarily on memorization.

3. Which of the following is the correct sequence through which information passes as it is processed by the human memory system?
   a. SM→WM→LTM   b. WM→SM→LTM   c. SM→LTM→WM   d. WM→LTM→ SM

   This question requires you to *learn a chronological relationship* among a series of concepts (e.g., SM, WM, and LTM).

4. Joan looked up a phone number, closed the phone book, and then repeated the number to herself as she dialed the phone. This phone number is being stored in _____.
   a. SM   b. WM   c. LTM   d. none of the above

   This question measures your ability to *understand and apply knowledge to a new, real-life situation* that was not presented in your textbook or lecture. It requires a deeper comprehension of the concept, which goes beyond mere memorization of its definition or characteristics.

5. WM is to LTM, as _____ is to _____.
   a. 7, unlimited   b. semantic, acoustic   c. relatively permanent, 30 seconds   d. all of the above

This is an analogy question, which measures your ability to *compare and contrast two concepts* (e.g., WM and LTM). This skill is based on—but goes beyond—the simpler ability of memorizing a concept's set of characteristics (from Question 2).

6. Which of the following students has given the *best* explanation of why Tom has already forgotten the name of the person to whom he was introduced only 3 minutes ago?
   a. Chang: "The name was never in Tom's WM."
   b. Monique: "The name was lost from Tom's LTM."
   c. Fritz: "Tom did not successfully transfer the name from his LTM to his SM."
   d. Juanita: "Tom did not successfully transfer the name from his WM to his LTM."

This question involves all the cognitive skills measured by the first five questions. It requires you to *evaluate knowledge you have acquired* so you can produce a logical decision on the basis of a thorough understanding of a relational concept (e.g., factors that affect the successful transfer of information from WM to LTM) that can be used to explain an example of complex human behavior (e.g., forgetting).

How well did you perform on this quiz? If you answered all the questions correctly, you possess the ability to **retain, understand, apply, compare, contrast,** and **evaluate** the information you will encounter in this class. Now all you need is the motivation to work hard so you can actualize your academic potential. If your performance on this quiz was less than spectacular—and you would like to avoid this type of performance on your tests in this class—then you should spend some time determining *why* you missed the questions you did. If you are like most students who take this quiz and perform below their expectations, you probably answered the first two or three questions correctly, but then began to experience difficulty as you attempted to answer the later questions that required you to apply, compare, contrast, or evaluate your knowledge. If this is the case, give careful consideration to your personal understanding of what it means "to study" a textbook assignment. If studying means making sure that your eyes see every word in a reading assignment and memorizing the important terms and their definitions, then I urge you to change your idea of what it means "to study." To answer the later questions on this quiz, you must assume an *active* approach to studying in which you ask yourself some of the following questions as you progress through your reading assignment.

1. Do I truly understand this information or have I just memorized it?
2. Can I apply this information to a "real life" situation?
3. Can I relate this information to other information in this assignment?
   a. Is it part of some type of sequence?
   b. Is it similar to other information and, if so, how is it similar?
   c. Is it different from other information and, if so, how is it different?
4. Can I use this information to evaluate the validity (i.e., truthfulness) of a statement?

When you ask yourself these questions as you read an assignment—and read actively to discover the answers—you will be engaging in a method of study that will increase your cognitive mastery of the material you are reading and increase the probability that you will perform well on tests. Take this exercise and its results seriously. As you study your textbook or lecture notes, think about the different kinds of questions that could be asked about the material you are studying. Anticipating these types of questions—and thinking about how you would answer them—is a powerful strategy that could help you master the material in this class *and* perform well on your tests.

29 CONTEXT AND MEMORY

Marty Klein

Lincoln, Nebraska

This in-class activity is a demonstration of the importance of context in enhancing recall. The activity is appropriate for courses in introductory psychology, memory, or cognition. It requires about 10 minutes in one class, some data analysis on the part of the instructor outside of class, and reporting of the results and accompanying discussion in a subsequent class. It is appropriate for any size class and involves all students.

CONCEPT
Memory is affected by a number of variables, some that enhance retention and some that promote forgetting. Arguably the most important factor in learning and memory is the meaningfulness of the material involved. One way to increase the meaning of material is to place that material in context. This activity illustrates that principle.

INSTRUCTIONS
Give half of the students in your class a piece of paper that contains the statement, "The context is kite flying." Indicate to these students that they are not to reveal the contents of this message to their classmates. Then read the following paragraph aloud, very slowly:

> A newspaper is better than a magazine. A seashore is a better place than the street. At first it is better to run than to walk. You may have to try several times. It takes some skill but is easy to learn. Even young children can enjoy it. Once successful, complications are minimal. Birds seldom get too close. Rain, however, soaks in very fast. Too many people doing the same thing can also cause problems. One needs lots of room. If there are no complications it can be very peaceful. A rock will serve as an anchor. If things break loose from it, however, you will not get a second chance.

Ask all the students to take out pencil and paper and write down as much of the paragraph just read as they can recall. Ask them to recall the sentences as precisely as they can. You may want to tell them that there were 14 sentences in the paragraph as a cue to their recall. Have those students who had been given the contextual statement in advance mark their papers so that you will be able to identify their responses. Before the papers are turned in, you might ask the students who were not given the context information to write, at the bottom of their paper, what they think the sentences might have been about. Collect all the papers.

You will need to analyze the data outside of class and report the differences at the next class period. Score each paper on a sentence-by-sentence basis, assigning one point for each sentence where the meaning is essentially the same. For example, a student might write "A rock can help" or "You should run not walk" or "Newspapers are best." Each of those would likely be scored as correct. With such a quantification scheme you can compare the two halves of the class in terms of recall. What you should find is a much higher recall score for the group that was given the piece of paper identifying the context of the sentences.

DISCUSSION   Obviously, knowing the context adds meaning to material that might otherwise appear as a set of unrelated statements. The context makes organization of learning possible. If organized properly, "one thing leads to another." What does this principle suggest about study strategies? Of course, context works in other ways to aid memory. Psychologists have long known that environmental context aids recall (Smith & Vela, 2001). Studies have shown, for example, that subjects' recall is best if they are tested in the same room where learning occurred as opposed to another room. State-dependent memory (Smith, 2006) and mood-dependent memory (Eich, Macauley, & Ryan, 1994) provide examples of other kinds of context that enhance recall. If you wish, you might extend the class discussion to the importance of context in perception and how it serves to enhance perceptual abilities.

Here is another example, similar to the kite flying paragraph, should you want to give your students another opportunity to test their recall. You could give this one to them with or without some of the students receiving the context in advance. You could just ask them to see if they can guess what these sentences are about.

> The procedure is actually quite simple. First you arrange items into different groups. Of course one pile may be sufficient depending on how much there is to do. If you have to go somewhere else due to lack of facilities that is the next step; otherwise, you are pretty well set. It is important not to overdo things. That is, it is better to do too few things at once than too many. In the short run this may not seem important but complications can easily arise. A mistake can be expensive as well. At first, the whole procedure will seem complicated. Soon however, it will become just another facet of life. It is difficult to foresee any end to the necessity for this task in the immediate future, but then, one can never tell. After the procedure is completed, one arranges the materials into different groups again. Eventually, they will be used once more and the whole cycle will then have to be repeated. However, that is part of life.

Again, there are 14 sentences. And have you guessed what these statements are about? They are about doing laundry.

REFERENCES AND SUGGESTED READING

Ashcraft, M. (2006). *Cognition* (4th ed.). Upper Saddle River, NJ: Prentice-Hall.

Eich, E., Macauley, D., & Ryan, L. (1994). Mood dependent memory for events of the personal past. *Journal of Experimental Psychology: General, 123,* 201–215.

Smith, S. M. (2006). Context and human memory. In H. L. Roediger III, Y. Dudai, & S. M. Fitzpatrick (Eds.), *Science of memory: Concepts* (pp. 111–114). New York: Oxford University Press.

Smith, S. M., & Vela, E. (2001). Environmental context-dependent memory: A review and meta analysis. *Psychonomic Bulletin and Review, 8,* 203–220.

Sternberg, R. J. (2005). *Cognitive psychology* (4th ed.). Belmont, CA: Wadsworth.

Thompson, R. F., & Madigan, S. A. (2005). *Memory: The key to consciousness.* Washington, DC: Joseph Henry Press.

Tileston, D. W. (2004). *What every teacher should know about learning, memory, and the brain.* Thousand Oaks, CA: Corwin Press.

30 INFORMATION PROCESSING CAPACITY: A VISUAL DEMONSTRATION OF THE MAGICAL NUMBER SEVEN

Fairfid M. Caudle

The College of Staten Island, City University of New York

This activity provides a visual demonstration of the well-known limitation on information processing capacity represented by the George A. Miller's phrase "the magical number seven, plus or minus two." It is appropriate for classes in introductory psychology, sensation/perception, and cognition. It is an in-class activity that requires 15 to 20 minutes of class time, involves all of the students, and can be demonstrated in classes of up to 90 students.

CONCEPT

The phrase "magical number seven, plus or minus two" refers to the limited capacity of short-term or working memory (Miller, 1956). This activity, unlike the auditory demonstrations typically included in introductory texts, uses visual stimuli to demonstrate this capacity and the value of chunking. Students are presented with an array of dots, arranged either randomly or in patterns. A graph of students' judgments of the number of dots in each array demonstrates the limits of information processing capacity and the facilitative effect of chunking. The demonstration also provides opportunities to explore aspects of experimental design and descriptive statistics.

MATERIALS NEEDED

In addition to chalk and a chalkboard, you will need 17 stimulus items, each constructed from a sheet of 8 ½ inch × 11 inch white paper and black or blue colored adhesive dots approximately ¾ inch in diameter. These are available in office supply stores. A total of 136 dots is needed.

Prepare the 17 stimulus items as indicated in Appendix 30.1. Each must consist of one sheet of paper with the number of dots indicated distributed either randomly or in a pattern. On the back of each sheet note lightly, for your own reference, the stimulus item number as well as the number and distribution of the dots. This will enable you to check that the sheets are in the proper sequence before beginning the demonstration.

The construction of stimulus items as described here has proved adequate for classes of up to 90 students. For larger classes, you may want to construct the stimulus items as slides for presentation by PowerPoint. However, if you choose this method, be certain that, after presenting each stimulus item, you can also present a blank PowerPoint slide.

You will find it helpful to prepare a summary sheet that indicates the random stimulus item numbers in order of increasing number of dots (e.g., Stimulus Item 6, having 1 dot; 3, having 2 dots; 12, having 3 dots; and continuing with remaining random Stimulus Items 1, 16, 14, 9, 11, 5, 4, 17, 2, 8, and 13) and the patterned item numbers in the same order (Stimulus Items 15, having 3 rows of 3 dots; 7, 2 rows of 5; and 10, 4 rows of 3). This will facilitate the construction of the results graph.

Preparation

On a table in front of you, arrange the stimulus items face down from Item 1 (on top) through Item 17 (on the bottom). Or, if presenting the stimulus items by PowerPoint, be sure that you can present the stimulus items in order, with "blank" slides between each. Ask the class to turn to a blank page in their notebooks and number from Line 1 through Line 17.

Say to the class: "I am going to show you some sheets of paper (or slides) with dots on them. For each sheet (slide), I will give you three beats to get ready, one beat to watch, and one beat to write down the number of dots you see on that sheet (slide). Write your answer for each sheet (slide) on a different line, going from Line 1 through Line 17. I will not be calling out line numbers, so just keep going until we finish. For each sheet (slide), I will say, 'dah, dah, dah, look, write.' " Demonstrate with hand motions how you will hold up a stimulus item or show a slide on "look."

Stimulus Presentation

Show each sheet by counting, at approximately 1 second per beat, "dah, dah, dah, look, write." As you say "look," hold up a stimulus item or show a PowerPoint slide. As you say "write," put the sheet face down or show a "blank" PowerPoint slide. Repeat for each stimulus item.

Recording Results

If you presented the stimulus items using PowerPoint slides, you will probably have to raise the projection screen at this point to make the chalkboard accessible. Draw a graph on the chalkboard. Label the vertical axis "Number of Persons Correct" and mark it in units of 10. Label the horizontal axis "Number of Dots" and number it from 1 to 14 (the maximum number of dots).

Referring to your summary sheet listing all the stimulus items, go through each item *in the order of increasing dots* and ask for a show of hands as to the number of students who wrote down the correct number. For example, say, "Item 6 had one dot. How many of you were correct?" Follow this with, "Item 12, two dots," and so on. It is helpful to know in advance how many are actually present so you can subtract the number of people wrong when almost everyone is correct. With a large class, divide the class into sections and have someone count each section. (If you want student responses to be anonymous, collect all the answer sheets, shuffle them, and pass them back out to the students, asking students to raise their hands in response to the answer sheet they now have.)

Using this procedure, record the number of persons correctly responding to random arrangements of 1 through 14 dots. For each stimulus item, count the number correct and plot a solid dot at the appropriate place on the graph. Connect the solid dots with solid lines to complete the graph. Then record the number of persons correctly responding to the three items with dots arranged in patterns. Indicate the number correct with small hollow circles and connect these with broken lines. Complete your graph with a key indicating that solid circles connected by a solid line correspond to random arrangements, whereas hollow circles connected with a broken line indicate pattern arrangements.

Typically, for random arrangements of dots, virtually the entire class is correct for 1 through 5 dots. Thereafter, the number of persons correct begins to decline, and does so precipitously for 10 through 14 dots. Your graph will not be perfect, but the trend should be clearly apparent.

Once you have constructed the graph for random arrangements, ask the class to interpret the graph. Identify the point where lots of people begin to make mistakes and relate this to the "magical number seven," which represents our information-processing capacity.

When dots are arranged in patterns, the number correct is always higher. Ask the class to compare the number correct for 9, 10, and 12 dots arranged in patterns with the number correct for 9, 10, and 12 dots distributed randomly. Ask for suggestions as to why the results are as they are. Introduce the concept of chunking to explain the dramatic increase in capacity when information is organized into patterns.

After discussing the main findings of the demonstration, you can extend the activity by having students analyze it in terms of design. Have them identify the independent variables (there are two: the total number of dots and the type of arrangement, random or pattern) and the dependent variable (number of persons correct) for the demonstration. Ask for someone to state a relationship between the independent and dependent variables that was illustrated by this activity. (As the number of dots increased, the number of persons correct decreased. However, the number of persons correct was higher when the dots were in a pattern.)

Continuing your discussion of variables, ask the class to identify possible uncontrolled variables that might have affected the outcome. These might include such things as distance from the stimulus items, viewing angle, movement of stimulus items as you held them up, inadvertent variations in viewing time, and so forth. Ask for suggestions as to how to control for these variables and describe laboratory instruments, such as the tachistoscope, that have been designed to enable increased control over such variables.

You can also point out how a very large number of individual responses (roughly 17 times the number of people who participated) can be summarized by means of a single graph. You may also wish to point out the analogy between dots in patterns and your final graph: Both are visual methods of organizing (chunking) individual pieces of information. You can also make the distinction between the visual presentation of data by means of a graph and the numerical presentation of data in a table. Note that both are valuable ways of making data manageable and understandable and point out other examples of each in your course textbook.

Finally, you may wish to extend the discussion by discussing real-life situations in which chunking of visual information into patterns is important. These might include occupations (e.g., air traffic controller or musician), sports (e.g., football or basketball), board games (e.g., chess), some video games, and activities of daily life (e.g., finding one's car in a large parking lot or finding items during a trip to a supermarket). Some examples of studies reporting visual chunking are noted in the References and Suggested Reading section.

REFERENCES AND SUGGESTED READING

Allard, E, & Burnett, N. (1985). Skill in sport. *Canadian Journal of Psychology, 9*, 294–312.

Chase, W. G., & Simon, H. A. (1973). Perception in chess. *Cognitive Psychology, 4*, 55–81.

Cohen, G. (1989). *Memory in the real world.* Hillsdale, NJ: Erlbaum.

Miller, G. A. (1956). The magical number seven, plus or minus two: Some limits on our capacity for processing information. *Psychological Review, 63*, 81–97.

Squire, L. R. (1992). *Encyclopedia of learning and memory.* New York: Macmillan.

Appendix 30.1

Stimulus Items

Item number	Number of dots	Distribution
1	4	Random
2	12	Random
3	2	Random
4	10	Random
5	9	Random
6	1	Random
7	10	Pattern (2 rows of 5)
8	13	Random
9	7	Random
10	12	Pattern (4 rows of 3)
11	8	Random
12	3	Random
13	14	Random
14	6	Random
15	9	Pattern (3 rows of 3)
16	5	Random
17	11	Random

31 PROCESSING MEANING ENHANCES RECALL

James J. Jenkins
University of South Florida

This activity, which requires little preparation, demonstrates an important finding concerning learning, memory, and cognition. The experiment is appropriate for introductory classes in psychology and in research methods. It is an in-class activity that requires 15 to 20 minutes of class time and involves all of the students. It can be conducted in any size class. In addition, it rapidly produces real data that can be used to illustrate simple nonparametric and parametric statistics such as the sign test and the t test for related measures.

CONCEPT

This simple experiment shows that tasks that involve processing the meaning of words aid in the recall of the words, whereas tasks that do not require such processing are not as effective. The activity also illustrates the recall method as a research technique, shows how memory depends largely on what people do with the words when they hear them, and illustrates experiments in which each participant is used as his or her own control group.

MATERIALS NEEDED

Make a list of 20 common nouns that are not related to each other in any obvious ways. Some should be one syllable; some should be two syllables or more. (An example list is given in Appendix 31.1.) Write each noun on a 3 × 5 card. On 10 of the cards write the letter A after the word, and on the rest write the letter B. Shuffle the cards so that the A's and the B's are well intermixed. Each student will need a sheet of paper and a pen. Now you are ready for the class.

INSTRUCTIONS

Have each student take a sheet of paper and number down the side from 1 to 20. Tell the students that they are going to hear a list of words that you will ask them to recall later but that first you want them to rate the words on two judgments. The letter that follows the word will tell them the judgment you want. If the word is followed by an **A,** you want them to write down how many syllables there are in the word. If the word is followed by a **B,** you want them to write whether they think the word is pleasant or unpleasant (**P** for pleasant and **U** for unpleasant). Put this information on the screen or chalkboard as a reminder.

Read the list of words at the rate of one word every 4 seconds or so. For example, "Table (pause), B (count 1, 2, 3, 4, to yourself), Ocean (pause), A, etc." When you have read the whole list, ask the students to turn over their papers. At this point say two or three general sentences about recall tasks or the importance of memory. (Your purpose here is to provide a little delay.) Then say, "I want you to try to recall all of the words you have just heard. You can recall them in any order you want. Just write the words in a straight column down the left hand side of the page. OK, go ahead." In 3 or 4 minutes they will have written all the words that they can recall.

Let the students score their own papers. Sort out the A cards and read the words to the class. Have each student total how many "A words" he or she recalled. Then make a frequency distribution on the screen or board. Ask the class how many recalled all 10 of the words, how many recalled 9, 8, and so on. Now, score the B words the same way. Make a frequency distribution right beside the first one. Some students will recall 8 or 9 of these 10 words, and the average is likely to be twice as high for the pleasant–unpleasant words as for the syllable-counted words.

To demonstrate the use of participants as their own control group, find out how many students recalled more A words than B words and how many recalled more B words than A words. Often no one falls in the first group, and everyone falls in the second.

DISCUSSION

Ask the class how to generalize from this experiment. What other tasks would work this way? What tasks would be good for remembering and which would be poor? Those that require thinking about the *meaning* of the word are generally good for recall. Here are some other tasks that I have used: "Is the word important or unimportant?" "What adjective goes with the noun?" "Would it be pleasant or unpleasant on a desert island?" In general, tasks concentrating on the *form* of the word are poor preparation for recall: "Is the word spelled with an e?" "How many letters are in it?" "Give me a word that rhymes with it." If you have more word lists ready, it is easy to test the students' ideas immediately. Finally, ask what the implications are for how one ought to study!

THEORETICAL BACKGROUND

Experiments of this sort, especially Hyde and Jenkins (1969) led Craik and Lockhart (1972) to advance a model of "levels of processing" in human memory. Their paper in turn was responsible for new attention to processing models of memory. At a conference on levels of processing in human memory (Cermak & Craik, 1979), there was a lot of disagreement about what "levels" really meant. Jenkins (1979) stressed the interaction between the kinds of processing involved in the original learning task and the kinds of processing required by the criterial measure of memory (recall, recognition, cued recall, etc.). An account of the history of this line of research and its importance in recent theorizing is given in Roediger, Gallo, and Geraci (2002).

REFERENCES AND SUGGESTED READING

Cermak, L. S., & Craik, F. I. M. (1979). (Eds.) *Levels of processing in human memory.* Hillsdale, NJ: Erlbaum.

Craik, F. I. M., & Lockhart, R. S. (1972). Levels of processing: A framework for memory research. *Journal of Verbal Learning and Verbal Behavior, 11,* 671–684.

Hyde, T. S., & Jenkins, J. J. (1969). Differential effects of incidental tasks on the organization of recall of a list of highly associated words. *Journal of Experimental Psychology, 82,* 472–481.

Jenkins, J. J. (1979). Four points to remember: A tetrahedral model of memory experiments. In L. S. Cermak & F. I. M. Craik (Eds.). *Levels of processing in human memory* (pp. 429–446). Hillsdale, NJ: Erlbaum.

Roediger, H. L., III (In press). Relativity of remembering: Why the laws of memory vanished. *Annual Review of Psychology.*

Roediger, H. L., III., Gallo, D. A., & Geraci, L. (2002). Processing approaches to cognition: The impetus from the levels-of-processing framework. *Memory, 10,* 319–332.

Appendix 31.1

Sample Word List

Book	A
Eagle	B
House	B
Table	A
King	A
Glasses	B
Tree	B
Spoon	A
Rug	B
Highway	A
River	B
Shoe	B
Lawn	A
Button	A
Kitten	B
Woman	A
Pepper	B
Lamp	B
Trouble	A
Hand	A

32 The Semantic Content of Long-Term Memory

George M. Diekhoff
Midwestern State University

This activity provides a convincing demonstration that what is stored in long-term memory is the meaning of the message, not a verbatim copy of the message. Students will also see how retrieval of information from long-term memory is a reconstructive process that includes a fair amount of confabulation, that is, recalling what must have been, not just what was actually experienced. The activity is appropriate for classes of any size in introductory psychology or for upper-division perception/cognition classes. It is an in-class activity that requires about 15 minutes of class time and involves all students.

CONCEPT

Errors in recalling items stored in short-term memory, though relatively rare, are usually acoustically similar to the correct items. For example, given the list TOAD, WALL, BOOK, and SKY, a participant in a short-term memory recall study might recall TOAD, BALL, BOOK, and SKY. The erroneously recalled item, BALL, sounds similar to the correct item, WALL, but the two items are semantically unrelated. This is taken as evidence that material is stored in short-term memory in an acoustic format. In contrast, errors in recall from long-term memory are more likely to be semantically similar to the correct items. Given the same list, a participant recalling from long-term memory might report: FROG, WALL, BOOK, and SKY. The erroneously recalled item, FROG, is acoustically dissimilar to the correct item, TOAD, but it is semantically related. This activity will demonstrate the tendency to store in long-term memory the deep structure (i.e., meaning) of a message rather than the surface structure (i.e., the specific words or physical stimulus characteristics) used in transmitting that meaning.

INSTRUCTIONS

At the beginning of a class period, read the following short passage from Nobel Prize winning author Doris Lessing's (1967) *Particularly Cats* to students:

> In the big sycamore at the bottom of the garden, a thrush builds a new nest every year. Every year, the little birds hatch out and take their first flights down into the jaws of waiting cats. Mother bird, father bird, comes down after them and is caught. The frightened chittering and squealing of a caught bird disturbs the house. Grey cat has brought the bird in, but only to be admired for her skill, for she plays with it, tortures it—and with what grace. Black cat crouches on the stairs and watches. But when three, four, five hours after grey cat has caught the thing and it is dead, or nearly so, black cat takes it and tosses it up and about, in emulation of the games grey cat plays. Every summer I rescue birds from grey cat. When this happens, grey cat is furious, puts her ears back, glares. When she brings a bird in she is proud. (p. 81)

The selection from *Particularly Cats* (copyright 1967, Doris Lessing) is reprinted by kind permission of Jonathan Clowes, Ltd., London, on behalf of Doris Lessing.

At the end of the class period, give each student a copy of the quiz (see Appendix 32.1) on the *Particularly Cats* passage or simply read the quiz to students and have them respond with a show of hands. The quiz contains three original sentences (2, 9, 10), three that contain semantic changes (4, 6, 12), three that retain the original meaning but contain syntax changes (1, 5, 8), and three that were not contained in the passage at all but were implied (3, 7, 11). Students are to determine for each sentence in the quiz if it is an exact duplicate of one contained in the passage (an "original" sentence) or if it is different in any way from the sentences in the passage (a "new" sentence).

Using a table like the one shown below, tabulate students' responses by recording the number of students who responded "original" and "new" to sentences of each of the four types. The asterisks in the table mark those cells that will contain the highest frequencies if your results match those typically found (Bransford, Barclay, & Franks, 1972; Sachs, 1967).

	Responses	
Type of sentence	Original	New
Original (2, 9, 10)	*	
Semantic Change (4, 6, 12)		*
Syntax Change (1, 5, 8)	*	
Implied (3, 7, 11)	*	

Students will be surprised at how often they identify sentences as "originals" that contain syntax changes or were merely implied by other sentences in the passage. Only sentences that involve an actual change in meaning are easily spotted as "new."

DISCUSSION

The fact that syntax changes are difficult to identify as "new" shows that sentence meanings, not the surface characteristics of those sentences, were stored in long-term memory. The difficulty that students have in identifying implied sentences as "new" illustrates the reconstructive nature of retrieval from long-term memory; that is, we tend to remember "what must have been" rather than what actually was.

You may want to discuss some or all of the following questions with students: What advantages might there be to the tendency to forget surface characteristics while retaining memory for meaning? What are some of the potential disadvantages? How does this fact of human memory influence students in scholastic situations? What impact might it have on the accuracy of eyewitness testimony in court? What does the tendency to confuse what actually happened with implications of those facts say about the accuracy of memory for temporally distant events (e.g., recall of the events of childhood)?

REFERENCES AND SUGGESTED READING

Ashcraft, M. (2006). *Cognition* (4th ed.). Upper Saddle River, NJ: Prentice-Hall.

Bartlett, F. C. (1932). *Remembering: A study in experimental and social psychology.* Cambridge, England: Cambridge University Press.

Bransford, J. D., Barclay, R., & Franks, J. (1972). Sentence memory: A constructive vs. interpretive approach. *Cognitive Psychology, 3,* 193–209.

Lessing, D. (1967). *Particularly cats.* New York: Simon & Schuster.

Sachs, J. S. (1967). Recognition memory for syntactic and semantic aspects of connected discourse. *Perception and Psychophysics, 2,* 437–442.

Schacter, D. L. (2002). *The seven sins of memory: How the mind forgets and remembers.* Boston: Houghton Mifflin.

Solso, R. L., MacLin, M. K., & MacLin, O. H. (2005). *Cognitive psychology* (7th ed.). Boston, MA: Pearson.

Appendix 32.1

Quiz on *Particularly Cats*

Directions: Place a checkmark next to each of the sentences below that appeared in the passage from Doris Lessing's *Particularly Cats*.

1. Every year thrushes build nests in the big sycamore at the bottom of the garden.

2. Every year, the little birds hatch out and take their first flights down into the jaws of waiting cats.

3. Each year, grey cat waits at the bottom of the sycamore tree.

4. The frightened chittering and squealing of a caught bird no longer disturbs the house.

5. Crouching on the stairs, black cat watches.

6. Mother bird, father bird, comes down after them, but they are not caught.

7. Black cat watches and waits for her turn.

8. But when three, four, five hours after grey cat has caught the thing and it is dead, or nearly so, black cat emulates grey cat's games, by tossing it up and about.

9. When this happens, grey cat is furious, puts her ears back, glares.

10. Grey cat has brought the bird in, but only to be admired for her skill, for she plays with it, tortures it— and with what grace.

11. Grey cat does not understand, no, not at all.

12. When she brings a bird in, she is ashamed.

CHAPTER 6
THINKING, PROBLEM SOLVING, AND LANGUAGE

Thinking, problem solving, and language are typically subsumed under the heading of cognitive processes, which also includes perception, learning, and memory, the subjects of earlier chapters. In this chapter you will find activities for critical thinking, selective attention, hindrances to problem solving including functional fixedness, and the effect of expectancies on language.

Activity 33 uses four ways of knowing (intuition, authority, rationalism, and empiricism) to engage students in a series of critical thinking exercises involving myths (e.g., that we use only 10% of our brains) and urban legends (e.g., that B. F. Skinner raised his daughter in a box and she later sued him). One of the goals of this activity is to help students understand psychology as a science.

Activity 34 deals with the concept of set or what is sometimes called *mental set*. Students are read a passage and expected to recall some information from it. But what should they recall? This activity shows how selective attention affects the processing of information, thus making some information available for subsequent retrieval while causing other information to be lost.

In Activity 35, students who may have never seen a long-playing record are asked to play one so that the music can be heard. But how can they do it with the materials they have been given—a pad of paper, a marker pen, rubber bands, a paper clip, a sewing kit, a roll of transparent tape, and so forth? This group exercise illustrates several issues associated with problem solving, including functional fixedness.

Perception is influenced by our expectancies, a point made in Activity 34. We tend to perceive our world in a way that is consistent with those expectancies. Activity 36 illustrates this point with regard to the perception of language, showing how the learned rules of spelling, grammar, and semantics provide the basis for our linguistic expectancies. Two demonstrations of the effects of expectancy on the perception of language are provided.

33 THE USE OF URBAN LEGENDS TO IMPROVE CRITICAL THINKING

Alva Hughes
Randolph-Macon College

Critical thinking involves an assessment of how we determine the truthfulness of information we encounter. As they evaluate urban legends, this activity encourages students to think critically about the way they make decisions about truth. The activity can also be used to launch a discussion of the value various cultures place on ways of knowing. This is an out-of-class activity that involves all students and can be used with any size class. It is appropriate for introductory psychology, cognition, and research methods classes.

CONCEPT

Although methods of assessing truth have been given a variety of labels, four basic approaches are usually covered in research methods texts: intuition, authority, rationalism, and empiricism (e.g., Graziano & Raulin, 2006). Introductory psychology text books typically have a more narrow focus and contrast intuition with empiricism (e.g., Myers, 2007). This activity can be tailored to fit the approaches discussed in any textbook. When we use intuition to make decisions about truth, we rely on the use of nonrational, nonconscious abilities. We go with our gut feeling. When we use authority to make decisions about truth, we rely on someone else's knowledge and expertise (this can be a good time to talk about the difference between knowledge in a peer-reviewed scientific journal versus knowledge obtained from a multitude of Internet sites). When we use rationalism to make decisions about truth, we rely on the rules of logic or on reason. Finally, when we use empiricism to make decisions about truth, we rely on objective observational techniques.

The information on methods of knowledge testing could be conveyed to students using the traditional lecture format; however, critical thinking is an active rather than a passive skill. The most effective way to teach students to use critical thinking is to have them actually apply each of the four methods of evaluating knowledge. The following assignment allows students to practice the four methods of knowing by evaluating a series of claims described as urban legends. Urban legends are stories that the storyteller believes to be true. The events in the story happened to "a friend of a friend" or were reported in the media and heard by someone once or twice removed from the teller (Brunvand, 1981). The stories include a high level of detail and often have a moral. Students use the ways of knowing to decide whether the claim is valid or whether it is an urban legend. These claims listed in Exhibit 33.1 were taken from Snopes.com, which investigates rumors and urban legends. An alternative would be to select claims from collections of urban legends (e.g., Brunvand, 1981, 2001, 2002), talk shows, or tabloids.

MATERIALS

1. Definitions of the four ways of knowing.
2. Urban legends or other claims. Exhibit 33.1 presents a list of sample legends based on those found on Snopes (http://www.snopes.com). Some of the statements

Exhibit 33.1. *Claims to Be Evaluated*

1. We only use 10% of our brains.
2. Vinyl lunchboxes contain unsafe levels of lead.
3. Psychologist B. F. Skinner's daughter was traumatized by being raised in a Skinner box and later sued her father.
4. Drug dealers are selling flavored crystal methamphetamine called *strawberry quick*.
5. Bananas will be extinct in 10 years.
6. Forty-five percent of the $20 bills in circulation in the United States are contaminated with cocaine.
7. Bubonic plague still exists in the western United States, but it does not cause epidemics.
8. Raisins can cause acute renal failure in dogs.
9. The stereotypical American image of Santa Claus originated in a Coca-Cola advertising campaign.
10. Tattoos laced with LSD are used to hook children on drugs.

should be true so that students will not be able to assume that all of the claims are false.

INSTRUCTIONS Present the students with a 20-minute lecture on the four methods of knowing. Following the lecture, assign the students to work in groups of two (or in larger classes you might want to use larger groups). Give each group the description of an urban legend, and ask the students to discover the truth about the legend using each of the four methods of knowing. Inform students that some legends cannot be tested empirically for ethical or practical reasons. If some students are assigned a legend that they cannot actually test, ask them to describe an experiment that could be used to validate the claim. Give students 1 week to complete the assignment.

DISCUSSION The class can discuss the usefulness of empiricism in validating claims. The discussion can include the fact that science uses all four ways of knowing. As scientists, we use intuition to generate hypotheses, and we often use authority by basing our decisions on reviews of existing research findings. We use logic and empiricism in designing experiments and in interpreting the results. The discussion can also include the fact that there are cultural differences in the value placed on empiricism and on authority. Traditional societies often place more emphasis on authority, whereas technological societies often emphasize empiricism and ignore the logic, intuition, and authority that also underlie science. Finally, the discussion can show students they now have the tools to validate information that they encounter as part of their daily lives. The assignment can help students to see why psychology is a science. It can also help them to see how the methods of psychology are related to life.

REFERENCES AND SUGGESTED READING Brunvand, J. (1981). *The vanishing hitchhiker.* New York: Norton.

Brunvand, J. (2001). *Too good to be true: The colossal book of urban legends.* New York: Norton.

Brunvand, J. (2002). *Encyclopedia of urban legends.* New York: Norton.

Graziano, A., & Raulin, M. (2006). *Research methods: A process of inquiry* (6th ed.). Boston: Allyn & Bacon.

Myers, D. (2007) *Psychology* (8th ed.). New York: Worth.

34 SET AND INFORMATION PROCESSING

Michael Wertheimer

University of Colorado at Boulder

This simple in-class activity demonstrates how selective attention affects the processing of information. It is appropriate for classes in introductory psychology, perception, and cognition and can be used in classes of any size. All students have the opportunity to participate. Approximately 15 minutes is required for the activity, but it can go longer and often does with a lively discussion.

CONCEPT

Human beings live in an environment that supplies enormous amounts of information. Cognitive processes are normally set to select some portion of this input and ignore other parts. What we choose to pay attention to is often referred to as *set*. Normally only those aspects of information input to which we are attuned are processed. The parts that get ignored typically remain inaccessible to further processing.

MATERIALS NEEDED

Students will each need a piece of paper and a writing instrument. You will need a narrative, including a set of numbers that is read aloud to the class. The particular numbers used are at your discretion (although the numbers should be fairly small and easy to process in the interest both of making the exercise realistic and of keeping the mental arithmetic that the students will engage in reasonably easy). Here is an example of a narrative that you might use:

> Assume that you're the engineer of a passenger train. At the first station, 20 passengers get on. At the next station, 5 passengers get off and 15 get on. At the next station, 10 passengers get off and 12 get on. At the next station, 7 get off and 10 get on. At the next station, 50 passengers get off and 5 get on. At the next station, 8 passengers get off and 3 get on.

INSTRUCTIONS

Slowly read the narrative to the class, pausing between sentences and after each number phrase. (The pause after each number phrase not only permits the students to perform the mental arithmetic, but also helps imply that the students should perform the mental calculations). After you have completed the narrative, ask the students to write down, on successive lines of a piece of paper, the numbers 1 through 5. Then ask the students to write the numbers that answer the following five questions after the numbers 1 through 5.

First question: "How old is the engineer of the train?" Second question: "How many stations were there?" Third question: "How many passengers are left on the train?" Fourth question: "Altogether, how many passengers have gotten off the train since the first station?" Fifth question: "Altogether, how many passengers have gotten on the train anywhere along its route?" Make sure that students have answered all of the five questions before you begin discussion of each question.

DISCUSSION

Most participants, if they have not encountered this demonstration (and probably it will be familiar to at least a few of them—that is one of the reasons for including the last two questions, which they are less likely to have run across before), will be startled by the first question and will react helplessly, wondering how in the world the information provided could give them any clue about the age of the engineer. When you remind the class of the first sentence of the narrative, "Assume that you're the engineer of a passenger train," many will groan or show other signs of insight: If the listener is the engineer of the train, then of course the answer is the listener's own age. In their initial processing of the information provided, the fact that the listener was to be considered the engineer of the train was regarded as inconsequential and hence did not make it into some students' memories.

As for the answer to the second question, most participants who go through the exercise the first time are so busy keeping track of the number of passengers on the train that they fail to register how many stations there are. The third question may be answered correctly by the students who were taken in by the set to keep track of the number of passengers on the train, but is apt to be missed by the participants in the know who therefore kept track of the number of stations but not the number of passengers.

The fourth and fifth questions are there to make the point that whether or not the students were aware of the trick nature of the exercise, they still were highly unlikely to engage in the cognitive processing that would have been necessary to answer them correctly, given their understanding of the task—even though they too are perfectly reasonable questions that could easily have been answered by anyone who was set to keep track of the relevant quantities.

You may wish to read the entire narrative again after all this, so that the students can try to keep track of all the information needed to answer all the questions—but none of the students will be able to do so, even with the best of intentions, without using paper and pencil. It is just about impossible to retain all four numbers mentally after each station. Modern cognitive models of attention make clear that we have a limited capacity to store and process incoming information; keeping track of more than one or two of these quantities results in information overload. The human cognitive system cannot do it without help. The point of the entire demonstration, of course, is that we attend selectively to all input and process it in only one or a few of the many ways in which it could be processed.

REFERENCES AND SUGGESTED READING

Goldstein, E. B. (2007). *Sensation & perception* (7th ed.). Belmont, CA: Wadsworth.

Kramer, A. F., Logan, G. D., & Coles, M. G. H. (Eds.). (1995). *Converging operations in the study of visual selective attention* (Monograph). Washington, DC: American Psychological Association.

Solso, R. L., MacLin, M. K., & MacLin, O. H. (2005). *Cognitive psychology* (7th ed.). Boston: Pearson.

Styles, E. A. (2005). *Attention, perception, and memory: An integrated introduction.* New York: Psychology Press.

Styles, E. A. (2006). *The psychology of attention* (2nd ed.). New York: Psychology Press.

35 FUNCTIONAL FIXEDNESS IN PROBLEM SOLVING

Douglas A. Bernstein
University of South Florida
University of Southampton

Sandra Goss Lucas
University of Illinois

One of the most interesting obstacles to problem solving is functional fixedness, the failure to think of using familiar objects in novel or unfamiliar ways to solve a problem. The most common textbook example of this phenomenon uses the two-string problem (in which a pair of scissors must be used as a pendulum to bring together the ends of two strings that are hanging too far apart to be reached simultaneously). This activity, which is appropriate for classes in introductory psychology and cognition, offers another problem that appeared many years ago on the Mr. Wizard television show. The in-class activity can be done as a whole class exercise or in small groups working separately. Students should be given 10 to 15 minutes to attempt to solve the problem, and discussion will probably take another 10 to 15 minutes.

CONCEPT
This demonstration helps students recognize how easily functional fixedness—a term coined by German psychologist Karl Duncker in 1945—and other cognitive habits can form obstacles to problem solving. The demonstration also helps reveal the effects of prior knowledge, stress, group processes, and gender stereotypes on problem solving.

MATERIALS NEEDED
Assemble an array of items including a sewing kit, a pad of $8\frac{1}{2} \times 11$ inch paper, a roll of transparent tape, a marker pen, and an old phonograph record that you don't mind damaging. To make the students' task more difficult, add to this core set of materials several other diverse and interesting—but, for this task, useless—items such as a tennis ball, a tool kit, an apple, paper clips, and rubber bands. If you plan to ask your students to solve this problem in small groups, you will need an identical set of materials for each group (although the records can differ for each group).

INSTRUCTIONS
Tell the students that the problem to be solved is to play the phonograph record so that the class can hear it, using only the materials displayed. Then show them the entire item array, being sure to use the pad of paper as a tray. Ask for suggestions for solving this problem, and let the class offer them. You can appoint one student to handle the materials according to student suggestions (e.g., "tape the point of the marker pen to the record"), or you can do this yourself.

If you want to make this a small-group project, the instructions remain the same, but in this case, your role is to stroll around the room observing progress while each group works on the problem with its own set of materials. To stimulate later discussion, you should take special note of the appearance of problem-solving obstacles, examples of gender bias, group process effects, and other phenomena. For example, you might notice that men tend to take the lead in the task or that older students, who are likely to have more knowledge of and experience with phonographs, might perform better on this task.

To demonstrate the effect of stress on problem solving, set a short time limit for solving the problem or, better yet, divide the class into several competing groups with a reward for the group that solves the problem first.

DISCUSSION   Because none of the items in the materials provided, except the record, is normally associated with record playing, it may take a while for the students to think of the following solution: Take a sheet of paper from the pad, roll it from one corner to form a cone, and tape the edge to hold that conical shape. Then tape a needle from the sewing kit to the outside of the narrow end of the paper cone so that its point extends an inch or so beyond the cone. Now take the cap off the marker pen and push the point of the pen firmly into the hole in the record (be sure to choose a pen that will fit snugly). By resting the back end of the pen vertically on a flat surface and turning its barrel, the record can be turned clockwise in a horizontal plane. While turning the record in this way, grasp the edge of the large end of the paper cone between thumb and forefinger and let the needle rest on the turning record. (It often helps to have two people working together: one to spin the record and the other to hold the cone.) It will not be high fidelity or stereo, but the sound will be amplified enough for everyone to hear. If the sound is too faint, exert a little downward pressure on the needle.

Most students have a difficult time solving this problem because they show functional fixedness about the items provided. For example, they may use the sewing kit case itself rather than opening it and using the needle. They may ignore the pad of paper, viewing it as simply something to hold the objects.

We have noticed that males often try to take over the problem-solving process. If a male says something like "I'm in engineering," the rest of the class will defer to his implied expertise. Sometimes a male will become the self-appointed leader of the group and ignore suggestions made by females. The instructor's observations of such group processes and other aspects of the problem-solving session often prompt discussions about how groups function, the role of expertise, the need for domain-relevant knowledge (students are becoming increasingly unfamiliar with the principles of the phonograph record and its amplification), and the persistence of incorrect problem solutions.

You might also ask one person in the class, or one in each group, to record the sequence of all suggestions made to solve the problem. Students can use copies of this record as the basis of a short paper comparing their problem-solving strategy and obstacles with those discussed in class or in the textbook. Students can also be encouraged to include comments or observations about their particular group's problem-solving attempts that especially intrigued them. It is often in this section that issues like gender stereotypes and narrowed attention will be discussed.

REFERENCES AND SUGGESTED READING

Defeyter, M. A., & German, T. P. (2003). Acquiring an understanding of design: Evidence from children's insight problem solving. *Cognition, 89,* 133–155.

Duncker, K. (1945). On problem solving. *Psychological Monographs, 58* (Whole No. 270).

German, T. P., & Barrett, H. C. (2005). Functional fixedness in a technologically sparse culture. *Psychological Science, 16,* 1–5.

German, T. P., & Defeyter, M. A. (2000). Immunity to functional fixedness in young children. *Psychonomic Bulletin & Review, 7,* 707–712.

Halpern, D. F. (Ed.). (1994). *Changing college classrooms: New teaching and learning strategies for an increasingly complex world.* San Francisco: Jossey-Bass.

Halpern, D. F. (2003) *Thought and knowledge* (4th ed.). Mahwah, NJ: Lawrence Erlbaum.

36 ROLE OF EXPECTANCIES IN THE PERCEPTION OF LANGUAGE

George M. Diekhoff
Midwestern State University

This activity will help students learn how expectancies established by the rules of grammar and semantics influence and even distort our perceptions of written and spoken language. The activity can serve to introduce the broader concept of top-down or conceptually driven information processing in perception. It is appropriate for classes of any size in introductory psychology or for upper-division perception/cognition classes. It is an in-class activity that requires about 10 minutes of class time and involves all students.

CONCEPT   It is generally true that perception is influenced by our expectancies and that we tend to perceive the world in a manner that is consistent with those expectancies. This is easily demonstrated in the perception of spoken and written language, in which the learned rules of spelling, grammar, and semantics provide much of the basis for our expectancies. These rules lead us to expect certain letter and word strings over others, and the accuracy and ease of the perception of linguistic stimuli are influenced by the degree to which they conform to our expectations (Miller & Isard, 1963). The following demonstrations illustrate the influence of expectancy on the perception of language and set the stage for a broader discussion of top-down processing, conceptually driven processing, and the subjectivity of perception.

INSTRUCTIONS   *Demonstration 1: Perception of written language.* Prepare a large sign or PowerPoint slide that reads:

Flowers bloom
in the
the spring.

(Read carefully! The word "the" appears twice in this stimulus.)

Tell students that you are going to show them a short message very briefly. Then, present the stimulus for no more than 3 seconds. Using a show of hands, ask students how many saw "Flowers bloom in the the spring." Invariably, one-half to two-thirds of the class will respond. Show students the stimulus again and point out their error.

Demonstration 2: Perception of spoken speech. Prepare several sentences that are grammatical and meaningful (e.g., "The dog looked warily over its shoulder and then gobbled down the hot dog."), grammatical but meaningless (e.g., "The door ate the sky loudly, but would not drop the ocean."), and ungrammatical and meaningless (e.g., "Door ocean the quickly sky over drop shoulder the nor warily and.").

Tell students that you will read each of several sentences slowly, but only once. Their task is to write down, verbatim, each sentence as it is read. Read the prepared sentences fast enough to force students to transcribe at a rapid pace, but slow enough to allow them to transcribe the grammatical/meaningful sentences accurately. Have students score the accuracy of their transcriptions by reading the sentences again and having students count the number of words copied correctly from each sentence. Compare the percentages of accurately copied words for each of the three types of sentences. Accuracy will be highest for grammatical/meaningful sentences, less accurate for grammatical/meaningless sentences, and least accurate for ungrammatical/meaningless sentences.

DISCUSSION

It is important that the observed effects be explained to students by showing that they are specific cases of a general principle. In the first activity, the second "the" in the sentence "Flowers bloom in the the spring" is often not perceived because the rules of grammar prohibit the word's occurrence twice in sequence. Perceptions conform to this grammar-induced expectancy and we see what we expect to see, not what is in front of our eyes.

In the second activity, perception of the grammatical/meaningful sentences is most accurate because neither the rules of grammar nor semantics are violated by these sentences. Our expectancies match with the stimuli, leading to accurate perceptions. Grammatical/meaningless sentences are less accurately perceived because, although the expectancies established by the rules of grammar are not violated, expectancies from semantics are. Finally, ungrammatical/meaningless sentences are perceived least accurately because these sentences violate all of our expectancies, those established through grammar as well as those established by semantics.

Further explanation can involve the theoretical mechanisms underlying the effects of expectancies on perception. Donald Hebb's theory of cell assemblies and phase sequences (Allport, 1955; Hebb, 1949) included the proposition that expectancies lead to a partial preactivation of the neural structures that underlie the perception of the expected stimulus. These preactivated structures then require less additional stimulus activation to come to full activation (i.e., perception). When one's expectancies (and corresponding patterns of neural preactivation) are inconsistent with the stimuli actually encountered, greater stimulus support is required to activate fully the neural structures underlying correct perceptions.

Some nonphysiological explanations have also been offered. Ulric Neisser, in his modified theory of analysis by synthesis (Neisser, 1967, 1976), proposed that language perception occurs when a preliminary analysis of an incoming message leads one to generate general hypotheses as to what will come next. These expectancies direct subsequent attentional processes to determine what will be picked up next. Linguistic stimuli that violate our expectancies are more difficult to perceive accurately because our expectancies direct our attention in a manner that is inconsistent with these unexpected stimuli.

In his feature analytic theory of pattern recognition, Jerome Bruner (1957) proposed that perception involves an analysis of the features of an incoming stimulus into a feature list. This feature list is taken to long-term memory, where a search is made for the most closely matching stored feature list. That stored feature list, when found, is activated and recognition occurs. Bruner also proposed that stored feature lists vary in their accessibility, and that accessibility is determined in part by our expectancies: Feature lists for stimuli that we expect to see are more accessible; feature lists for unexpected stimuli are less accessible. Expectancies established by grammar, semantics, and other factors influence the accessibility of stored feature lists in this way, making it harder to perceive ungrammatical or nonsensical linguistic stimuli and easier to perceive grammatical and meaningful linguistic stimuli.

More recently, network models of cognitive structure have attempted to explain the influence of expectations on perception as being a result of "spreading activation" from one concept node to another through the cognitive structure. Though the terms used have changed, the fundamental ideas about how expectancies shape perception have been quite consistent over the years.

Although the activities described here illustrate most directly the influence of grammar- and semantics-established expectancies on the perception of language, you may want to discuss with students other kinds of perceptions that are shaped by expectancies established in other ways. How might prejudices shape interpersonal perceptions? How might a scientist's expectations for the outcome of an experiment influence his or her interpretation of the data? Moving from perception to memory, how might eyewitness testimony be affected by the wording of the attorney's questions?

In addition to examining the distorting effects of expectancies on perception, you might also encourage students to think about the potential benefits that derive from this influence. Expectancies can make perception more accurate and less effortful. After all, most of the time the world that we encounter does not violate our expectancies, it is consistent with those expectancies.

In conclusion, students will discover from these activities and subsequent discussions that we do not always see things the way we do because "that's the way they are." Instead, sometimes we see things the way we do because "that's the way *we* are."

REFERENCES AND SUGGESTED READING

Allport, F. H. (1955). *Theories of perception and the concept of structure.* New York: Wiley.

Biederman, I. (1972). Perceiving real-world scenes. *Science, 177,* 77–80.

Biederman, I., & Cooper, E. E. (1991). Priming contour-deleted images: Evidence for intermediate representation in visual object recognition. *Cognitive Psychology, 23,* 393–419.

Bruner, J. S. (1957). On perceptual readiness. *Psychological Review, 64,* 123–152.

Hebb, D. O. (1949). *The organization of behavior.* New York: Wiley.

Matlin, M. W. (2004). *Cognition* (6th ed.). Hoboken, NJ: John Wiley & Sons.

Miller, G. A., & Isard, S. (1963). Some perceptual consequences of linguistic rules. *Journal of Verbal Learning and Verbal Behavior, 2,* 217–228.

Neisser, U. (1967). *Cognitive psychology.* New York: Appleton-Century-Crofts.

Neisser, U. (1976). *Cognition and reality.* San Francisco: Freeman.

CHAPTER 7
MOTIVATION AND EMOTION

This chapter emphasizes discussion exercises on several issues of motivation and emotion that are especially relevant to college students. These activities cover the topics of aggression, sexual orientation, and the range of anxieties common among college students as revealed in a survey of student worries.

Aggression is a topic that is often treated in units on motivation or social psychology. In this book we have placed it in the former category. Activity 37 is a discussion exercise based on an in-class questionnaire that covers most of the principal issues in aggression such as harm to living versus nonliving things, accident versus intention, instrumental versus hostile aggression, actual damage versus no physical damage, self-defense, passive aggressiveness, killing for sport, and so forth.

Activity 38 is a small-group, discussion-based exercise that shows students the difficulty of defining sexual orientation. The activity identifies several factors that may be important in identifying sexual orientation, such as age, context, forms of behavior, emotional attachment, and sexual fantasy content.

Anxieties are a normal part of student life. Students worry about their health and appearance, romantic relationships, social acceptance, money, grades, and what they will do after they graduate. Activity 39 uses a 35-item "student worries" questionnaire to serve as a basis for class discussion on these highly relevant issues.

37 DEFINING AGGRESSION

Ludy T. Benjamin, Jr.

Texas A&M University

This is a discussion activity (based on a questionnaire) that explores the topic of aggression but also provides insights into the nature of psychological constructs and operational definitions. It is appropriate for any class where aggression is part of the subject matter or in courses treating the issue of definition and measurement of psychological constructs. In an introductory psychology course it is perhaps most appropriate in the units on motivation and emotion or social psychology. This is an in-class activity that typically requires 30 to 45 minutes. It involves all students in the class, and can be used, albeit differently, in large and small classes.

CONCEPT   This activity is designed to generate class discussion on the definition of aggression and related issues of causation and control. It exposes students to a large number of issues involved in defining aggression and helps them to understand the complexity of such a construct and, thus, the reasons why their classmates and psychologists disagree about its meaning.

Aggression is a topic included in virtually every textbook on introductory psychology. Some books discuss aggression in the section on motivation and emotion, whereas others cover it as part of social psychology. Most include it in reference to research on humans, but discussion of some animal studies of aggression is also common. Related concepts such as violence, anger, frustration, and assertiveness are also common topics.

Although textbook coverage of aggression is almost guaranteed, a definition of the term is not. In a nonrandom sample of 10 introductory psychology books (selected from my bookcase), 5 provided an explicit definition of aggression but the others left the meaning embedded in a series of paragraphs and so required the reader to serve as lexicographer. Considering the complexity of the term *aggression*, it is not surprising that these authors might choose to avoid espousing a particular definition.

In this activity, aggression is used as an example of a typical construct in psychology, permeated with a host of subtle meanings and not-so-subtle disagreements that make it difficult to reach a consensual definition (other similarly difficult constructs include intelligence and self-esteem). Aggression is a topic that is of keen interest to students. Anecdotal evidence for the fascination with this subject can be drawn from the prevalence of aggression as a theme in movies and television, the growing popularity of violent sports, and the interest many people show in reports of violent crime. As I write this, it is only 1 week since the mass murder of 32 students and professors at Virginia Tech University.

The exercise described here can be used in a number of classes, including introductory psychology or anywhere you treat the topic of aggression. It should be used prior to any lecture on aggression and before the students have read their textbook coverage of the subject. This activity works best in a class of 50 students or fewer, but by altering the data reporting procedures it can be used in much larger classes, although discussion obviously will suffer in large classes. The activity takes about 50 minutes but could be made shorter or longer. The instructor's role in this exercise is to serve as a tabulator of the data and as moderator of the discussion. In very large classes—for example, 200 students or more—the questionnaire can be used to collect data from the class in advance of a lecture on aggression in which the lecturer introduces the data from the class in an aggregated form.

MATERIALS NEEDED

You will need to make enough copies of the aggression questionnaire shown in Appendix 37.1 to provide one to each student in the class.

INSTRUCTIONS

At the beginning of the class, give each student a copy of the aggression questionnaire which contains 26 numbered statements. Instruct the students as follows: "Read each statement and decide whether or not you believe the situation described is one of aggression." Wording of this instruction is critical so as not to bias the responses. Avoid using phrases like "aggressive act" or "aggressive behavior," because one of the issues to be discussed is whether some overt behavior needs to occur in aggression. Tell students to circle the number of each statement that describes aggression. Tell them they should respond according to their own beliefs and not how they think they should respond or how they think most people would respond. Compliance with this request can be enhanced by telling the students not to put their names on the questionnaires. Indeed, there is no reason in this exercise to know how a particular person responded. You may want to have the students indicate their sex on the questionnaire if you are interested in looking at potential sex differences in the definition of aggression. Such differences, if obtained, would undoubtedly add to the interest in the discussion.

Allow the students about 5 minutes to complete the questionnaire. Most, if not all, of the students will finish before that time (indeed, many will finish in 3 minutes or less), so you should be ready to proceed when the last person has finished. Collect the questionnaires, shuffle, and redistribute them to the class so that each student gets a copy. Most students will be given a questionnaire other than their own, but it is unimportant if they get their own copy back. This procedure allows students to report on the responses that may or may not be their own, thus eliminating a potential source of embarrassment.

Record the data on the board by reading the number of each statement aloud and asking students to raise their hands if the item is circled on the questionnaire they are holding. It is important to know the exact number of questionnaires in this exercise to know when you have unanimity. For example, with a class size of 34, total agreement would come from a score of 34 or a score of 0. A unanimous score is rare and typically occurs only on those few items in which there seems to be no intent to harm. Tabulating the data on the chalkboard can be accomplished quickly, usually in less than 5 minutes, so that the bulk of the class time can be devoted to discussion. If the class is large—for example, more than 50 students—collect the questionnaires for tabulation of the data outside of class, and then use the data in a subsequent class.

DISCUSSION

Use the questionnaire results to get the students talking about how aggression is defined. You might begin with those items for which there is greater agreement and proceed to those on which the class is evenly divided. Note that the 26 statements are quite diverse and are intended to span the gamut of issues related to aggression: harm to living versus nonliving things (Statements 9 and 23), accident versus intention (8 and 21), instrumental aggression (26), actual damage versus no physical damage (10, 13, and 18), self-defense (3, 13, and 14), duty or job responsibility (3, 4, 19, 20, and 22), predation and instinctual behavior (1, 2, and 25), survival (1, 6, and 16), acts involving animals other than humans

(7, 16, 17, and 18), covert acts (11 and 14), passive-aggressiveness and inaction (12 and 15), self-injury (24), and killing for sport (17 and 25).

Help students grasp these issues by grouping the related items in the discussion. For example, Statements 16 and 17 make an interesting comparison. The latter is more often viewed as aggressive, and a similar pattern emerges in Statements 1 and 25. In both pairs, students distinguish between killing for food and killing for sport. Many will argue that food seeking justifies the act and would not label it aggression. Debate on these items and many others is typically lively and opposing viewpoints are common. If alternative views are not forthcoming on some issues, you may wish to play the role of devil's advocate. Ask how a fly might answer Question 1.

If there is time, or in a separate lecture in the next class period, you can present some of the definitions of aggression proposed by psychologists. Consider the following examples:

1. "A form of antisocial behavior that is directed against another person or persons, intended to cause harm or injury to the recipient of the aggression" (Sternberg, 2004, p. A-24).
2. "Hostile action directed against another member of one's species, usually intended to do physical or social harm or, for hostile intent, to limit the target's actions" (Gleitman, Reisberg, & Gross, 2007, p. G-1).
3. "Any behavior that is intended to cause harm to others (whether or not harm actually results)" (Zimbardo, Weber, & Johnson, 2003, p. 572).
4. "Behavior that is intended to harm another living being who does not wish to be harmed" (Kosslyn & Rosenberg, 2004, p. G-1).
5. "Verbal or physical behavior aimed at harming another person" (Sdorow & Rickabaugh, 2002, p. 502).
6. "Behavior that is intended to injure another person (physically or verbally) or to destroy property" (Atkinson, Atkinson, & Hilgard, 1983, p. 321).
7. "A response that delivers noxious stimuli to another organism" (Buss, 1961, p. 3).

The first six definitions require intent, but the last one does not. Definitions 1, 5, and 6 limit aggression to humans, with no mention of other species. Definition 6 is the only one that recognizes that aggression can be directed at property, thus kicking wastebaskets and smashing tennis rackets (see the questionnaire) could qualify. All definitions talk about behaviors, actions, or responses but are unclear as to whether inaction can be aggressive or not. Definitions 5 and 6 specifically mention that aggression can be verbal behavior. Definition 4 seems to exclude masochists. Definition 3 makes it clear that only the intent to harm is required; that is, it can still be aggression if no harm is done but the intent to harm was present. Providing these definitions to students helps them to understand that, like themselves, psychologists also have some difficulty in agreeing on what does or does not constitute aggression.

Students in my classes consistently have rated this activity high in terms of satisfaction and as an exercise in learning. Written comments indicate that a number of them believe that it serves to sharpen their critical thinking skills. A few miss the point and want to be told the "real" definition of aggression after the exercise is over, but that kind of reaction is quite rare.

You can use this exercise as a basis for discussion or as a lecture on the causes of aggression. Questions for discussion include the following: Is aggression instinctual? Is aggression a natural reaction to conditions such as frustration, conflict, and pain? Is aggression learned or innate? Consider contrasting the views of Konrad Lorenz, novelist William Golding (as espoused in his *Lord of the Flies*), and B. F. Skinner. If aggression is learned, what sources seem important? This last question presents a good opportunity to discuss aggression in the media, particularly television and video and computer games, and what effect they may have on the behavior of viewers (see Anderson & Bushman, 2002, and Freedman, 2002, for conflicting views). Other topics of interest include aggression in athletics, competitiveness versus aggressiveness, assertiveness versus aggressiveness, the positive role of aggression, violent crime, the relation of prejudice to aggression, and methods for the control of aggression.

REFERENCES AND SUGGESTED READING

Anderson, C. A., & Bushman, B. J. (2002). Human aggression. *Annual Review of Psychology, 53*, 27–51.

Atkinson, R. L., Atkinson, R. C., & Hilgard, E. R. (1983). *Introduction to psychology* (8th ed.). New York: Harcourt Brace Jovanovich.

Benjamin, L. T., Jr. (1985). Defining aggression: An exercise for classroom discussion. Teaching of Psychology, 12, 40–42.

Buss, A. (1961). *The psychology of aggression*. New York: Wiley.

Freedman, J. (2002). *Media violence and its effect on aggression: Assessing the scientific evidence*. Toronto, Ontario, Canada: University of Toronto Press.

Gleitman, H., Reisberg, D., & Gross, J. (2007). *Psychology* (7th ed.). New York: W. W. Norton.

Kosslyn, S. M., & Rosenberg, R. S. (2004). *Psychology: The brain, the person, the world* (2nd ed.). Boston: Pearson.

Krahé, B. (2001). *The social psychology of aggression*. Philadelphia: Taylor & Francis.

Sdorow, L. M., & Rickabaugh, C. A. (2002). *Psychology* (5th ed.). New York: McGraw-Hill.

Sternberg, R. J. (2004). *Psychology* (4th ed.). Belmont, CA: Wadsworth.

Zimbardo, P. G., Weber, A. L., & Johnson, R. L. (2003). *Psychology: Core concepts* (4th ed.). Boston: Allyn and Bacon.

Appendix 37.1

Questionnaire

1. A spider eats a fly.
2. Two wolves fight for leadership of the pack.
3. A soldier shoots an enemy at the front line.
4. The warden of a prison executes a convicted criminal.
5. A juvenile gang attacks members of another gang.
6. Two people fight for a piece of bread.
7. A person viciously kicks a cat.
8. A man, while cleaning a window, knocks over a flowerpot which, in falling, injures a pedestrian.
9. A girl kicks a wastebasket.
10. Mr. Bradley, a notorious gossip, speaks disparagingly of many people of his acquaintance.
11. A woman mentally rehearses a murder she is about to commit.
12. An angry daughter purposely fails to write to her mother, who is expecting a letter and will be hurt if none arrives.
13. An enraged boy tries with all his might to inflict injury on his antagonist, a bigger boy, but is not successful in doing so. His efforts simply amuse the bigger boy.
14. A woman dreams of harming her antagonist but has no hope of doing so.
15. A senator does not protest the escalation of bombing to which she is morally opposed.
16. A farmer beheads a chicken and prepares it for supper.
17. A hunter kills an animal and mounts it as a trophy.
18. A dog snarls at a mail carrier but does not bite.
19. A physician gives a flu shot to a screaming child.
20. A boxer gives his opponent a bloody nose.
21. A Girl Scout tries to assist an elderly woman but trips her by accident.
22. A bank robber is shot in the back while trying to escape.
23. A tennis player smashes his racket after missing a volley.
24. A person commits suicide.
25. A cat kills a mouse, parades around with it, and then discards it.
26. A high school student running to the cafeteria for lunch bumps into a classmate, causing her to fall down.

Adapted from Johnson (1972); Kaufman (1970); and Krech, Crutchfield, Livson, Wilson, and Parducci (1982).

38 Exploring the Concept of Sexual Orientation Through Classroom Discussion

Mark G. Hartlaub

Texas A & M University—Corpus Christi

Using a small-group format, this activity was created to help students understand the difficulties in defining sexual orientation. Once they have completed the exercise, students will be able to list and briefly discuss several factors relevant to defining sexual orientation. This in-class activity is appropriate for classes in introductory psychology, social psychology, and human sexuality. It involves all students in the class, can be used in classes of any size, and requires one class period to complete.

CONCEPT

Although psychologists generally realize how difficult it is to define sexual orientation, students often do not. This activity will allow you to introduce students to the concept of sexual orientation and then extend the discussion into various aspects of sexual orientation, starting with the measurement or definition of sexual orientation (see Sell, 1997). Kinsey's continuum model (Kinsey, Pomeroy, & Martin, 1948), which offers essentially two categories, can be contrasted with other, more complex models such as that by Storms (1980), which offers four categories.

This activity also allows students to see and understand why psychologists cannot give unequivocal answers to some questions, such as how many people are homosexual and how many are heterosexual. One popular human sexuality textbook states that approximately 93.8% of males are exclusively heterosexual and about 2.4% are exclusively homosexual, whereas approximately 95.6% of females are exclusively heterosexual and approximately less than 1% are exclusively homosexual; the rest fall in between, depending on the definition one uses (data from Laumann, Gagnon, Michael, & Michaels, 1994, quoted in Hyde & DeLamater, 2006). It is often a surprise to students to hear that there is a gray area in defining sexual orientation.

This activity is designed to allow students to explore, via small-group and classroom discussion, factors that may be important in defining sexual orientation, such as age, forms of behavior, emotional attachment, sexual fantasy content, and present contextual situation.

MATERIALS NEEDED

If the class is relatively small, this exercise can be done via small groups. If so, you will need several copies of a group worksheet that lists brief descriptions of various individuals. On the other hand, if the class is very large (< 75), then the descriptions can be presented via PowerPoint for the entire class to view and each student can either work with a nearby student or work individually. An abbreviated copy of the form I have used is shown in Appendix 38.1, although any individual instructor can create brief scenarios that present difficulties in defining sexual orientation.

Begin the activity by informing students of the task ahead. If the class allows small-group work, encourage the students to move the desks to create groups. Once groups of four or five students are created, either invite the groups to elect a spokesperson or select one yourself. Give each group leader/recorder a worksheet with spaces provided for the names of the group members (see Appendix 38.1). If done with a large class, present the scenarios via PowerPoint and have the students either work in pairs or as individuals, thinking about each vignette and writing down their answers.

Give the student groups approximately 10 to 15 minutes in which to work. The spokesperson of each group shares the short description of each hypothetical individual with the other members, and then, as a group, the members try to decide where the person should fall on a 7-point continuum ranging from *definitely homosexual* to *definitely heterosexual,* and why the person belongs there. This scale is similar to the 7-point scale used by Kinsey (Kinsey et al., 1948). Once the group members have discussed each of the individuals, they try to define the terms *homosexual* and *heterosexual*. I stress that although it may be difficult to do, their definitions should be consistent with the decisions they made concerning each of the individuals they have just discussed. (Obviously, students in large classrooms will do this individually.)

Once all the groups have finished or nearly finished, they should return their seats to their original positions and a class discussion can begin. Essentially, the class will discuss in turn each of the brief descriptions on the handout. Ask group leaders to share their group's response with the class. If students worked individually, simply ask for volunteers to share their ratings. Once they give a ranking (e.g., "One to the left of *definitely heterosexual*"), always ask, "Why?" Record key comments and factors mentioned by the groups on the chalkboard, overhead projector, or on PowerPoint for the entire class to see.

I almost always have at least one group that takes a relatively extreme stance such that if any person ever engages in homosexual behavior, they are necessarily *definitely homosexual.* I try not to be confrontational in my classes; I often respond with a question such as, "What about a person who is exclusively homosexual yet has one heterosexual encounter? Is that person, then, heterosexual?" Alternatively, I often change the descriptions to make a point. For example, when discussion centers on the young boy who wishes to marry an adult male, groups tend to answer with something like "We [the group] said you can't make a decision. He's too young." I respond, "What if he were 15 years old?" "What if he were 25 years old?" These questions help to illustrate the importance of age as a context when interpreting statements of attraction.

Finally, the group (or individuals) shares its definitions of homosexuality and heterosexuality with the rest of the class. Have the group (or individuals) turn in their worksheets once the class period is finished. Although I usually only glance at these briefly, turning in the sheets helps students feel they are being held accountable for their discussion.

This activity can be very helpful in teaching students important factors associated with defining sexual orientation. Evaluations have shown that students find this exercise both valuable and enjoyable. The effect of the small-group discussion was assessed by asking students in two sections of a general psychology class ($N = 49$) to write down as many factors as they could think of in 4 minutes that could influence how sexual orientation is defined both before the small-group exercise was begun and after it was completed. A correlated-groups t test showed that participants were able to list significantly more factors after they had participated in the exercise ($M = 6.3$) than before the exercise ($M = 3.4$),

$t(48) = -6.79$, $p < .01$. This indicates that the small-group exercise was effective in exposing students to several factors that influence the definition of sexual orientation that they did not know when the exercise was begun.

Clearly, as a result of this activity students were better able to understand how difficult it may be to offer a clear-cut answer to questions concerning sexual orientation; rather than an instructor *telling* them it is difficult, they *experience* how difficult it is. Because sexual orientation is such a highly charged issue for some students, this is a good exercise to help begin investigation of the topic, because it encourages discussion and critical thinking without putting students on the defensive.

REFERENCES AND SUGGESTED READING

Bailey, J. M., & Zucker, K. J. (1995). Childhood sex-typed behavior and sexual orientation: A conceptual analysis and quantitative review. *Developmental Psychology, 31*, 43–55.

Bogaert, A. F., & Liu, J. (2006). Birth order and sexual orientation in men: Evidence for two independent interactions. *Journal of Biosocial Science, 38*, 811–819.

Coleman, E. (1987). Bisexuality: Challenging our understanding of human sexuality and sexual orientation: In E. E. Shelp (Ed.), *Sexuality and medicine* (Vol. 1, pp. 225–242). New York: Reidel.

Dworkin, A. (1987). *Intercourse.* New York: Free Press/Macmillan.

Hyde, J. S., & DeLamater, J. D. (2006). *Understanding human sexuality* (9th ed.). Boston: McGraw-Hill.

Kinsey, A. C., Pomeroy, W. B., & Martin, C. E. (1948). *Sexual behavior in the human male.* Philadelphia: W. B. Saunders.

Laumann, E. O., Gagnon, J. H., Michael, R. T., & Michaels, S. (1994). *The social organization of sexuality: Sexual practices in the United States.* Chicago: University of Chicago Press.

Sell, R. L. (1997). Defining and measuring sexual orientation: A review. *Archives of Sexual Behavior, 26*, 643–658.

Storms, M. D. (1980). Theories of sexual orientation. *Journal of Personality and Social Psychology, 38*, 783–792.

Appendix 38.1

Sexual Orientation Exercise

Group members: _____

_____

_____

_____

Directions: Read the brief descriptions of people. As a group, try to decide whether the person should be considered a homosexual or a heterosexual. Once you have finished, synthesize your answers and define a homosexual and a heterosexual.

A. Person A is a man who is married and has three children. Approximately once a month he engages in impersonal sex with another man in a public restroom or bathhouse.

Definitely Homosexual ____ ____ ____ ____ ____ ____ ____ Definitely Heterosexual

B. Person B is a 58-year-old man who lives alone. He has never been married, nor has he had any sexual contact of any kind. He occasionally buys pornographic magazines, which depict male-to-male sexual contact, although he does not enjoy these very much.

C. Person C is a 29-year-old woman. She was sexually active with men from the time she was 19 until she was raped at 24. She has had no sexual contact since that time. She is no longer interested in sex with men, but says she would consider a sexual relationship with another woman.

D. Person D is a 44-year-old woman who has been married for 20 years. Occasionally during intercourse with her husband she imagines engaging in sex with another woman. She has never had any sexual partner besides her husband.

E. Person E is a woman who shares an apartment with another woman. They have not had any sexual contact other than an occasional hug and kiss when greeting or departing.

F. Person F is a 5-year-old boy who enjoys watching basketball. When asked whom he wants to marry he answers, "LeBron James."

G. Person G is a 28-year-old man who has been sent to prison. From the time he was 20 until he was sent to prison, he engaged in intercourse with his girlfriend approximately twice weekly. Now he engages in intercourse with other male inmates approximately twice weekly. He plans to continue his sexual relationship with his girlfriend once he is released from prison.

Definition of homosexuality:

Definition of heterosexuality:

39 ASSESSING STUDENT WORRIES

Patricia Smoot McDaniel
Jefferson College

James Eison
Southeast Missouri State University

This activity involves a topic of interest to students that can be used as the vehicle for introducing discussions of emotion, methodology, or testing. Advance preparation is minimal, and no prior knowledge of psychological theory is necessary. This in-class activity is appropriate for courses in introductory, health, and abnormal psychology, as well as courses in psychological testing, and is suitable for classes of any size.

CONCEPT

Worry is an abstract concept with which most people are all too familiar; it affects all of us to some extent throughout our lives. Many definitions of worry suggest its stifling effects. For example, Maultsby (cited in Benson, 1981) described worry as an "unproductive, useless and intense form of fear" (p. 66), and Borkovec (1985) defined worry as "a chain of negative and relatively uncontrollable thoughts and images" (p. 59). Although college students have been used widely in psychological research, surprisingly little is known about the specific nature or extent of their worries. However, college student worries and stress have been associated with alcohol consumption for tension reduction (Kieffer, Cronin, & Gawet, 2006) and as predictors of students' depressive symptoms (Dyson & Renk, 2006).

Readers of introductory, abnormal, and health psychology texts are undoubtedly familiar with the concept of *stress*. Such texts typically discuss the topic in detail and describe how psychologists have attempted to measure this construct. The Holmes and Rahe Schedule of Recent Experiences (cited in Gatchel & Baum, 1983) and the Hassles Scale (Kanner, Coyne, Schaefer, & Lazarus, 1981) are two commonly used methods of assessing stress. Although stress is often analyzed extensively, the subject of *worry* has been addressed less often. Perhaps this is a result of the scarcity of inventory or assessment devices to measure worries.

MATERIALS NEEDED

You will need one copy of the Worries Survey (see Appendix 39.1) and one copy of the Worries Survey Answer Sheet (see Appendix 39.2) for each student in the class.

INSTRUCTIONS

The Worries Survey (Eison & McDaniel, 1985) is an unpublished, 35-item self-report questionnaire developed from a pilot study to assess college student worries. The questionnaire consists of five statements for each of the following seven worry dimensions: (a) school, (b) romance and relationships, (c) health and appearance, (d) career development, (e) social acceptance, (f) money, and (g) time. These dimensions were identified from responses to an open-ended questionnaire that was previously completed by several hundred college students. Normative data, gathered from 533 university students enrolled in biology, psychology, sociology, economics, nursing, English composition, history, and business courses, appears in Table 39.1.

Table 39.1. *Student Worry Survey: Norms*

				Dimension and Corresponding Survey Item				
Percentile rank	School (1,8,15,22,29)	Romance and relationships (2,9,16,23,30)	Health and appearance (3,10,17,24,31)	Career development (4,11,18,25,32)	Social acceptance (5,12,19,26,33)	Money (6,13,20,27,34)	Time (7,14,21,28,35)	Total (1–35)
100	80	76	66	80	80	80	76	452
90	59	46	45	51	35	53	50	297
80	51	32	37	40	27	42	42	244
70	45	26	31	32	21	35	34	219
60	40	21	26	25	18	30	29	192
50	35	17	21	22	14	25	25	173
40	31	13	18	18	11	20	21	152
30	25	10	14	14	9	15	18	128
20	21	7	10	9	7	11	14	105
10	16	3	5	5	4	6	9	79

Note. *N* = 533.

Students complete the Worries Survey according to instructions provided, responding to each item in two ways: frequency is recorded on a 5-point scale ranging from 0 *(never)* to 4 *(always)*, and intensity is measured on a 5-point scale ranging from 0 *(never)* to 4 *(a great deal)*. Frequency scores are multiplied by intensity scores to create a total discomfort score for each item. You may wish to provide directions for scoring on the answer sheet (as seen in Appendix 39.2) or at a later time (when a modified answer sheet is used). Students typically complete and score the Worries Survey in 25 minutes.

DISCUSSION

The Worries Survey was designed as both a research instrument and a pedagogical device to promote student self-analysis and stimulate classroom discussion of worries (e.g., definitions, causes and sources, effects, correlations with other indices of health, methods of control, and so on). By scoring their own papers, students are able to identify the specific worry items or worry dimensions causing them greatest concern. Individual comparisons with the normative data enable students to interpret their scores relative to other university respondents and to create a personal worry profile.

In addition to the previously described uses of the Worries Survey, analysis of this assessment technique is useful in itself. You may wish to ask students the following questions to initiate class discussion: What are the advantages/disadvantages/limitations of self-report survey instruments? How reliable or valid is normative data gathered from another university? Are student concerns exceptional or similar to those of other societal groups? How do characteristics of this survey instrument (i.e., its development and method of score interpretation) affect its legitimacy?

We have used the Worries Survey with several other survey instruments to study the relation between college student worries and other measures of health and adjustment (McDaniel & Eison, 1986); copies of this study are available from the second author.

REFERENCES AND SUGGESTED READING

Benson, S. (1981, February). Dr. Max Maultsby says: Stop worrying and get on with your life. *Ebony*, pp. 66–70.

Borkovec, T. (1985, December). What's the use of worrying? *Psychology Today*, pp. 59–64.

Dyson, R., & Renk, K. (2006). Freshmen adaptation to university life: Depressive symptoms, stress, and coping. *Journal of Clinical Psychology, 62,* 1231–1244.

Eison, J., & McDaniel, P. S. (1985). *The development of a student worry survey.* Unpublished manuscript.

Ellis, A., & Harper, R. (1975). *A new guide to rational living.* Hollywood, CA: Wilshire.

Hauck, P. A. (1975). *Overcoming worry and fear.* Philadelphia: Westminister.

Gatchel, R. J., & Baum, A. (1983). *An introduction to health psychology.* Reading, MA: Addison-Wesley.

Kanner, A. D., Coyne, J. C., Schaefer, C., & Lazarus, R. S. (1981). Comparison of two modes of stress measurement: Daily hassles and uplifts versus major life events. *Journal of Behavioral Medicine, 4,* 1–39.

Kieffer, K. M., Cronin, C., & Gawet, D. L. (2006). Test and study worry and emotionality in the prediction of college students' reasons for drinking: An exploratory investigation. *Journal of Alcohol & Drug Education, 50,* 57–81.

Maultsby, M. (1975). *Help yourself to happiness through rational self-counseling.* New York: Institute for Rational Living.

McDaniel, P. S., & Eison, J. (1986). *The relationship between college student worries and other measures of health and adjustment.* Unpublished manuscript.

Zaritsky, J. S. (1990). "What I worry about." Meeting the needs of the community college student. *Community Review, 10,* 19–24.

Appendix 39.1

Worries Survey

Directions: Below is a list of common worries taken from interviews and surveys with individuals like yourself. Please read each statement carefully. On the answer sheet provided, use the following rating scales to indicate the frequency with which you worry about each item and the intensity or degree of discomfort created by each worry.

FREQUENCY	INTENSITY
0—never	0—never
1—seldom (i.e., once or twice a year)	1—barely noticeable
2—sometimes (i.e., once or twice a month)	2—a slight amount
3—often (i.e., once or twice a week)	3—a moderate amount
4—always (i.e., once or twice a day)	4—a great deal

Answer honestly and candidly without spending too much time thinking about any one item. Pick the response that best indicates how you actually feel and not how you think you *should* feel.

1. I worry about being able to get into the classes I need or want.
2. I worry about spending more time alone than I prefer (e.g., not having someone to date or friends to spend time with).
3. I worry about maintaining a desirable body weight.
4. I worry about whether I have really chosen the right major.
5. I worry about trying too hard to please other people.
6. I worry about making financial ends meet.
7. I worry about having too much to do and too little time to do it.
8. I worry about not studying effectively.
9. I worry about starting new relationships with people.
10. I worry about not being able to break bad habits (e.g., quit smoking or drinking, etc.).
11. I worry about the problems associated with changing my major or my future career plans.
12. I worry about being liked by my friends.
13. I worry about not having enough money for both essentials and recreation.
14. I worry about spending too little time with people I care about.
15. I worry about my performance on tests.
16. I worry about making existing relationships (e.g., marriage or other relationships) successful.
17. I worry about not eating properly and/or exercising regularly.
18. I worry about not being successful in my major.
19. I worry about getting along with other students.
20. I worry about not having enough money to pay for my education.
21. I worry about not balancing properly the amount of time spent at school, work, and other activities.
22. I worry about being able to handle my course work and my assignments.
23. I worry about remaining in an emotionally unfulfilling relationship.
24. I worry about looking and dressing my best.
25. I worry about finding a job in my major field upon graduation.
26. I worry about getting along with my professors.
27. I worry about not knowing how to manage money wisely.
28. I worry about not making enough time for rest and relaxation.
29. I worry about my grades.
30. I worry about coping with the ending of a serious relationship.
31. I worry about becoming seriously ill.
32. I worry about being professionally successful.
33. I worry about being a good family member.
34. I worry about being a financial burden to my family.
35. I worry about not having enough time, quiet time, for myself.

Appendix 39.2

Worries Survey Answer Sheet

Scoring Directions: For each of the 35 items, multiply the number in the *F* column by the number in the *I* column. Place this value in the space to the right of each *I* column. Add up the resulting $F \times I$ values in each of the seven columns (labeled *a* through *g*) and combine the seven scale totals to produce a total worry score.

F *I*	*F* *I*	*F* *I*	*F* *I*	*F* *I*	*F* *I*	*F* *I*
(1) ___ ___	(2) ___ ___	(3) ___ ___	(4) ___ ___	(5) ___ ___	(6) ___ ___	(7) ___ ___
(8) ___ ___	(9) ___ ___	(10) ___ ___	(11) ___ ___	(12) ___ ___	(13) ___ ___	(14) ___ ___
(15) ___ ___	(16) ___ ___	(17) ___ ___	(18) ___ ___	(19) ___ ___	(20) ___ ___	(21) ___ ___
(22) ___ ___	(23) ___ ___	(24) ___ ___	(25) ___ ___	(26) ___ ___	(27) ___ ___	(28) ___ ___
(29) ___ ___	(30) ___ ___	(31) ___ ___	(32) ___ ___	(33) ___ ___	(34) ___ ___	(35) ___ ___

Scale totals: ___   ___   ___   ___   ___   ___   ___
              a   b   c   d   e   f   g

Total score: _____

CHAPTER 8
DEVELOPMENTAL PSYCHOLOGY

The six activities in this chapter span the gamut of human development from infancy to older adulthood. There is even an activity that looks at development in rat pups in their first year of life. Topics covered include genetic screening, parenting styles in relationship to stages of child development, adolescent identity, and attitudes toward older adults.

Although the emphasis of Activity 40 is on genetic screening and the possibilities for using such genetic information, students acquire a better understanding of gene–environment interactions as a result of this focused discussion. This exercise allows students to discuss what implications genetic screening might have in their own lives as parents.

Activity 41 offers students the opportunity to observe development firsthand using a litter of rat pups. Students observe the pups in their first month of life, recording information about the development of motor skills, grooming, exploration, socialization, and weaning. Because of the rapid maturity of rats, students are able to see the marked changes in behavior from hairless, blind pups to young rats that are running, jumping, and interacting with their littermates. Detailed instructions for the observations are provided.

Human development from birth to age 8 is the subject of Activity 42. Students are asked to create a developmental chronology of motor and verbal behaviors from a checklist provided to them. Students are also required to identify those behaviors that they believe are a result of maturation and those they believe require some training. These exercises are used as the basis for a class discussion.

Working in small groups in Activity 43, students choose a stage of parenthood they would like to explore and are responsible for arranging a small panel of parents to meet with the class to discuss their parenting styles and issues for that stage of parenthood. One goal of these panels is to show students the changing role of parenthood as it relates to the changing developmental stage of their children.

The focus of Activity 44 is on adolescent identity. Drawing on the work of Piaget, Erikson, Kohlberg, and Gilligan, this set of three discussion-based activities explores the social, cognitive, and moral aspects of identity in adolescence.

In Activity 45, students are asked to interview four of their peers (outside of class) in terms of their attitudes and beliefs about older adults. The results of these surveys are aggregated to provide data for a class discussion, including a focus on negative stereotypes about aging and the consequences of those stereotypes for older and younger adults.

40 Bringing Genetic Screening Home: Are We Moving Toward Designer Babies?

Richard Ely

Boston University

This simple classroom demonstration has proven to be an effective way of making the implications of genetic screening feel very real. This in-class activity should follow a presentation that addresses the influence of genes on behavior, as well as a background description of prenatal screening, including mention of screening for entities like Down syndrome. The activity involves 10 students in discussion-starter roles but mostly involves the entire class in a focused discussion. We have used this demonstration in our general psychology course. It is also suitable for courses in developmental psychology, health psychology, and biopsychology. The activity typically consumes the entire class period.

CONCEPT
This simulation activity allows students to experience what it would be like to be given information about their unborn baby on the basis of genetic screening. The activity allows them to explore how they would react to such knowledge. By doing so, students can come to a better real world understanding of the concept of genetic susceptibility. They also gain knowledge about gene–environment interactions. Most important, they explore the ethical issues surrounding the use of information gained from genetic screening.

MATERIALS NEEDED
You will need ten 3- × 5-inch cards and 10 envelopes.

INSTRUCTIONS
Begin by asking how many students would like to know in advance the sex of their unborn baby. Then ask them why they answered the way they did. Students who do not want to know in advance often say that it will reduce the joy, excitement, and surprise. Those who do want to know often say they would like to be able to be better *prepared*. You can build on this response by asking students what they mean by being *prepared*. This introductory discussion serves as a warm-up for what is to follow.

After the introductory discussion, distribute the envelopes randomly to students in the class. Each envelope contains a prenatal diagnosis, a statement about the genetic disposition of the developing fetus. They are numbered 1 though 10 to allow you to orchestrate the type of effect desired. The effect is a product of both the nature of the content of each diagnosis, as well as its placement relative to the diagnoses that precede or follow it (explained later).

Students who receive an envelope are asked to stand up and read out loud the diagnosis. Be as creative as you would like in the selection of diagnoses, as well as in their wording. We have chosen to word the diagnoses in the second person (e.g., "Your baby is likely to grow up to be . . ."). However, wording the diagnoses in the first person is also effective (e.g., "My baby is likely to grow up to be . . ."). The following is the list of 10 items that we have used regularly:

1. Your baby is likely to grow up to be very neurotic.
2. Your baby is likely to grow up to be very extroverted.
3. Your baby is likely to grow up to be autistic.
4. Your baby is likely to grow up to be a genius.
5. Your baby is likely to grow up to be a genius and be very neurotic.
6. Your baby is likely to grow up to be musically very talented but also be poor at verbal tasks.
7. Your baby is likely to grow up to be dyslexic.
8. Your baby is likely to grow up to be a homosexual.
9. Your baby is likely to grow up to be just average.
10. Your baby is likely to grow up to be just like you.

Specific diagnoses with which students are unfamiliar should be explained. For some diagnoses (e.g., dyslexia, autism), it may be beneficial to provide an initial explanation that mimics the highly specialized language that physicians and clinicians sometimes use. By using this professional jargon, students are able to experience the difficulties expectant parents sometimes encounter in trying to understand what they are being told. Later you can provide follow-up explanations that use more straightforward language. After students understand all the diagnoses, ask them to consider and discuss how they would feel if they were to receive each diagnosis. Would their child-rearing practices change, knowing what they know in advance? Would they try to alter some outcomes more than others?

The diagnoses used in this exercise tap four distinct areas. First, some diagnoses (e.g., tendencies toward neuroticism and extroversion) focus on heritable personality attributes (Jang, Livesley, & Vernon, 1996; Loehlin, McCrae, & Costa, 1998). Given this information, explore the degree to which students believe that it would be possible or advisable to modify the expression of certain personality traits. Many students will agree that parents should try to reduce or temper a genetic disposition toward neuroticism. In contrast, there is likely to be little support for the notion that parents should try to modify a genetic disposition toward extroversion. Making these views explicit can also lead to a discussion of how various cultures differentially value assorted personality traits (Schmitt, Allik, McCrae, & Benet-Martinez, 2007).

Second, some diagnoses identify the tendency to excel or falter in a number of cognitive domains that have been shown to be influenced to a greater degree than others by genes. These domains include intelligence, verbal ability, and musical ability (Drayna, Manichaikul, de Lange, Snieder, & Spector, 2001; Gupta & State, 2007; Hawke, Wadsworth, & Defries, 2005; Plomin & Spinath, 2004). Students should be asked to consider the degree to which they would try to alter or foster genetic dispositions in these domains. For example, would students be more willing to pay for music lessons for a child who had a genetic predisposition to be musically talented than for one who did not have such a predisposition? Would they push a child who had a genetic disposition toward being a genius to excel at academics? Would they do this even if the child not only showed little interest in academics but actively pursued sports to the detriment of academics?

A third category is represented by only one diagnosis, the genetic tendency to become a homosexual. This is a complex topic about which many students are likely to have strong feelings. The instructor should review the evidence that sexual orientation appears to be mediated by genes (Bailey, Dunne, & Martin, 2000; Kirk, Bailey, Dunne, & Martin, 2000). Students should then be encouraged to discuss in as frank a manner as possible how they would respond to a prenatal diagnosis indicating that there was a strong tendency for their son or daughter to become a homosexual. By asking specific questions, like those that follow, the discussion is likely to become more focused: How much would they read into the cross-gender play (i.e., girls pretending to be boys and boys pretending to be girls) that is relatively common in early childhood (Linday, 1994)? Would they try to prevent such play (Sandnabba, 1999)? How would they discuss sexuality with their child as he or she approached puberty?

The fourth area is represented by the two diagnoses *just average* and *just like you.* The *just like you* diagnosis is particularly relevant in light of recent advances in cloning (Wilmut & Highfield, 2006). Both the *just like you* and the *just average* diagnoses raise interesting questions about identity, self-concept, and parenting. To what degree do we seek to be unique? In what ways do we want to replicate ourselves? These two diagnoses can be tied to the other diagnoses to help bring closure to the overall discussion. For example, would a student be more likely to want her child to be *just like her* if she were a genius? Or would a student want his child to be *just average* if he were highly neurotic or dyslexic?

Throughout the exercise, the instructor should stress what is meant by genetic disposition, particularly as it is captured in the wording of the diagnoses (e.g., "Your baby is *likely* to grow up to be . . ."). The instructor should emphasize the importance of understanding that most behaviors, particularly complex behaviors, are the product of the interaction of genes and environment (Moore, 2001; Rutter, 2006). Likewise, in any offspring, the total effect of the genotype is likely to generate dispositions toward what many would consider to be both positive as well as negative attributes. Diagnoses 5 and 6 are designed to demonstrate this notion.

Finally, the social, political, and ethical implications of genetic screening should be raised (Beckwith, 2002; Hay, 2003; Kitcher, 1997; Sternberg, Grigorenko, & Kidd, 2005). By making the implications of genetic screening personal and specific, this exercise makes such a discussion more meaningful. Again, asking students specific questions can promote a more focused discussion. Some sample questions include the following: Should prenatal screening for some disorders (e.g., autism) be mandatory? Alternatively, should prenatal screening for other behaviors (e.g., personality traits, sexual orientation) be prohibited? To what degree would the wide-scale availability and use of comprehensive prenatal screening create a de facto eugenic society? You might point out that recent evidence suggests that prenatal screening for sex followed by selective abortion has been identified as the reason for the low male-to-female ratio of births in India (Jha et al., 2006).

In general, students are quite moved by this exercise and, in our experience, the discussion has always been thoughtful and reflective. They are also likely to come away from this experience with a better understanding of how genes and environment interact. Stress to the students that in their role as (future) parents, they will be providing much of the social environment that their children will encounter. Lastly, be sensitive to the cultural and religious implications that such an exercise is likely to generate. Discussing these in a straightforward and balanced manner is in itself often enriching.

If the groupings identified in the Discussion section were not explicitly explained in the classroom discussion, ask students if they can generate a way in which they would group the diagnoses. Then ask them to rank-order their groupings and to justify both their groupings and their ranking. We would anticipate that students would either group diagnoses as we grouped them, or they would group them in clusters that shared comparable levels of social and cultural desirability (e.g., genius status and extroversion grouped together and ranked as less likely to be modified than dyslexia and neuroticism).

As a final exercise, provide the students with the list of diagnoses. Ask them to use the diagnoses to formulate a policy statement that would be directed toward their state or federal legislators. They should address the following two questions: (a) What would be the risks and benefits of wide-scale use of comprehensive prenatal screening? (b) To what degree should the government fund such screening or mandate the funding of such screening?

Bailey, J. M., Dunne, M. P., & Martin, N. G. (2000). The distribution, correlates and determinants of sexual orientation in an Australian twin sample. *Journal of Personality and Social Psychology, 78,* 524–536.

Beckwith, J. (2002). *Making genes, making waves: A social activist in science.* Cambridge, MA: Harvard University Press.

Drayna, D., Manichaikul, A., de Lange, M., Snieder, H., & Spector, T. (2001). Genetic correlates of musical pitch recognition in humans. *Science, 291,* 1969–1972.

Gupta, A. R., & State, M. W. (2007). Recent advances in the genetics of autism. *Biological Psychiatry, 61,* 429–437.

Hawke, J. L., Wadsworth, S. J., & Defries, J. C. (2005). Genetic influences on reading difficulties in boys and girls: The Colorado Twin Study. *Dyslexia, 12,* 21–29.

Hay, D. A. (2003). Who should fund and control the direction of human behavior genetics? Review of Nuffield Council on Bioethics 2002 Report, Genetics and Human Behavior: The Ethical Context. *Genes, Brain and Behavior, 2,* 321–326.

Jang, K. L., Livesley, J. W., & Vernon, P. A. (1996). Heritability of the Big Five personality dimensions and their facets: A twin study. *Journal of Personality, 64,* 577–591.

Jha, P., Kumar, R., Vasa, P., Dhingra, N., Thiruchelvam, D., & Moineddin, R. (2006). Low male-to-female sex ratio of children born in India: A national survey of 1.1 million households. *Lancet, 367,* 211–218.

Kirk, K. M., Bailey, J. M., Dunne, M. P., & Martin, N. G. (2000). Measurement models for sexual orientation in a community twin sample. *Behavior Genetics, 30,* 345–356.

Kitcher, P. (1997). *The lives to come: The genetic revolution and human possibilities.* New York: Touchstone.

Linday, L. A. (1994). Maternal reports of pregnancy, genital, and related fantasies in preschool and kindergarten children. *Journal of the American Academy of Child and Adolescent Psychiatry, 33,* 416–423.

Loehlin, J. C., McCrae, R. R., & Costa, P. T. (1998). Heritabilities of common and measure-specific components of the Big Five personality factors. *Journal of Research in Personality, 32,* 431–453.

Martin, C. L. (1995). Stereotypes about children with traditional and nontraditional gender roles. *Sex Roles, 33,* 727–751.

Moore, D. S. (2001). *The dependent gene: The fallacy of "nature vs. nurture."* New York: W. H. Freeman.

Plomin, R., Defries, J. C., Craig, I. W., & McGuffin, P. (Eds.). (2003). *Behavioral genetics in the postgenomic era.* Washington, DC: American Psychological Association.

Plomin, R., Defries, J. C., McClearn, G. E., & McFuffin, P. (2001). *Behavioral genetics* (4th ed.). New York: Worth Publishers.

Plomin, R., & Spinath, F. M. (2004). Intelligence: Genetics, genes, and genomics. *Journal of Personality and Social Psychology, 86,* 112–129.

Rutter, M. (2006). *Genes and behavior: Nature–nurture interplay explained.* Malden, MA: Blackwell Publishing.

Sandnabba, K. N. (1999). Parents' attitudes and expectations about children's cross-gender behavior. *Sex Roles, 40,* 249–263.

Schmitt, D. P., Allik, J., McCrae, R. R., & Benet-Martinez, V. (2007). The geographic distribution of Big Five personality traits: Patterns and profiles of human self-description across 56 nations. *Journal of Cross-Cultural Psychology, 38,* 173–212.

Sternberg, R. J., Grigorenko, E. L., & Kidd, K. K. (2005). Intelligence, race, and genetics. *American Psychologist, 60,* 46–59.

Wilmut, I., & Highfield, R. (2006). *After Dolly: The uses and misuses of human cloning.* New York: W. W. Norton.

41 ANIMAL OBSERVATION: THE MAMA RAT PROJECT

Barbara F. Nodine
Arcadia University

Observation of a litter of rat pups, from birth to one month can easily be made part of an introductory psychology course of any size, because students make the observations outside of class time and the animals are housed behind a window. The project offers clear instructions to students on how and what to observe, with a sufficient variety of choices that students can select those areas for observation and written paper that are of the greatest interest to them. This activity is also appropriate for classes in animal behavior/comparative psychology, developmental psychology, and research methods.

CONCEPT

Few creatures are more appealing than puppies, kittens, foals, and babies. Watching the young of a species develop is engaging and illuminating. Conceptual material on development and ethology is traditionally presented in lectures for introductory psychology students. But lectures and readings are passive ways of learning material that could be better taught with some student participation. Psychology instructors find that student observation of the birth and development of a litter of rat pups enriches the teaching of concepts of development and ethology.

This activity requires students to make 4 weeks of observations of the birth, development of motor skills, socialization, and weaning of a litter of rat pups. Another alternative is to have four litters of pups, each 1 week apart in age, so that the observation time can be compressed. Students organize and summarize their observations in a paper and relate them to the concepts taught in the course. Concepts that might be taught in conjunction with the observations are the trends or directions of motor development—cephalocaudal, proximodistal, and mass-specific—exemplified by crawling, walking, running, and jumping. Species-specific behaviors might be observed to occur in nest building, retrieving young, feeding, grooming, or weaning. After making observations of 4 weeks of growth, students will have detailed, personally collected descriptions that make the concepts taught in the course meaningful and real. The purposes of this activity are to have students (a) learn to make objective, detailed observations; (b) learn to prepare a written summary of those observations; and (c) learn to write an interpretation of those results using concepts from development and ethology taught in the course.

Besides being a worthwhile teaching technique, this activity has some very practical appeal for the instructor. Rats mature rapidly enough for use in this type of course. There is no manipulation of the environment; the animals simply live in their home cage. Students see the mother give birth to a litter of totally dependent, blind, hairless pups and

---

Note. Bernard Mausner designed this project to be part of the introductory psychology course at Beaver College (now Arcadia University). It has been used for many years and has been modified over time.

4 weeks later observe her litter looking fully developed, running, jumping, interacting with litter mates, and eating solid food. The activity is well suited to introductory courses because the requirement for apparatus is minimal. As many as 100 students can easily observe one litter cage because they can determine their own flexible observation schedules. In addition, sophisticated research skills are not needed by the student—only skills of observation. Admittedly, simple observation is more difficult than it seems, but the student will be developing a basic skill useful in psychology as well as other subjects.

PREPARATION OF CLASS

Materials needed include a pregnant female rat, a large, clear plastic cage for mother and litter when delivered, and a room with see-through mirrors or windows. Using a window or some other barrier will prevent students from being tempted to tap on or open the cage to awaken the animals or disturb them in any way. Also, to keep distraction to a minimum, a darkened room with a red light over the cage would allow the animals to behave as though they were in their natural setting yet allow student observation. Another possibility, if the equipment is available, is to use a webcam and computer to stream the video, around the clock, to a university Web site. This arrangement would provide a schedule that is very flexible for student use.

Preparation of students for participation in this activity will take only a few minutes of lecture time, and all observations will be made on the student's time. The student handout reproduced in the following pages explains the activity completely with the exception of the text material or readings for your course. The specific focus of the activity will depend on what you emphasize in your lectures and on the reading you select. For example, you may wish to limit the potential wealth of observations by having students concentrate on the mother's behavior, or motor trends, or the socialization of the pups. Cross-species comparisons might be made by using gerbils or hamsters.

Student papers can be modified to meet your own goals. You might want to require graphs or tables of results. Library search and use of references beyond those required could be encouraged. Length limits for the paper of two or three pages are feasible, as are longer papers. Usually, the students must select some of their observations and reject others in order to write coherent papers.

Read the statement from the American Psychological Association entitled "Guidelines for Ethical Conduct in the Care and Use of Animals." You may want to request a free copy of that statement to post in your classroom or in the animal observation room. Write to APA Order Department, P.O. Box 2710, Hyattsville, MD 20784-0710, or you can print a copy from APA's Web site at http://www.apa.org/science/anguide.html.

Student Handout

Introduction. One of the major goals of this project is to show how the course of development follows an orderly sequence both in humans and other mammals. Another is to observe the behavior of mothers before birth and with their pups. You are probably more interested in children than rats, but children develop much too slowly for the time we have available. Rats go through childhood in 6 weeks and are sexually adult in 12 weeks; the developmental process is short in length but is similar in many respects to that exhibited by humans. As you watch baby rats develop, you will gain experience in making behavioral observations, relating those observations to theoretical principles, and writing a short paper describing your observations and conclusions.

The theoretical interest of the project lies in two areas. The first is that of "instinct," or species-characteristic behavior. One of the readings on ethology gives you some background for the ideas you will be examining in this area. Maternal behavior is often given as an example of an instinct. You will have a chance to watch a rat mother preparing for the birth of her pups and caring for them. You will then be able to check what you see against the criteria for species-characteristic behavior in the readings.

The other area is development. You will have a chance to observe the orderly changes in appearance and behavior of the pups as they get older and to check these observations against the principles of development described in your readings and in class.

Instructions for observation. You will observe the external anatomy and behavior of a litter of rat pups from the time they are born until they are weaned about a month later. You will also observe the behavior of the mother from the last few days of her pregnancy until weaning. Pregnant rats usually build nests a few days prior to parturition. With luck, you may be present while a female is delivering.

You should observe the rats for 15 minutes per day, 3 days a week, for 4 weeks—that is, 12 observation periods lasting a total of 3 hours. If all of the rats are asleep, you will have to stay longer than 15 minutes or come back at another time. The animals are located behind a one-way viewing window. Rats are most active during the night, so they are being maintained on a reversed light/dark cycle. Because they are relatively insensitive to red light, such illumination simulates their nighttime, which begins at 8:00 a.m. and ends at 5:00 p.m. Try to make all of your observations at about the same time each day. Do not turn on the lights in the observation room. You must allow a few minutes for your eyes to adapt to the very dim light in the room.

The most useful way to record your observations is to make a large table or chart on several pages of your notebook (or as an Excel file if you have a laptop computer) with columns for each behavior. An example of the format for such a chart is shown in appendix 41.1. During each period you should be sure to record descriptions of at least several of the items about mother or pups from the list on Exhibit 41.1. The more information you record, the easier it will be to write your final paper. Date every observation so that you see a progression and know the milestones, such as birth, eyes opening, beginning walking, first eating solid food, or weaning.

It sometimes helps to discuss your observations with someone else in the class to increase the precision of your descriptions. You may find that you did not notice some details. After talking with someone else you may be able to record your next observations with greater exactness.

Observation of mothers. Your observation periods will be divided between watching the mothers and watching the pups. In observing the mothers you should look for the follow-

Exhibit 41.1. *Behavioral Categories for Description of Mother Rat and Pups*

Mothers	Nest building
	Grooming self, grooming pups (especially anal licking)
	Exploration
	Nursing
	Retrieving
	Rejecting pups at weaning
	Walking
	Feeding
Pups	Sleeping (solitary, social)
	Feeding
	Suckling
	Solid food—eating behavior
	Drinking
	Locomotion: Stages include trunk movements or wiggling, twitching, freezing, sniffing, orienting, hopping, crawling with forepaws, righting movements, rising to erect position, walking, running, climbing, rising and swaying, jumping.
	Sensory behavior: Describe indications of response to visual, auditory, odor, and tactile cues.
	Elimination: urination, defecation, anal licking.
	Vocalization: quality of sounds (if audible), stimuli to sound production
	Grooming: face washing, licking, scratching (which paws, location of area scratched)
	Exploration: sniffing objects, making lateral head movements, digging in nesting materials
	Social behavior: Describe at each stage—huddling, mutual sleeping postures; fighting over nursing position; general social activity such as running, jumping, chasing, wrestling, mutual grooming; fighting, including description of posture, length of encounter, acting of "victor" and "loser"; pseudo-sexual behavior, sniffing and licking of genitals, mounting.

Stages of growth and physical development should be outlined on the basis of exact descriptions of skin (later fur), appearance of coloration, apparent length and weight, and time of opening of eyes.

ing categories of observations (as listed in Exhibit 41.1): nest building, retrieving the young, grooming the young, self-grooming, nursing, sleeping, feeding, walking. The last four activities you should observe simply to see the postures and movements characteristic of an adult rat so you can compare those behaviors in the pups. The mothers' behaviors of major interest are those that involve the litter (nest building, retrieving, grooming, and nursing). You should see changes in those behaviors during the 4 weeks because at the end of that period, the litter will be weaned and may be living away from the mother.

When you observe a behavior such as grooming, record in as much detail as you can exactly how the mother does it. How does she hold the pups? Does she hold them differently at different ages? What parts of the body are involved? Is this grooming similar to her grooming of herself or to the pups' grooming of one another? When observing nursing you should also record details such as how much time it takes, what postures are displayed, what the ages of the pups are, and what the method of weaning is. Each behavior that you observe will present many aspects that you should describe precisely. If possible, try to establish your own set of subcategories for these behaviors. Remember that besides obtaining a complete description of the behavior, you are also interested in describing changes in that behavior over the 4-week period. Examples of criteria for several categories of behavior are given in Exhibit 41.2.

Observation of pups. Spend two thirds of each observation period observing the pups in any single cage. Observe the same cage during all 12 observation periods so you gain an

Exhibit 41.2. *Sample Criteria for Behavioral Categories*

Nest building	Mother rat pushes bedding material with nose, holds it in forepaws, heaps it in corner of cage (How high? How tidy or regular? What proportion of the bedding materials in the cage is included in the heap?). Mother lies on heap, creating a depression in the center. Mother works at edges of heap. Mother picks up her tail and encircles her body with it.
Grooming self	Mother lies on back, paws extended, licks and bites at fur (Where?). Mother scratches at head behind ears with fore or rear paws (Which?). Mother rubs against sides of cage. (Describe as precisely as possible position of mother while she is licking.)
Feeding behavior	Mother lies on side, belly extended (describe position exactly). Pup struggles for position on mother's belly with wriggling movements of trunk and treading movements of forepaws. Pup holds on to nipple, engages in coordinated sucking movements and treading of forepaws. Pup struggles to maintain position, squeals if displaced by mother's movements or by other pups. (Time the length of suckling for several pups.) Describe actions as pup disengages when it is sate.

appreciation of the behavioral and anatomical development of rat pups. Exhibit 41.1 provides a partial list of items to observe. For each item you must record in careful detail the components of each behavior. How do they sleep? In what position? Related to the litter in what way? How does walking develop? What parts of the body make what kind of movements? Do the pups walk the way the mother walks?

Be careful not to record your feelings or interpretations; simply record what you see. "The mother is taking time for herself" or "She hates her babies now that they are older" are *not* good observations. "Mother is sleeping on opposite side of cage from nest" or "Mother walks away from pups during nursing" are appropriate observations because they do not project human ideas onto the animals.

Instructions for paper. Your paper has two components: (a) a chronological summary of your observations and (b) an interpretation or discussion of the important concepts demonstrated by your observations. Assume that your paper will be read by another member of the class who could not do the observations but who read the same material you did.

Summary. In making your summary, first arrange all 12 observations of mother and pups in order and read through them to see the chronology of feeding changes, mobility, grooming, condition of the nest, and so forth. You are to summarize material both about the mothers and the pups. A summary requires the omission of some of the details and the selection of more important observations. If your 12 observation periods show a continuous, detailed picture of growth for only some of the behaviors listed on Exhibit 41.2, then emphasize those behaviors and ignore others. You will see that the quality of your summary depends on the quality of your observations. A graphic or tabular summary of your observations is helpful to the reader. Remember, there are many details to be read about and understood, so give the reader all the help you can.

Also remember that you are providing scientific data rather than a report on your own feelings. For example, even if you had a strong emotional reaction to seeing a mother rat give birth, you should not include a report on that in this paper (you might want to write an entirely different kind of essay for your English class on your feelings of pity, terror, or sympathy as you watched a mother rat give birth).

Interpretation. The purpose of this section of the paper is to link the observations you have described in the summary with the theoretical ideas and concepts discussed in the readings and in class. In a sense you are telling the reader why it was worthwhile to have made these observations. You should take several of the theoretical concepts about trends in development or about species-specific behavior and look for data in your observations that would help to explain or illustrate these concepts. One example might be the concept that motor behavior progresses from mass responses to specific or differentiated responses. Look at your observations. Can you find examples of mass responses? (Generalized twitching might be one.) Can you find examples of specific responses? (Handling solid food is one.) Now check the frequency with which mass responses and specific responses occur early in the pup's development and later in development. Does the concept fit your observations? Are there more mass responses early and more specific responses later?

Do something like this for two or three other concepts. The more ably you relate observations to concepts, the more you will understand how scientists are able to draw conclusions of importance from observational data.

REFERENCES AND SUGGESTED READING

Maimon, E. P., Belcher, G. L., Hearn, G. W., Nodine, B. F., & O'Connor, F. W. (1981). *Writing in the arts and sciences.* New York: Winthrop Publishers.

Papalia, D. E. (2006). *A child's world: Infancy through adolescence* (10th ed.). New York: McGraw-Hill.

Shaffer, D., & Kipp, K. (2007). *Developmental psychology: Childhood and adolescence* (7th ed.). Belmont, CA: Wadsworth.

Siiter, R. J. (1999). *Introduction to animal behavior.* Belmont, CA: Wadsworth.

Whishaw, I. Q., & Kolb, B. (2004). *The behavior of the laboratory rat.* New York: Oxford University Press.

See also:

http://ratgrowth.homestead.com

http://hometown.aol.com/RistoRat/ratbabies.html

http://www.dapper.com.au/links.htm

Appendix 41.1

Sample Chart

Date of observation	Mother's behavior	Pups' physical development	Locomotion	Sensory development	Social behavior	Miscellaneous

42 EARLY MOTOR AND VERBAL DEVELOPMENT

Peter S. Fernald
University of New Hampshire

L. Dodge Fernald
Harvard University

This activity is appropriate for classes in introductory psychology, child psychology, or any course that treats the developmental sequence in infancy and childhood. It can be used in a class of any size and requires approximately 30 minutes, although it can go longer with more discussion. This in-class activity is a good lead-in to a discussion about the developmental sequence, the distinction between abilities that are acquired through training and those that are acquired through maturation, and early intelligence testing.

CONCEPT

Several principles of human development, especially the cephalocaudal and proximodistal sequences and the role of maturation, are illustrated. Students should have some prior knowledge of the cephalocaudal and proximodistal sequences either through assigned reading or lecture.

MATERIALS NEEDED

Write the list of motor and verbal abilities on the chalkboard, or show them on a PowerPoint slide, or give a copy of the list to each student in the class.

Order of Development	Motor and Verbal Abilities
_____	Walks alone; says several words
_____	Describes the difference between a bird and a dog
_____	Turns head to follow moving object
_____	Names penny, nickel, and dime
_____	Climbs stairs; says many words
_____	Laces shoes
_____	Sits alone for one minute; says "da-da"
_____	Tells how a baseball and an orange or an airplane and a kite are alike
_____	Puts on shoes
_____	Tells time to quarter-hour
_____	Runs; uses simple word combinations
_____	Walks while holding onto something

INSTRUCTIONS

Ask the students to rank the various abilities according to their developmental sequence, beginning with 1, which indicates the first ability to develop, and ending with 12, the last ability to develop. After the students have completed this task, tell them the proper sequence, which is 3, 7, 12, 1, 5, 11, 9, 6, 4, 2, 10, 8. Then, to help students understand the sequence more clearly, put the list in its rearranged but correct order from first ability to develop (top) to last ability to develop. The list, with approximate ages, should appear as follows.

2 months	Turns head to follow moving object
9 months	Sits alone for 1 minute; says "da-da"
1 year	Walks while holding on to something
1 year 3 months	Walks alone; says several words
1 year 6 months	Climbs stairs; says many words
2 years	Runs; uses simple word combinations
3 years	Puts on shoes
4 years	Laces shoes
5 years	Names penny, nickel, and dime
6 years	Describes the difference between a bird and a dog
7 years	Tells time to quarter-hour
8 years	Tells how a baseball and an orange and an airplane and a kite are alike

DISCUSSION

Ask the students the following question: In what ways are cephalocaudal and proximodistal development indicated in the sequence just described? Coax out of the students some examples illustrated in the sequence. An example of cephalocaudal development is that a baby turns his or her head to follow a moving object before he or she walks. The baby also puts on his or her shoes before he or she learns to lace them, a sequence that suggests proximodistal development.

Next, tell the students to put the letter *M* beside those abilities they believe are acquired chiefly through maturation and a *T* beside those that clearly involve training. Then ask them a second question: Is there any trend or pattern with regard to the abilities that develop primarily through maturation and those for which training is also required? Elicit through discussion the following points: The first three abilities develop chiefly through maturation with regard to the motor task, but training is involved with each of the verbal tasks; the last six abilities all involve some training. Thus, it would appear that training (learning) assumes greater importance for abilities occurring later in the developmental sequence.

Finally, invite students to construct an intelligence test for infants and young children, birth through 8 years, and ask them a third question: Would it be appropriate to use some of these items in such a test? Again, through discussion, elicit the following ideas. *Intelligence,* defined in general terms, is the ability to adjust to one's environment. Placed in the correct order, the items represent a progressive increase in capacity to adapt to and deal with the environment. In fact, several of the tasks are included in standard intelligence tests. Note also the changing nature of intelligence as one ascends the age scale, from a largely motor ability very early in life to greater verbal emphasis later on. Adult intelligence tests involve mostly verbal abilities.

REFERENCES AND SUGGESTED READING

Papalia, D. E. (2006). *A child's world: Infancy through adolescence* (10th ed.). New York: McGraw-Hill.

Shaffer, D., & Kipp, K. (2007). *Developmental psychology: Childhood and adolescence* (7th ed.). Belmont, CA: Wadsworth.

43 Parent Panels: Bringing the Parent Into Understanding Childhood and Adolescence

Janet Morahan-Martin

Bryant University

This activity illustrates the changing role of parenthood according to the developmental stage of children. It is appropriate for classes in introductory psychology as well as child, adolescent, and adult development psychology classes. The activity involves one to six class sessions and requires advance preparation by students. It can be used by classes of any size but works best with classes of small to medium size if all students participate.

CONCEPT

Parents play a critical role in the lives of children and adolescents. Frequently, however, parents are relegated to a lesser role. Typically, in coverage of childhood and adolescence in texts, the study of parents focuses on genetics, modeling, and child-rearing patterns leading to adaptive traits or psychopathology in children. By implication, the emphasis is on how the parent molds or shapes the child. Although these approaches are valuable, I believe they do not adequately examine normal, healthy parenting or the interactive quality of parenting. The parent panels presented here provide a method of directly introducing parents to an undergraduate course. As the parents discuss their approaches to parenting, they bring to life the issues that parents face in raising their children. I have found using parent panels to be a particularly valuable method in teaching undergraduates who are not parents themselves.

Child rearing is an interactive process. The parent shapes the child and the child shapes the parent. Children continually change as they grow. As the child changes, so must the parent. The parent must adjust to the shifting needs of the child. Parenthood is thus a developmental process. Galinsky documented six stages of parenthood in her books *Between Generations* (1981) and *The Six Stages of Parenthood* (1987). Each stage of parenthood is characterized by themes and tasks that are largely determined by the child's developmental needs. These stages include expectant parents; parents of infants, toddlers, school-age children, and adolescents; and parents whose children are leaving home. Because these stages are the theoretical basis of the parent panels described here, a brief outline of the relevant issues for each stage is presented.

During pregnancy, parents are in the first, or image-making, stage. The expectant parents accept the pregnancy and prepare for the birth and parenthood. They build images of what the child will be like and what sort of parents they hope to be. Expectant parents also evaluate change in the relationships with their partners, parents, and friends. With the birth of the baby, parents enter the second, or nurturing, stage, which continues for about 1½–2 years, when the child begins to say no. The key task of this stage for the parents is becoming attached to their baby. The parents face a changing sense of self because they must balance the needs of the baby with their own needs. They change in their relationship to each other and other significant people in their lives. During this stage, the parents compare the actual experience of parenting with their images of birth, their child, and themselves as parents. The third, or authority, stage of parenthood lasts from the time the child is about 2 until he or she is about 4 or 5 years old. As the child begins to become autonomous, the parents' task shifts from nurturing to asserting responsible power and authority. The parents must determine acceptable limits for the child and how to enforce those limits and communicate with their child. In doing so, they must deal with their own often-shattered images of their not-so-perfect child and of themselves as the not-so-perfect parents. Also, they must deal with the child's sex role identity.

From the time that a child is about 4 or 5 until the approach of adolescence, the parent is in the fourth, or interpretive, stage. As the child's world expands beyond the safety of home and school, the parents' major task is to interpret the world to their child. This involves interpreting themselves to their child and interpreting and developing the child's self-concept as well as helping the child form values. The parents also must answer the child's questions about his or her expanding world and provide the child with access to the skills and information needed. The fifth, or interdependent, stage includes the child's teenage years. Parents must come to terms with the shock of their child becoming a teenager, and their images of themselves as parents must be reevaluated. Once again, the parent must renegotiate many of the issues of the authority stage: control, communication, understanding, and avoiding a battle of wills. They must deal with the child's sexuality and accept the teenager's identity and form new bonds with their almost-grown child. The sixth, or departure, stage happens when the child leaves home. This period is characterized by evaluations. As the parents prepare for the departure of the child, they review the child's years with them and reevaluate the entire parenting process. When the child actually leaves, the parents redefine their identities as parents of grown children, reexamine other important relationships, and measure their accomplishments and failures.

INSTRUCTIONS The parent panels are scheduled after coverage of the appropriate developmental age of the child. Early in the semester, students choose the stage of parenthood they would like to present and form work groups on the basis of the stage they have chosen. These study groups are responsible for finding parents for the parent panel as well as conducting the session on the day of the parent panels.

Prior to the day of the panel presentation, all students are required to read about the developmental stage(s) of parenthood to be presented. Galinsky's *Between Generations* (1981) or *The Six Stages of Parenthood* (1987) is recommended. Additionally, each student in the study group for this parent panel is expected to conduct an interview with at least one parent of an appropriately aged child and write a paper summarizing the issues raised in this interview and whether the parent interview confirms the themes of parenthood raised in their readings. It is important that instructors discuss ethical issues involved in interviewing and require informed consent of interviewees.

Students in the study group that is responsible for a given developmental age group are responsible for conducting the class on the day of the parent panel. However, it is recommended that the instructor introduce himself or herself to all of the parents who have volunteered to participate and briefly explain the purpose of their participation in the parent panel. On the day of the parent panel, the parents and members of the study group all sit facing the class. The parents, and their children, if present, are introduced to the class by a member of the study group, who then briefly presents the issues of parenting that are relevant to the group and the findings from the interviews that the group conducted with other parents. The parents are encouraged to ask or comment on the presentation.

Members of the study group then begin asking the parents about their experiences parenting a child of this developmental age. The study groups have previously been informed about open-ended questions and techniques for promoting discussion. Questions typically focus on the best and worst things about parenting a child of this developmental age; how the parents have changed; adjustments in their relationships with the child, their mate, other siblings, and their own parents, and in their life in general. Discussion among parents is encouraged, as are questions from the rest of the class. About 5 to10 minutes at the end of the period is reserved for the parents to make comments and to again thank the parents for their participation.

The size and duration of each parent panel can vary. I have typically allotted one 50-minute class period for each of the developmental stages, and each panel has 4 to 6 parents. However, this can be abbreviated to two or three panels per class period, with fewer parents in each age group. Having more than one parent for each age group is strongly advised; students often comment later on the differences among parents within each stage as well as among stages.

An alternative approach that involves the whole class is to assign readings, and, based on the readings, have all students in the class write a paper based on least one or more interviews with parents and prepare questions to ask parents. Parent panels can be chosen by the instructor.

DISCUSSION

Discussion is used to summarize the issues raised in the panel discussions. The focus is on developmental themes apparent from the parent panel and on contrasting the issues and themes of parents in this developmental age with parents in previous groups. Differences among styles of parenting are highlighted, as are the interactions between parent and child.

REFERENCES AND SUGGESTED READING

Bartz, K. W. (1978). Selected childrearing tasks and problems of mothers and fathers. *The Family Coordinator, 27,* 209–214.

Freed, A. O. (1985). Linking developmental, family and life cycle theories. *Smith College Studies in Social Work, 55,* 169–182.

Galinsky, E. (1981). *Between generations: The stages of parenthood.* New York: Berkeley Books.

Galinsky, E. (1987). *The six stages of parenthood.* New York: Perseus Publishing.

Rhodes, S. I. (1977). A developmental approach to the life cycle of the family. *Social Casework, 58,* 301–311.

Schaefer, C. E., & DiGer, T. F. (2000). *Ages and stages: A parent's guide to normal child development.* New York: Wiley.

Unell, B. C., & Wyckoff, J. L. (2000). *The 8 seasons of parenthood.* New York: Crown.

44 THREE TASKS OF ADOLESCENT IDENTITY: COGNITIVE, MORAL, AND SOCIAL

Mary Moore Vandendorpe

Lewis University

This three-part discussion is designed to bring abstract theories concerning adolescent development to life, and is suitable as an in-class activity for introductory and developmental psychology. It can be modified to fit available class time; allow 20 minutes if it is an instructor-directed discussion emphasizing Piaget and Erikson. No materials are needed and any size class can participate. Large classes may be broken into small discussion groups to facilitate student participation.

CONCEPT

The cognitive theory of Jean Piaget, the moral theories of Lawrence Kohlberg and Carol Gilligan, and the concept of social age-graded norms are key constructs for the study of adolescence. According to Erik Erikson (1954), the formation of identity is aided by development in these areas. More recent discussions of these theories often use the concept of schema, a customary way of thinking about things, rather than the concept of stage (Gibbs, 2003).

Piaget (1972) postulated that formal operational thought requires an ability to think hypothetically and to generate logical rules for abstract problems. Both Kohlberg (1986) and Gilligan (1982) proposed that adolescents become capable of moral reasoning and look beyond simple rewards and punishments. Kohlberg's theory is based on considerations of justice and equity and seems applicable to most men. Gilligan's theory describes moral decisions as being based on relationships and responsibilities and seems to be more descriptive of women. In our society, age-graded norms are not highly visible because there is no single, universally recognized rite of passage. Adolescents are frequently caught between the norms for children and the norms for adults. As societies become more fragmented, conflicting norms and ideals complicate the formation of identity.

These developments make the adolescent's search for his or her own identity a difficult struggle. Cognitive changes allow the teenager to generate several potential identities and to evaluate them in a reasonably logical manner. The adolescent can question beliefs and roles handed down by the family and society while still remaining sensitive to expectations about what his or her appropriate behavior should be. A successful resolution of identity depends on the ability to coordinate all of these elements.

INSTRUCTIONS

The activity is composed of three applications of the theories and a conclusion:

1. After presenting the definition of the formal operations stage, introduce what I call the *"One Leg Scenario."* Ask the students, "Suppose that from this moment on, every human baby is born with only one leg. What would have to change?" Elaborate on the sit-

uation according to class questions; for example, state that the one-legged babies are normal in every other way. Then ask for ideas about what would have to change. The students quickly suggest changes in clothing, as well as in architecture. They often decide, for example, that stairs would disappear; the discussion will also include ideas of what cars and sports would be like. How would people travel—using crutches, riding on scooters, or just hopping on the one leg? Have the class consider how such an event might change our ideas of normality and might introduce new targets of discrimination. In conclusion, point out the characteristics of formal operations that usually become evident from the students' contributions: hypothetico-deductive reasoning and consideration of every aspect of the problem. This can also be a lead-in to discussions about divergent thinking and problem solving.

2. Kohlberg's (1986) moral dilemma concerning Heinz and the druggist is cited in almost every text, but in my classes, two other moral dilemmas have been more realistic and interesting to undergraduates. They are exceeding the speed limit and cheating in school. Other topics that have been successful are abortion and underage drinking.

Instruct the class to generate every reason that they can imagine for and against these behaviors. It is useful to ask them to suggest what other students might say, rather than give their own reasoning. Divide the class into small groups and have each group classify each reason according to its level of morality for both Kohlberg's (1986) and Gilligan's (1982) theories. Each group can describe an appropriate approach to encourage moral growth in an adolescent. I often do the speeding example as a large group exercise and then have the small groups discuss the second "dilemma." Discuss the difference between moral reasoning and moral behavior.

3. Students may not realize the impact of *norms* on our lives. Age-graded norms can be demonstrated by asking the students how a high school freshman is expected to act and how a college senior is expected to act. Students usually volunteer descriptions in terms of drinking, driving, relationships and classroom behavior. The major point, that norms are often age graded and that they have a strong, often unrecognized effect on our lives, needs little elaboration. Point out that norms make it easier to know how to behave: they can be efficient and comfortable.

DISCUSSION   The discussion should point out how the abilities to negotiate cognitive, moral, and social tasks influence the development of identity. To emphasize themes of change and consistency, ask the students to write 10 answers to the item "I am . . ." in two sets—one for themselves currently and one for when they were 12 years old. Ask the students to describe the changes in their identity—such as viewpoint, sense of moral responsibility, and perception of self—that have occurred over time and also to note the similarities that have remained. Have them apply the theories discussed in this activity to their own development. Make the point that highly industrialized Western cultures typically prize individuality, whereas traditional cultures more often value interdependence and cooperation (Hoover, 2004).

A second area of discussion relates to the strong attraction many adolescents feel for ideologies. My classes have analyzed the ways in which growing analytical ability, a stronger moral sense, and the comfort of norms can make young people vulnerable to ideological groups: political and religious extremists, cults, gangs, and social and military organizations.

Students can write responses to these exercises, discussing an example of their own thinking, how norms have influenced them, or how identity may change over time.

REFERENCES AND SUGGESTED READING

Erikson, E. (1954). *Childhood and society.* New York: W. W. Norton.

Gibbs, J. C. (2003). *Moral development and reality: Beyond the theories of Kohlberg and Hoffman.* Thousand Oaks, CA: Sage.

Gilligan, C. (1982). *In a different voice: Psychological theory and women's development.* Cambridge, MA: Harvard University Press.

Hoover, K. R. (Ed.). (2004). *The future of identity: Centennial reflections on the legacy of Erik Erikson.* Lanham, MD: Lexington Books.

Kohlberg, L. (1986). *The stages of ethical development from childhood through old age.* San Francisco: Harper & Row.

Piaget, J. (1972). Intellectual evolution from adolescence to adulthood. *Human Development, 15,* 1–12.

Thomas, R. (2004). *Comparing theories of child development* (6th ed.). Belmont, CA: Wadsworth.

45 INVESTIGATING ATTITUDES TOWARD OLDER ADULTS

Paul E. Panek

The Ohio State University at Newark

This activity demonstrates that attitudes toward aging are mixed, that is, positive as well as negative attitudes are associated with the aging process and older adults. It is appropriate for classes in life-span developmental psychology, introductory psychology, and social psychology. This activity has both an out-of-class component and an in-class component. Depending on class size and whether all students or a selected number of students participate in the in-class component, the activity requires 15 to 30 minutes of class time.

CONCEPT

Adults over 65 years of age are the fastest growing part of the United States population, a situation produced both by the size of the baby-boomer generation and the changes in medical science that have extended life expectancy. What are the implications of this change in America's population makeup in terms of politics, economics, the job market, and family obligations?

Society's attitudes toward the aging process and older adults, though moderated by a number of factors (e.g., previous exposure to older adults, stimulus characteristics of older target persons, age of respondents) have generally been described as mixed (Chasteen, Schwartz, & Park, 2002; Kite, Stockdale, Whitley, & Johnson, 2005). That is, people associate both positive and negative stereotypes with aging (Fiske, Cuddy, Glick, & Xu, 2002). Butler (1969) coined the term *age-ism* to describe the negative attitudes expressed by many toward older adults. In the following activity, students investigate the attitudes of their peers toward older adults and develop hands-on experience in research methodology. This activity has been demonstrated to be effective with college undergraduates (Panek, 1984).

INSTRUCTIONS

Give students a brief introduction regarding attitudes toward the aging process and older adults. Then tell them that each of them will research the attitudes of his or her peers toward older adults. Instruct each student to ask four other students (not in the class) the three terms or words that come to mind when they hear the term *old person*. Ask them to record the age of the person responding. Have each student prepare an overall list of responses and a frequency count of each response after interviewing the four participants. After all students have collected their data, ask them to present their findings on the board. Prepare a master list of the terms and their frequency on the board as each student presents his or her findings. On the basis of your master list, present the overall summary table of the terms and the frequency count of each term. Ask class members to discuss openly the connotation of each term: positive (e.g., wisdom), negative (e.g., senile), or neutral (e.g., easy to please). Base the final determination of the connotation of each term on a majority vote of the entire class. Place a P (positive), O (neutral), or N (negative) next to the term, based on how the class voted.

If there is enough diversity in the ages of the out-of-class respondents, it might be instructive to look for any differences in the patterns of responses generated by students of different ages, for example, 40-year-olds versus 20-year-olds. Or if you want to ensure some age diversity in the sample, ask students to seek out respondents from particular age groups, perhaps in shopping malls or other public venues.

DISCUSSION

Using a similar procedure with a class of college undergraduates, 60% of the responses regarding the term *old person* were negative, 30% were positive, and 10% were neutral (Panek, 1984). This activity can be quite effective in generating classroom discussion regarding attitudes toward the aging process and older adults. Discussion topics might include such questions as, Where do aging stereotypes come from? What role does the media play? How well trained are medical personnel in psychological and physical issues of aging? What environmental barriers exist for older persons? In what ways do such negative stereotypes serve as barriers to older people? How could young adults be made more aware of social barriers that affect older adults? What cross-cultural differences exist in terms of attitudes toward aging? For example, how do the attitudes compare in the United States versus China? How might negative aging stereotypes be changed in the United States? At what age are aging stereotypes learned? Kwong See and Heller (2005) have found that children as young as 5 years demonstrate negative stereotypes about older adults.

In addition to helping students become more aware of attitudes toward older adults, this activity has a number of secondary benefits. These include greater classroom discussion and participation, an illustration of research methodology, and an increase in students' desire to undertake other research projects.

It is important that students understand that there are very real consequences as a result of negative stereotypes about older persons. For example, it has been shown that such stereotypes about older adults have resulted, too often, in their not being the targets of legislation for health promotion and disease prevention programs (Ory, Kinney, Hawkins, Sanner, & Mockenhaupt, 2003). Ory et al. (2003) have written that "ageist stereotypes are pervasive in U.S. society and harmful to older adults' psychological well-being, physical and cognitive functioning, and survival" (p. 164). Thus the importance of this topic for psychology and for our students cannot be overstated.

REFERENCES AND SUGGESTED READING

Butler, R. N. (1969). Age-ism: Another form of bigotry. *The Gerontologist, 14,* 243–249.

Chasteen, A. L., Schwartz, N., & Park, D. C. (2002). The activation of aging stereotypes in younger and older adults. *Journal of Gerontology, 57B,* 540–547.

Fiske, S. T., Cuddy, A. C., Glick, P., & Xu, J. (2002). A model of (often mixed) stereotype content: Competence and warmth respectively follow from perceived status and competition. *Journal of Personality and Social Psychology, 82,* 878–902.

Kite, M. E., Stockdale, G. D., Whitley, B. E., & Johnson, B. T. (2005). Attitudes toward younger and older adults: An updated meta-analytic review. *Journal of Social Issues, 61,* 241–266.

Kwong See, S. T., & Heller, R. (2005). Measuring ageism in children. In E. Palmore, L. Branch, & D. Harris (Eds.), *The encyclopedia of ageism* (pp. 210–217). Binghamton, NY: Haworth Press.

Panek, P. E. (1984). A classroom technique for demonstrating negative attitudes toward aging. *Teaching of Psychology, 11,* 173–174.

Ory, M., Kinney, H. M., Hawkins, M., Sanner, B., & Mockenhaupt, R. (2003). Challenging aging stereotypes: Strategies for creating a more active society. *American Journal of Preventive Medicine, 25,* 164–171.

CHAPTER 9
PERSONALITY

The activities in this chapter begin with an investigation of personality theories. Students will explore their implicit personality theories, the nature of projective approaches to personality assessment, the illusion of personal control over chance events that often accounts for superstitious behavior, the nature of bogus assessments of personality, and the psychology of the self as portrayed in psychology and in literature.

This chapter starts with a look at the topic of personality theory. Activity 46 helps students identify their implicit theories of personality. It encourages them "to think about their personal theory of personality and to consider how it relates to prominent personality theories in the field of psychology." This activity helps students address the question, "What is personality?" and to understand why there are so many different theories of personality in psychology.

The projective approach to assessing personality is the subject of Activity 47. Data from a sentence-completion test for two fictional individuals provides the basis for discussing their personalities. Further, the activity explores the use of personality tests as assessment devices in personnel decisions.

Ellen Langer has shown that some people believe they can exert control in situations where the outcome is wholly dictated by chance, a phenomenon labeled *the illusion of control.* In Activity 48, students play a game of chance in which they make predictions about their probability of winning. Typically their estimates far exceed their actual chances. Discussion ties the results of the activity to issues such as superstitions and compulsive gambling.

Activity 49 illustrates what is often called the Barnum effect in personality testing. Using a bogus personality test that is, in fact, not scored, students are given identical feedback about their personalities and asked how accurate the test seems in describing their personality. Discussion of the results focuses on the similarity of such Barnum statements to newspaper astrology columns. A principal goal of the exercise is to involve students in a discussion of how reliable and valid measures of personality might be constructed.

Activity 50 brings literature into the classroom by having students read one of two novels by Wallace Stegner: *A Shooting Star* or *Crossing to Safety.* The focus of the exercise is on an understanding of self and how self is viewed in personality psychology. This activity links psychological conceptions of the self with the self as portrayed in the two Stegner novels.

46 WHAT IS PERSONALITY? A PERSONAL APPRAISAL

Kenneth W. Kerber

This activity helps students identify and examine their implicit personality theories and makes personality theories concrete and understandable. It is appropriate for classes in introductory psychology, personality, social psychology, and personal adjustment. No prior knowledge of psychology is necessary. Advance preparation is minimal, and the activity is appropriate for classes of all sizes. This can be done in-class or outside of class with a writing assignment.

CONCEPT

The field of personality often is associated with comprehensive personality theories such as those developed by Sigmund Freud, Gordon Allport, and Raymond Cattell. Even a partial listing of current theories of personality would include scores of noted theorists and their viewpoints. The tremendous variety of personality theories can be made more understandable for the introductory psychology student by grouping these theories into broad categories such as the psychodynamic, humanistic, cognitive, trait, and learning approaches. Although interrelated, these approaches to personality use different concepts to achieve an understanding of human behavior and mental processes.

In his theory of personal constructs, Kelly (1963) viewed persons as scientists. He argued that each of us, like a scientist, attempts to predict and control events. We continually evaluate our experiences and use our interpretations of reality to understand and control the world around us. According to this viewpoint, each of us has our own theory of human personality, because people form a major part of the reality that we attempt to understand and control.

This activity encourages students to think about their personal theory of personality and to consider how it relates to prominent personality theories in the field of psychology. The exercise and resulting discussion can serve as an introduction to more detailed material about major types of personality theories.

INSTRUCTIONS

Introduce this activity with a brief discussion of the term *personality*. Distinguish among popular meanings of the word, such as social skill, charm, or attractiveness, and the meaning of the term for psychologists—that is, not our public impression but our essential nature as human beings.

Give each student a sheet of paper with the following instructions at the top: "Below are some concepts that may be important to you in the way you think about your own personality and the personalities of the people around you. Think about each item and check the three items that are most important regarding your view of human personality." Below these instructions, provide a list of terms such as the following:

_____ external environment
_____ temperament
_____ interpretation of experience

_____ conscious awareness
_____ childhood experiences
_____ rewards and punishments
_____ abilities
_____ organization of reality
_____ the self
_____ unconscious motives
_____ observable behavior
_____ enduring characteristics
_____ expectations
_____ subjective feelings
_____ sexual instincts

After the list, add the following instructions: "In the space below, explain why you chose the three items that you checked."

The list shown here was designed to contain three concepts associated with each of five major approaches to personality: psychodynamic (childhood experiences, unconscious motives, sexual instincts); humanistic (conscious awareness, the self, subjective feelings); cognitive (interpretations of experience, organization of reality, expectations); trait (temperament, abilities, enduring characteristics); and learning (external environment, rewards and punishments, observable behavior). The concepts that the terms on your list illustrate should coincide with those you will discuss in class or that will be covered in associated reading assignments. Try to select terms that match the students' psychological sophistication.

Students can finish the handout in class or as a homework assignment. On completion, have them discuss the concepts they chose and why. As part of the discussion, point out the association between particular concepts and different approaches to personality as a way of introducing major types of theories. Encourage students to consider how their personal view of human personality relates to major theories in psychology. In fact, this exercise can provide the basis for a paper in which students explain more fully their own view of personality in relation to the work of psychological theorists.

DISCUSSION

You can use this activity to address several important questions about the study of personality, including the following: What is personality? What is a personality theory? Why have psychologists proposed so many different personality theories? Is one theory correct and the others wrong? Have factor analytic approaches to personality answered that question (e.g., the Big Five, see Goldberg, 1990)? What functions are served by personality theories in psychology? Does the average person actually develop his or her own theory of personality? If so, how does this activity differ from that of a psychologist formulating a new theory? What functions are served by personal theories of human behavior? Are there good reasons why each of us should evaluate our own view of human personality?

In the end, it is probably quite reasonable to conclude, along with Hall, Lindzey, and Campbell (2001), that no single definition of personality can be applied with any generality, and that personality is defined by the particular concepts used by the theorist. With these conclusions in mind, it makes sense to introduce students to personality theories with an activity based on important psychological concepts.

Human personality is precisely the kind of complex subject matter about which theorists—and students—can easily disagree. You can enhance students' understanding of the enormous difficulties faced by a personality theorist if you involve them in the theorist's task, even for a short time. By encouraging students to struggle with the complexity inherent in defining personality, you can make the study of personality theories more interesting and perhaps more memorable.

For other teaching activities that explore implicit personality theory see Embree (1986) and Wang (1997).

REFERENCES AND SUGGESTED READING

Benjamin, L. T., Jr. (1983). A class exercise in personality and psychological assessment. *Teaching of Psychology, 10,* 94–95.

Embree, M. C. (1986). Implicit personality theory in the classroom: An integrative approach. *Teaching of Psychology, 13,* 78–80.

Goldberg, L. R. (1990). An alternative "description of personality": The Big-Five factor structure. *Journal of Personality and Social Psychology, 59,* 1216–1229.

Hall, C. S., Lindzey, G., & Campbell, J. B. (2001). *Theories of personality* (4th ed.). New York: Wiley.

Haslam, N., Bastian, B., & Bissett, M. (2004). Essentialist beliefs about personality and their implications. *Personality and Social Psychology Bulletin, 30,* 1661–1673.

Kelly, G. A. (1963). *A theory of personality: The psychology of personal constructs.* New York: Norton.

McAdams, D. P. (1995). What do we know when we know a person? *Journal of Personality, 63,* 365–396.

Moskowitz, G. B., & Tesser, A. (Eds.). (2005). *Social cognition: Understanding self and others.* New York: Guilford Press.

Schultz, D. P., & Schultz, S. E. (2004). *Theories of personality* (8th ed.). Belmont, CA: Wadsworth.

Wang, A. Y. (1997). Making implicit personality theories explicit: A classroom demonstration. *Teaching of Psychology, 24,* 258–261.

47 THE SENTENCE COMPLETION TEST: ASSESSING PERSONALITY

Peter S. Fernald
University of New Hampshire

L. Dodge Fernald
Harvard University

This is an excellent vehicle for discussing the nature and application of personality testing for classes in introductory psychology, personality, personal adjustment, psychological testing, or industrial–organizational psychology. Students are exposed to a real test in an engaging yet safe and ethical way. Advance preparation is minimal, and no prior knowledge of psychology is necessary. The activity is appropriate for classes of any size.

CONCEPT

The theory of projective testing is demonstrated with the sentence completion test described here. In addition, several concepts relevant to the study of personality and personality assessment are considered, namely, projection, situational versus dispositional responses, interjudge reliability, test validity, problems in interpreting test responses, and caution in the use of personality tests.

MATERIALS NEEDED

You will need a handout for each student that contains the sentence completion responses of both Al and Bill, candidates for a position in a business firm, and 12 questions about their responses (shown in Appendix 47.1).

INSTRUCTIONS

Tell the students to read the sentence completions of Al and Bill and answer the 12 questions that follow the sentence completions. It is not important that the students answer all of the 12 questions. Give them 8 minutes (or at the very most 10 minutes) to analyze Al's and Bill's responses. Allow at least 15 to 20 minutes for what is certain to be a very spirited discussion.

DISCUSSION

Ask the students to consider the sentence fragment "People think of me . . ." and to indicate whether they would add or eliminate words to make it more projective. Also, ask them to indicate how they would make it less projective. The fragment could be made more projective by eliminating several words and vice versa. To illustrate, the fragments "People . . ." or "People think . . ." provide for more projection, whereas the fragment "People think of me only when I am . . ." allows for less projection. As a further illustration of how eliminating or adding words can control the amount of projection, consider the sentence fragments "Everyone . . ." and "Everyone is born free and. . . ."

Point out to the students that a word count indicates Bill is more verbose than Al in his sentence completions. Then ask them if they believe Bill is more verbose than Al in other situations, for example, those involving report writing, or during committee meetings, cocktail parties, dinner, or personal conversations. Any psychologist who uses assessment techniques for placement or selection is interested in the extent to which test behavior can be generalized to other situations. Possibly Bill is verbose only in sentence completion tests or in situations in which he is being assessed. He may be a man of few words at cocktail parties, committee meetings, and elsewhere. If this were true, Bill's verbosity would be considered a situational response. If, on the other hand, Bill were verbose in most situations, then his verbosity would be considered a dispositional response or a personality trait.

Personality assessment is complicated by the fact that many human activities are largely situational. The skilled examiner knows when he or she can generalize to other situations and is very cautious when speculating about behavior in situations bearing little or no resemblance to the test situation. When test responses closely parallel behavior in the situation of interest, the test is said to be a valid assessment instrument.

Ask the students if they would expect examiners to agree on their interpretations of sentence completions. Then, after listening to some of their reactions, explain that examiners sometimes are in agreement and sometimes are not, depending on the kind of interpretations requested, among other things. Undergraduate students are not trained examiners, but responses of 64 students to the 12 questions about Al and Bill illustrate the point:

	Al	Bill
1.	—	64
2.	56	8
3.	32	32
4.	—	64
5.	60	4
6.	10	54
7.	52	12
8.	55	9
9.	—	64
10.	1	63
11.	2	62
12.	35	29

Note the lack of agreement as to who is more self-centered (Question 12). The term *self-centered* is not easily defined, and discussion of it typically reveals that one's value system bears directly on one's definition. On the other hand, there is little disagreement regarding the definition of *verbose* (Question 1); merely counting the words will determine the more verbose individual. Accordingly, one might describe the answer to Question 1 as a close-to-the-data interpretation. Many factors contribute to interjudge reliability (i.e., agreement among examiners), but the two primary ones are close-to-the-data interpretations and terms with clear definitions.

Suppose Al and Bill were being considered for the position of junior accountant, a position requiring close adherence to office and accounting procedures established by the senior accountant. Ask the students to indicate whom they would select and have them explain the reasons for their choice. Then try to elicit from the discussion the following points: Bill's test performance suggests a willingness to conform to rules and authority. This is apparent in his completions of Sentences 9 and 10 and in his adherence to the test instructions. His sentence completions suggest that he took the test seriously.

Al's last four sentence completions, on the other hand, indicate otherwise. And in sentence 3, Al deviates from the test instructions by writing an entirely new sentence. Last, Al demonstrated little concern for usual writing standards in his use of "if" in Sentence 12 and "to" in Sentences 8 and 10 and his omission of a period in Sentence 3. On the basis of these observations, one might tentatively conclude that Bill is more likely to conform to the senior accountant's office and accounting procedures. On the other hand, some of Bill's characteristics might create a very disagreeable relationship between him and the senior accountant. For example, it may be that Bill conforms only to rules that make sense to him, and that he is reluctant, perhaps more reluctant than Al, to accept certain office procedures outlined by the senior accountant. Again, note the problem of generalizing from test performance to other situations (i.e., the problem of test validity).

Point out that most students consider Al both more impulsive and more spontaneous than Bill. Then ask the class whether these terms are synonymous, and if not, what the implications of using one but not the other to describe Al are. Students generally agree that the terms *impulsive* and *spontaneous* are not synonymous, yet they disagree as to which word better describes Al's sentence completions, especially for Sentences 13 through 16. Is Al impulsive, spontaneous, or just fed up with the test? The word a psychological examiner uses may have important implications in employment and other situations. Who wants to hire an impulsive employee?

Ask the students if they would have reservations about making an important selection decision solely on the basis of sentence completions, and then make sure the ensuing discussion includes the following point: Any trained psychologist would have grave reservations about using only one selection device, whether it be a sentence completion test or some other assessment instrument. One reason is that some of the findings from the sentence completions may not be indicated by other tests. Another reason is that many other factors, such as general intelligence, training in mathematics or accounting, and previous work experience, are doubtless of equal or greater importance for performing well in the business position described.

REFERENCES AND SUGGESTED READING

Anastasi, A., & Urbina, S. P. (1997). *Psychological testing* (7th ed.). Upper Saddle River, NJ: Prentice-Hall.

Funder, D. C., & Ozer, D. J. (1997). *Pieces of the personality puzzle: Readings in theory and research.* New York: W. W. Norton.

Wallen, R. W. (1956). *Clinical psychology: The study of persons.* New York: McGraw-Hill.

Appendix 47.1

Responses to the Sentence Completion Test*

Directions. Below are the sentence completions of Al and Bill, candidates for a position in a business firm. Your task is to read their sentence completions and then answer the 12 questions that follow.

1. My mother . . .
   Al: is the nicest person on earth.
   Bill: is my ideal in most respects and as devoted to me as I am to her.
2. My father . . .
   Al: is a good fellow.
   Bill: was an admirable, lovable, honest, and righteous friend.
3. Brothers and sisters . . .
   Al: I have many.
   Bill: are wonderful companions, standing by each other whatever happens.
4. Our family . . .
   Al: is not very close.
   Bill: functions as a unit, where all participate in decisions, based on the fact we love each other.
5. Other people usually . . .
   Al: like me.
   Bill: like me, respect me, and work well with and for me.
6. People think of me as . . .
   Al: a good fellow.
   Bill: a leader with my feet on the ground—one who is substantial and sincere.
7. If people only knew . . .
   Al: my ability.
   Bill: how to build relationships, the world would be a happier place.
8. People are slow to . . .
   Al: to realize my ability.
   Bill: judge unfairly.
9. If I had my way . . .
   Al: I would be a success.
   Bill: we'd all believe in and live by certain basic principles.
10. I will do anything to . . .
    Al: to be on top.
    Bill: serve God and my fellow man.
11. My greatest ambition . . .
    Al: to be in good health and financial security.
    Bill: is to succeed.
12. I get down in the dumps when . . .
    Al: if I am sick.
    Bill: someone very dear to me lies at death's door.
13. I suffer most from . . .
    Al: the atomic bomb.
    Bill: the failures of others.

---

*Note. Sentence completions reprinted from Wallen (1956).

14. Nothing is so frustrating as . . .
    Al: a traffic jam.
    Bill: being apparently unable to come up with the right answer on the spur of the moment.
15. I failed . . .
    Al: to cross the street.
    Bill: to get an order because I temporarily lost sight of the prospect's interests.
16. What gets me in trouble is . . .
    Al: robbing banks.
    Bill: sometimes expecting other people to react or go into action as quickly as I do.

Referring to Al's and Bill's sentence completions above, answer the following questions.

1. Who is more verbose, Al or Bill?
2. Who is more spontaneous?
3. Who is more flexible in thought and action?
4. Who stresses the importance of human relationships?
5. Who is more impulsive?
6. Who is more cautious and methodical?
7. Who is more aggressive?
8. Who makes jokes and ridicules when frustrated?
9. Who is more of an idealist?
10. Whose righteousness might alienate some of his associates?
11. Who is more dependable and conscientious?
12. Who is more self-centered?

48 THE ILLUSION OF CONTROL
Stephen J. Dollinger
Southern Illinois University at Carbondale

All you will need is a deck of standard playing cards and a dollar bill to conduct this quick, easy activity on the illusion of personal control. Students need no prior knowledge, and the demonstration can be done in a single class session. The activity is appropriate for classes of any size in introductory psychology, research methods, or personality, and it leads to a lively discussion of superstitious behavior and gambling.

CONCEPT

This activity involves a simulation that illustrates research methodology in experimental personality psychology and serves as a preliminary introduction to lecture material on the topic of illusion of control. Langer (1975) showed that people often believe that they can exert control in totally chance situations. Examples of this are apparent in lotteries, horse races, or ESP tasks. This illusion is most likely to be evident when a chance situation incorporates cues from similar skill situations, cues that suggest that skill factors might be effective in determining the outcome of the chance. For example, one's odds of winning the lottery do not change by virtue of one's choosing or being assigned a ticket; nevertheless, many people feel more confident when they feel that they are in a position of active, rather than passive, participation. The concept of illusory control becomes especially interesting in light of such phenomena as compulsive gambling, superstitions, and mania (Ayeroff & Abelson, 1976; Benassi, Sweeney, & Drevno, 1979; Burger & Schnerring, 1982; Golin, Terrell, & Johnson, 1977; Stern & Berrenberg, 1979).

MATERIALS NEEDED

You will need a standard deck of 52 playing cards and a $1 prize. At least four participants (preferably about 20 participants) are needed to conduct the simulation.

INSTRUCTIONS

As you enter the classroom, take the dollar bill from your wallet and, holding it high, announce that the class will begin with a brief card game. State that the person drawing the highest-valued card will win the dollar.

Tell the students that you are going to give each one a card but they are not to look at their cards until instructed to do so. Hand a card to the first person, direct the second to draw his or her own card, and alternate in this way until everyone has a card (i.e., giving half the students their cards and allowing the other half to choose their cards). Now ask the students, before looking at their cards, to use a percentage figure and write down what their level of confidence is that they will win. After all participants have received a card and written down their subjective probability of winning, have the students look at their cards and determine who the winner is. Now have a class member calculate a composite result of the two groups' (choice and no choice) responses.

In keeping with the illusion-of-control phenomenon, subjects choosing their own cards are likely to show a higher confidence estimate (e.g., group mean = 55%) than those whose card was assigned (no-choice group mean = 45%). Both groups are typically markedly overconfident when the base rate odds are considered (11% probability with 9 participants in the class; 5% probability with 20 participants in the class, etc.).

DISCUSSION I use this simulation, as well as a discussion about the Illinois State Lottery and its workings, as a lead-in to lecture material on the illusion of control. Likely your state has a lottery as well—39 states do as of 2007—and learning about its operation and varied games will aid you in discussing the implications of this activity.

This simulation has been effective in eliciting intently focused attention and enthusiastic participation in the lecture material and its implications. For example, it elicited a number of comments about the personal relevance of the phenomenon (see Cramer & Perreault, 2006; Langens, 2007). You can also bring up factors that contribute to the illusion of control, such as superstitions. What kinds of superstitions do students use when taking final exams or playing in an important sporting event? Have these superstitions ever been connected to the actual outcome, or has the belief in them actually helped to assuage some of the anxiety inherent in such situations? Ask students to consider the contradictions between the illusion of control held by gamblers and race-track bettors and the loss of control from which compulsive gamblers suffer (see Griffiths, 2006; Wohl, Young, & Hart, 2007). The argument is often made that success in racetrack betting does require certain knowledge of the situation (what the horses are like, how they run in certain conditions, how the jockeys have been doing lately, and so on). How true is this, and can other types of gambling make a similar claim (Williams & Connolly, 2006)?

REFERENCES AND SUGGESTED READING

Ayeroff, F., & Abelson, R. P. (1976). ESP and ESB: Belief in personal success at mental telepathy. *Journal of Personality and Social Psychology, 34,* 240–247.

Benassi, V. A., Sweeney, P. D., & Drevno, G. E. (1979). Mind over matter: Perceived success at psychokinesis. *Journal of Personality and Social Psychology, 37,* 1377–1386.

Burger, J. M., & Schnerring, D. A. (1982). The effects of desire for control and extrinsic rewards on the illusion of control and gambling. *Motivation and Emotion, 6,* 329–335.

Cramer, K. M., & Perreault, L. A. (2006). Effects of predictability, actual controllability, and awareness of choice on perceptions of control. *Current Research in Social Psychology, 11,* 111–126.

Golin, S., Terrell, F., & Johnson, B. (1977). Depression and the illusion of control. *Journal of Abnormal Psychology, 86,* 440–442.

Goodman, J. K., & Irwin, J. R. (2006). Special random numbers: Beyond the illusion of control. *Organizational Behavior and Human Decision Processes, 99,* 161–174.

Griffiths, M. (2006). An overview of pathological gambling. In T. G. Plante (Ed.), *Mental disorders of the new millennium: Behavioral issues* (Vol. 1, pp. 73–98). Westport, CT: Praeger Publishers.

Langens, T. A. (2007). Regulatory focus and illusions of control. *Personality and Social Psychology Bulletin, 33,* 226–237.

Langer, E. J. (1975). The illusion of control. *Journal of Personality and Social Psychology, 32,* 311–328.

Stern, G. S., & Berrenberg, J. L. (1979). Skill-set, success outcome, and mania as determinants of the illusion of control. *Journal of Research in Personality, 13,* 206–220.

Williams, R. J., & Connolly, D. (2006). Does learning about the mathematics of gambling change gambling behavior? *Psychology of Addictive Behaviors, 20,* 62–68.

Wohl, M. J. A., Young, M. M., & Hart, K. E. (2007). Self-perceptions of dispositional luck: Relationship to *DSM* gambling symptoms, subjective enjoyment of gambling, and treatment readiness. *Substance Use & Misuse, 42,* 43–63.

49 PERSONALITY TESTS

Nancy Felipe Russo

Arizona State University

This activity illustrates what is often called the Barnum effect *in personality testing, that is, an individual's tendency to believe in the validity of personality descriptions that are vague enough to apply to virtually everyone. It is appropriate for classes in introductory psychology, research methods, psychological testing, and personality. This activity can be used in any size class and involves all the students in the class. It requires about 10 minutes in one class period and 20 to 30 minutes in a subsequent class.*

CONCEPT

This exercise is based on an article by Bertram Forer (1949) and shows the fallacy of using personal agreement as a validation method. It effectively demonstrates how easy it is to agree with vague statements, in this case, statements that are supposed to be an accurate indication of an individual's personality. This is sometimes called the *Forer effect*, the *personal validation fallacy*, or the *Barnum effect* ("There's a sucker born every minute.").

MATERIALS NEEDED

You need a one-page adjective checklist personality test and a personality summary sheet and rating scale for each member of the class. Both items are provided as part of this activity.

INSTRUCTIONS

This activity involves deception, so you need to recognize that before you use it. The deception, however, is minor, and is not likely to cause any discomfort for the students. Tell the class that you are going to administer a personality test to the class. You might want to give the test a name, such as the "Thompson Personality Inventory." Announce that students can choose to participate or not. Pass out the copies of the personality checklist (see Appendix 49.1) and ask students who are participating to fill it out. Normally it takes students 3 to 5 minutes at most to complete the checklist. Remind students that their names are supposed to be on the personality test before they hand it back to you. Announce that you will score the tests and bring the results to the next class period.

Once in your office you should make a list of the students who turned in the test. One way to do that is simply to cut off the name on the top of the test and save those names. The tests should be disposed of, perhaps in a shredder. There is no reason for the instructor to look at how the students filled out their checklists. In fact, that information should be considered private.

For each of the students who took the personality test, you will need to prepare a results sheet to hand to that student in class (see Appendix 49.2). That sheet is a series of statements meant to describe the personality of that particular student. In fact, however, all students will get the same results sheet. That is, the personality description for every student will be identical. For each of the personality descriptions, fold the paper in half so that the information is inside and write the student's name on the outside. In small classes you can pass out the sheets to individual students. In larger classes (if you have assigned seats) you can arrange the forms by row, pass them down each row, asking students to take the one with their name on it. Should students be absent, ask that their forms be passed to the end of the row so you can collect them. **Important:** Before you pass out these results, tell students that this information is private and that they should keep their eyes on their own paper and not be looking at the personality assessments of others. Ask students not to open their personality descriptions until you tell them to do so.

Tell students that the Thompson Personality Inventory identifies individuals as one of 24 personality types, each type identified by a letter of the alphabet (in this case, all forms indicate the personality type is Type C). At this point, ask students to open their personality descriptions and read them. And add that when they have done that they should fill out the rating scale at the bottom of the sheet. (At the bottom of the form is a rating scale on which students rate how well they feel the personality description matches how they see their own personality.)

Ask for a show of hands for each number on the rating scale (e.g., "How many of you circled 5?" "How many circled 4?"). Count the hands and put the number on the board. Typical results are that most students rate the test as a 4 or 5 (a very good description of their personality), whereas very few students will circle 1, 2, or 3.

Tell students that if they wish they can share their personality description with others in the class. And allow a few minutes for forms to be passed and read. The class will quickly discover that everyone has the same personality description. As that happens, tell the class that indeed everyone has the same personality description and that you did not bother to score the data from the checklist, that you disposed of those tests without reading any of the results, and that the Thompson Personality Inventory does not exist.

DISCUSSION

You might begin class discussion by asking why there was such widespread agreement that the test was a valid test. How might this activity reveal the way in which astrologers or graphologists work? Ask students what they would say to therapists who say they are good diagnosticians because their clients agree with their observations?

You might follow this exercise with a lecture on personality testing. How are such tests constructed and validated? What are the controversies in modern personality research? Consider how testing might differ with trait or factor approaches to personality. What agreements and disagreements exist across these various approaches and theories?

REFERENCES AND SUGGESTED READING

Boyce, T. E., & Geller, E. S. (2002). Using the Barnum effect to teach psychological research methods. *Teaching of Psychology, 29,* 316–318.

Burger, J. M. (2008). *Personality* (7th ed.). Belmont, CA: Thomson Wadsworth.

Dickson, D. H., & Kelly, I. W. (1985). The "Barnum effect" in personality assessment: A review of the literature. *Psychological Reports, 57,* 367–382.

Forer, B. (1949). The fallacy of personal validation: A classroom demonstration of gullibility. *Journal of Abnormal and Social Psychology, 44,* 118–123.

Goldfried, M. R., & Kent, R. N. (1972). Traditional versus behavioral personality assessment: A comparison of methodological and theoretical assumptions. *Psychological Bulletin, 77,* 409–420.

Layne, C. (1998). Gender and the Barnum effect: A reinterpretation of Piper-Terry and Downey's results. *Psychological Reports, 83,* 608–610.

MacDonald, D. J., & Standing, L. G. (2002). Does self-serving bias cancel the Barnum effect? *Social Behavior and Personality, 30,* 625–630.

Piper-Terry, M. L., & Downey, J. L. (1998). Sex, gullibility, and the Barnum effect. *Psychological Reports, 82,* 571–576.

Schultz, D. P., & Schultz, S. E. (2005). *Theories of personality* (8th ed.). Belmont, CA: Thompson Wadsworth.

Appendix 49.1

Name: _____

Instructions: For each of the items below, place a check mark in the blank for those that describe you as you *usually* are.

_____ Active	_____ Adaptable
_____ Aggressive	_____ Attractive
_____ Ambitious	_____ Considerate
_____ Assertive	_____ Contented
_____ Capable	_____ Cooperative
_____ Confident	_____ Curious
_____ Determined	_____ Daring
_____ Dominant	_____ Good Natured
_____ Efficient	_____ Loyal
_____ Enterprising	_____ Mannerly
_____ Forceful	_____ Mature
_____ Independent	_____ Mischievous
_____ Industrious	_____ Peaceable
_____ Initiating	_____ Praising
_____ Intelligent	_____ Relaxed
_____ Opportunistic	_____ Talkative
_____ Persevering	_____ Trusting
_____ Persistent	_____ Understanding
_____ Planful	_____ Warm
_____ Resourceful	_____ Wholesome

Appendix 49.2

Summary for Personality Type C

You have a great need for other people to like and admire you. You have a tendency to be critical of yourself. You have a great deal of unused capacity that you have not turned to your advantage. Although you have some personality weaknesses, you are generally able to compensate for them. Your adjustment to the opposite sex has presented some problems for you. More disciplined and self-controlled outside, you tend to be worrisome and insecure inside. At times you have serious doubts as to whether you have made the right decision or done the right thing. You prefer a certain amount of change and variety and become dissatisfied when hemmed in by restrictions and limitations. You pride yourself on being an independent thinker and do not accept other's statements without satisfactory proof. You have found it unwise to be too frank in revealing yourself to others.

How effective do you believe the personality test was in revealing your personality? Please CIRCLE one of the numbers below.

1	2	3	4	5
No correspondence at all				Perfect correspondence

$\overset{\square}{50}$ Interpreting the Self Through Literature: Psychology and the Novels of Wallace Stegner

Dana S. Dunn
Moravian College

This activity uses two novels by Wallace Stegner to examine the subjective nature of the self. Students enrolled in personality, developmental psychology, life-span development, or introductory psychology, read and discuss A Shooting Star *or* Crossing to Safety, *novels that examine stress/coping and aging/integrity, respectively, among other psychological themes. The activity allows students to explore the interpretive links between psychology and literature during class discussion or when writing about the self as an out-of-class assignment. A class of 30 to 40 students can participate by commenting on a novel in class; above 40 students, smaller group discussions can precede a general class discussion. Regardless of class size, students can write about a novel outside of class.*

CONCEPT

Teachers sometimes forget that psychology, like literature, is fundamentally an interpretive enterprise; one beginning and ending with the self. Whether reacting to a book or reflecting on their own experiences, students interpret these realities through subjective perceptions. This activity allows students to consider interpretation and self-perception by discussing psychological aspects of the self presented in two novels by Wallace Stegner. Students examine stress and coping, as well as self-denigration, by reading and discussing *A Shooting Star* (Stegner, 1996). In contrast, *Crossing to Safety* (Stegner, 2006) highlights issues of aging, integrity, and the meaning of self across the life-span. Your goal as the instructor is to demonstrate that the interpretive qualities of self-psychology are relevant to discussing literature, Stegner's novels in particular.

MATERIALS NEEDED

Students will need to purchase a copy of *Crossing to Safety* or *A Shooting Star*. Both novels are available in reasonably priced paperback editions.

INSTRUCTIONS

Wallace Stegner (1909–1993) was an American novelist whose work mined timeless topics of self and character, such as love, confronting adversity, friendship, sacrifice, personal integrity, and forgiveness (Benson, 1996). I use his novels in a teaching activity on the self for two of my classes: *Crossing to Safety* in a class on contemporary approaches to the study of the self and *A Shooting Star* in a course on stress, coping, and health. Both novels lend themselves to sustained discussion of the interpretive qualities of the self, as well as issues of human development and behavior more broadly defined. As a means to apply concepts drawn from units on development, aging, personality, and social psychology, this activity could also be used in the introductory psychology course. Indeed, having introductory psychology students read and discuss a novel in light of course concepts is fine way to illustrate the applicability of psychological theories and concepts to other areas of study.

To begin the activity, draw a distinction between subjective (self-psychology) and objective (personality psychology) psychological accounts of the self (Brown, 1997). Self-psychology is phenomenological in orientation; how we perceive the world, people, and events is of greater interest than the actual state of these entities. Personality psychology focuses on establishing the objective qualities of the self, as well as determining whether people can provide accurate accounts of their thought and behavior.

To forge links among self, interpretation, and literature, give students brief directions on how to approach either novel. While reading the novel, for example, students can adopt the perspective of a main character portrayed in the work. Tell students to follow a book's narrative as if it were a representation of their own experience. Short summaries of each novel and directions for discussion follow.

SUMMARY OF *A SHOOTING STAR*

A Shooting Star is the story of an intelligent woman, Sabrina Castro, who is financially independent but emotionally bankrupt. Caught between a loveless marriage and a rigid family upbringing, she yearns to start her life anew, but that hoped-for beginning is an ill-fated affair with a married man followed by a retreat to her childhood home, where her aging mother and a prideful ancestry reign. A slow spiral of self-denigration ensues and, before hitting bottom, Sabrina realizes that she must rebuild her life on the remnants of the old one: The pull of one's past life is inevitable, there is no way to completely start over again.

Class discussion concerning *A Shooting Star* can focus on the frequently self-imposed nature of stress in American society; we often place ourselves in unhappy circumstances to satisfy societal expectations (e.g., overwrought materialism; marriage for wealth or prestige, not love). Lazarus and Folkman's (1984) stress and coping model is useful in discussing this work because it is transactional and phenomenological: Stress occurs as a result of the fit between the person and the perceived environment. The idiosyncratic nature of stress allows students to empathize with the main character's experience, while simultaneously considering alternatives. Self-respect and self-responsibility are key themes in the novel, and they take on new meanings when examined in stressful contexts.

SUMMARY OF *CROSSING TO SAFETY*

Departing from an exclusively individualistic focus, *Crossing to Safety* is about two married couples who share a very long but sometimes difficult friendship. Both wives are afflicted with human ills—one has polio, the other an unquenchable drive to control the destinies of those around her. The latter character, in fact, gathers the couples together for one last time, as cancer is ending her life. Charity Lang's death, like her life and that of her family, must be carefully orchestrated to the last. The bittersweet reunion of the two couples allows the narrator, Larry Morgan, to review the pleasures, pains, subtle rivalries, and shared successes of this 40-year friendship and what in those years lends meaning to life.

Students are frequently drawn to the opposing marital styles displayed by the two couples. Superficially, one marriage seems idyllic and mutually supportive, whereas the other appears to be static, carefully scripted, and based on dependence. Closer reading and discussion of the text reveals that both marriages share many similarities beneath the surface, but that one cannot adequately summarize human relationships by pointing to a few differences. Aging, distance, and reconciliation imposed by time, experience, and acquired perspective matter a great deal to self-understanding. Students initially ask, "How could these people remain friends?" Subsequently, the question becomes, "How could they not be friends?"

I find it very useful to guide discussion of this novel by focusing on generativity, or what psychological goods one individual (or generation) leaves behind for another. Each of the husbands and wives gives something of themselves to the others in the course of the friendship. Invite students to reflect on their own lives to date, asking them to identify what theme or message in their own experiences could be worth sharing with others. To emphasize the role this generativity plays in the self and its interpretive mission, I discuss McAdam's (1993) work on personal myth and autobiography, in which the concept serves to pull together life themes. The great virtue of *Crossing to Safety* is that the reader sees generativity played out in the lives of the characters; their complex, variegated lives serving as examples to readers. The novel also delivers the poignant message that reflection on aging, long life, and existential meaning can be a grace, not merely a duty or ending.

DISCUSSION

Great fiction inspires and teaches its readers (Coles, 1989). Indeed, storytelling is an important human activity, as we come to know ourselves through the stories we tell (McAdams, 1993; McAdams, Josselson, & Lieblich, 2006). It is also true that we can see and learn about ourselves through reading, discussing, and interpreting the stories of others. Literature, of course, is excellent fodder for understanding the self; any story will contain issues of human development, drama, or comedy. Ironically, perhaps, few psychology courses use novels, let alone link their themes to interpretive views of the self.

This activity links psychological topics with literature by exploring the views of the self portrayed in these two Wallace Stegner novels. Why the self? Because character, author, and reader meet in the course of reading and discussing a novel: How people think about themselves becomes apparent in their interpretations of the actions of others. This occurs inevitably, as students interpret the motivations, personalities, and individual natures of characters by relating them to their *own* selves.

The discussion usually takes one or two class periods. Always begin by reminding the students that their purpose is to explore the subjective nature of the self by discussing their reactions to the story told in the novel. If you, as the instructor, have read and thought about the novels in advance, you will be able to bring a set of discussion questions that link course topics to plot, characters, and themes. How should readers feel about Sabrina, her character, and the choices she makes? What would they do in her place? Why? Do not rely on these questions unless or until free-wheeling, student-led discussion lags. The novelty of discussing books in psychology classes results in a very lively discussion.

Emphasize to students that there are no right answers or correct interpretations of these novels. Doubtless, as class discussion will reveal, there are interpretations that are more tenable given a novel's plot and the intent of the psychology course where the book is being read. This lack of objectivity is also to be expected, indeed welcomed, given the subjective nature of the self.

Finally, there is something oddly refreshing about reading and teaching a novel in a psychology class. Students do not expect to encounter novels in social science courses, nor are they used to discussing them the way most authors intend: as interpretations of life. Invariably, students are often surprised when they enjoy the novels and learn that sustained discussion about literature is an agreeable, enlightening exercise. It is also a valuable exercise because it allows students to see and think beyond the arbitrary disciplinary boundaries separating the study of mind from that of prose.

WRITING COMPONENT

Two writing exercises can be used to explore themes pertaining to the self in these novels. First, ask students to write a book review of either novel, slanting the review toward a course topic. For example, if *Crossing to Safety* were read in a course on human development or life-span development, the requisite themes in the novel could be reviewed in light of relevant psychological data or theory on adult friendship, aging, and even death, as well as the topic of generativity (McAdams, 1993). Encourage students to adopt a persona as they write their reviews; whether they choose to write from the perspective of a book critic or academic psychologist affects the tone of the review, as well as insights drawn therein.

A second writing assignment could be a more focused character study of one or more of the main features from either novel. Any such character study should rely heavily on a model or theory from psychology to bolster the interpretation. If one were to study Sabrina Castro's character in *A Shooting Star*, the aforementioned transactional model of stress and coping would be a useful touchstone. Students can readily write an analysis of a protagonist's character by seeing how well this model of stress explains a character's reactions in the course of the novel.

REFERENCES AND SUGGESTED READING

Benson, J. J. (1996). *Wallace Stegner: His life and work*. New York: Viking.

Brown, J. D. (1997). *The self*. New York: McGraw-Hill.

Coles, R. (1989). *The call of stories: Teaching and the moral imagination*. Boston: Houghton-Mifflin.

Josselson, R., Lieblich, A., & McAdams, D. P. (Eds.). (2002). *Up close and personal: The teaching and learning of narrative research*. Washington, DC: American Psychological Association.

Lazarus, R. S., & Folkman, S. (1984). *Stress, appraisal, and coping*. New York: Springer.

McAdams, D. P. (1993). *The stories we live by: Personal myths and the making of the self*. New York: William Morrow.

McAdams, D. P., Josselson, R., & Lieblich, A. (Eds.). (2006). *Identity and story: Creating self in narrative*. Washington, DC: American Psychological Association.

Stegner, W. (1996). *Remembering laughter*. New York: Penguin Books.

Stegner, W. (1996). *A shooting star*. New York: Penguin Books.

Stegner, W. (1997). *Recapitulation*. New York: Penguin Books.

Stegner, W. (2006). *Angle of repose*. New York: Penguin Books.

Stegner, W. (2006). *Crossing to safety*. New York: Penguin Books.

CHAPTER 10
PSYCHOLOGICAL
DISORDERS AND
TREATMENTS

Among the plethora of active learning possibilities, activities for psychological disorders and their treatments are not plentiful because of the difficulty of creating meaningful exercises for the classroom. This chapter, however, contains some exceptionally good examples, including two that bring a humanities element to the psychology classroom. Topics covered include treatment planning based on varied psychological approaches, a self-change project using behavior modification techniques, learning progressive muscle relaxation as a means of stress management, creating productive solutions to conflicts in the case of Romeo and Juliet, and making legal determinations of insanity in the murder trial of Hamlet. You have much to choose from!

Activity 51 uses the brief case history of a fictional woman, Ellen, age 32. The students are asked to describe appropriate courses of psychological treatment for Ellen based on various perspectives such as a biomedical approach, a behavioral approach, a cognitive approach, or a psychoanalytic approach.

In Activity 52, students work in groups, applying cognitive–behavioral techniques to change personal behaviors that they have selected for modification. Groups are formed based on common goal choices. This self-change activity is primarily an out-of-class project, including small-group meetings, and requires abut 8 weeks to complete.

Stress and stress management are the subjects of Activity 53, which involves teaching students a method of progressive muscle relaxation. A principal goal of the activity is to make students aware of how they experience tension and relaxation, and to offer them a way that can help them relax and reduce their experience of stress.

Shakespeare's *Romeo and Juliet* is the backdrop for Activity 54, a role-playing and discussion exercise that focuses on conflict resolution. The activity emphasizes the search for productive rather than destructive solutions, thus avoiding the tragic outcome of these classic lovers. The activity ends with a set of provocative and productive questions that are guaranteed to generate a lively and fascinating class discussion.

The Shakespeare theme is continued in Activity 55 in a mock trial to determine whether Hamlet was insane when he killed Polonius. The activity requires considerable preparation, but for the instructor who is willing to venture the work, there is the promise of an incredibly valuable and exciting class experience. Many lessons can be learned, and students are exposed to the role played by forensic psychologists and the deliberative group processes of juries.

51 PARADIGMS ON THE ETIOLOGY AND TREATMENT OF ABNORMAL BEHAVIOR

Janet Morahan-Martin

Bryant University

This activity demonstrates the role of paradigms in explaining and treating abnormal behavior. It can be used with classes in introductory psychology, abnormal psychology, and clinical and counseling psychology. The activity is done during class, requires participation of all students, and can be used with any size class. It takes at least 30 minutes.

CONCEPT

Paradigms are the theoretical frameworks scientists use to explain reality (Kuhn, 1996). The specific paradigm or model psychologists hold plays a powerful role in how they view human behavior, affecting the questions they ask, the causes they attribute to certain behaviors, and the way they treat abnormal behaviors. Paradigms also reflect assumptions that they hold about behavior. For example, psychologists adhering to a biological paradigm of behavior would attribute abnormal behavior to abnormalities in the functioning of the body, would stress the importance of genetics and the nervous and endocrine systems, and would advocate somatic treatments such as psychoactive medications. In contrast, psychologists adhering to a behavioral paradigm would attribute abnormal behavior to faulty learning, would stress the importance of models of conditioning, and would advocate behavioral interventions such as contingency management or systematic desensitization.

As psychologists, we have been trained to understand how paradigms affect our judgments and assumptions about behavior; however, for students, this concept can be confusing and difficult to understand. To the introductory students especially, this idea may reinforce a belief that psychologists never agree and therefore are incompetent and don't know what they are talking about. To upper-level students, the role paradigms play may be more obvious. However, students may still find it hard to understand their own implicit assumptions about the causes of behavior as well as what constitutes normal and abnormal behavior.

This activity illustrates the role of paradigms in human behavior and can furthermore be used to reveal to the students their own assumptions about normal and abnormal behavior and to introduce a discussion on the history of abnormal psychology.

MATERIALS NEEDED

You will need a copy of the case handout (see Appendix 51.1) for each student or else you can display the case on a PowerPoint slide for all the students to see.

INSTRUCTIONS

Have the class read the case and answer the questions. This may be done with the entire class participating, or the class may be broken into smaller groups that first discuss the case and then present their answers to the entire class.

DISCUSSION

After eliciting answers from the class, ask the students to attempt to classify their answers according to the psychological paradigms being used in the course. It is useful to focus on the causes of behavior that are not attributed and to ask why this is the case. For example, students frequently do not question whether the cause of Ellen's behavior may be physical. This can be an opportunity to stress that problems in behavior may be physical in origin. A discussion of how treatment follows cause can be elicited by asking the class whether the treatments they recommended followed from the causes that they attributed to Ellen's behavior. The discussion can then focus on what assumptions about normal and abnormal behavior the students have made in their answers. Finally, this discussion can be used to introduce a survey of the history of abnormal psychology by questioning why no one suggested that Ellen is possessed by the devil or that she is experiencing masturbatory insanity or an imbalance of bodily fluids.

REFERENCES AND SUGGESTED READING

Benjamin, L. T., Jr. (2007). *A brief history of modern psychology.* Malden, MA: Blackwell Publishing.

Davison, G. C., & Neale, J. M. (2000). *Abnormal psychology* (8th ed.). New York: Wiley.

Halgin, R. P., & Whitbourne, S. K. (2007). *Abnormal psychology* (5th ed.). New York: McGraw-Hill.

Kuhn, T. S. (1996). *The structure of scientific revolutions* (3rd ed.). Chicago: University of Chicago Press.

Prilleltensky, I. (1990). The politics of abnormal psychology: Past, present, and future. *Political Psychology, 11,* 767–785

Schultz, D. P., & Schultz, S. E. (2008). *A history of modern psychology* (9th ed.). Belmont, CA: Wadsworth/Thomson Learning.

Thomas, R. M. (2001). *Folk psychologies across cultures.* Thousand Oaks, CA: Sage.

Appendix 51.1

The Case of Ellen

Ellen S. was referred to the clinic shortly after her "miscarriage." She was a 32-year-old woman who was employed as an administrative assistant for Mr. Johnson. She and Mr. Johnson had recently terminated their 2-year-old love affair because Mr. Johnson was unwilling to divorce his wife because of his children.

Although medical tests indicated that she was not actually pregnant, Ellen had shown classic symptoms of early pregnancy during the 3 months when she believed she was pregnant. She ceased menstruation, was chronically fatigued and nauseated, and had gained weight.

Ellen was raised by fundamentalist religious parents with whom she still lived. She had been told repeatedly about the sins of sex and alcohol. Her affair with Mr. Johnson was her first relationship.

Assume you are Ellen's therapist:

1. What issues do you think are important to the development of Ellen's problems?
2. How would you treat Ellen?

52 A MODULE FOR A SELF-DIRECTED BEHAVIOR CHANGE PROJECT

Janet Morahan-Martin

Bryant University

In this activity, students, working in groups, apply cognitive–behavioral techniques to change self-chosen behaviors. It is appropriate for classes in introductory psychology, clinical and counseling psychology, personal adjustment, and health psychology. The activity is primarily conducted outside of class time; it extends over several weeks and includes small-group meetings outside of class. It can be used with classes of any size.

CONCEPT

An activity requiring students to change their behavior is an excellent method of the direct application of the principles of psychology. Such programs, often called *self-modification* or *self-change* projects, have been successfully used in a variety of courses, including introductory psychology, counseling, cognitive–behavioral techniques, adjustment, health psychology, self-modification (Dodd, 1986; Rakos & Grodek, 1984), stress management (Deffenbacher & Shephard, 1994), and academic skills (Brigham, Moseley, Sneed, & Fisher, 1994). Most self-modification projects use cognitive–behavioral techniques, although some have involved the application of other paradigms as well.

The format for self-modification projects described here involves (a) frequent reporting of the steps involved in the project and weighing these steps into the final project grade; (b) bringing in outside advisers on the major group of projects to lecture on that topic; and (c) forming support and discussion groups of students involved in similar projects.

MATERIALS NEEDED

Watson and Tharp's (2007) *Self-Directed Behavior: Self-Modification for Personal Adjustment* may be useful. The authors detail behavioral and cognitive techniques for self-change and guide the reader step by step through the entire process of self-change. The chapters are general to any type of behavioral self-change, but are supplemented by frequent examples as well as a section at the end of many chapters that provides specific ideas for common projects, involving topics such as anxiety, assertiveness, smoking, alcohol and substance abuse, depression, exercise, social skills and relations, stress management, study skills, time management, and weight management. Included at the end of each chapter is a series of specific graduated steps in planning and implementing a self-change program.

INSTRUCTIONS

Have the students form groups according to their goal choices, with each group working on a different area. Groups should meet weekly throughout the semester for about 15 to 20 minutes to discuss their progress. This can be done in class or out of class. It is important that instructors discuss ethical treatment of privileged information that may emerge in group meetings.

Divide the activity into three phases. In the first phase, have students specify a goal for change and conduct a 2- to 3-week baseline observation period. While still in this period, have them start the second phase: planning the initial contract. Allot a span of about 5 weeks for the implementation of their contract. In the third phase, students plan and implement termination.

At each phase, specific steps adapted from Watson and Tharp (2007) are incorporated into the syllabus and required as written assignments of the students. These help shape the final paper by gradually taking the students through the required approximations and skills necessary for each aspect of the project.

Prompt feedback from the instructor and from other students should be provided at each step to students in the self-modification groups. Completion of each step is weighted in the project grade along with the final paper. Student feedback indicates that requiring weekly or biweekly steps is worth the extra time and work involved because it builds commitment; keeps the students up to date; provides outside comments on their progress, which in turn helps them to modify their program; and provides the basis for the final written paper.

The following is a description of the process in its three phases.

I. Specify goal and conduct observation
   A. Goal setting
      1. List five personal goals you would like to achieve.
      2. Choose a specific goal and subgoals and write an initial contract.
         a) Plan ahead for obstacles by evaluating the pros and cons of change and evaluating self-efficacy beliefs.
         b) Build commitment by anticipating tempting situations and making public commitments.
   B. Baseline observation period
      1. Plan and implement the specific methods that will be used during this time. Behaviors must be recorded daily and include antecedents, behaviors, and consequences. A structured diary, frequency count, or rating scale must be used. This will last about 2 or 3 weeks.

II. Formal contracts
   A. Planning
      1. On the basis of your observations, identify and evaluate the antecedents of your behavior and the consequences of your behavior.
      2. Identify antecedents of your desired and undesired behavior and devise a specific plan to increase or decrease stimulus control using at least two of the following: self-instructions, narrowing antecedent controls, reperceiving antecedents, changes in the chain of events, thought stopping, and precommitment.
      3. Develop specific plans to reach your behavioral goals and subgoals using each of the following techniques at least once: substituting new thoughts and behaviors, shaping, overt and covert modeling, and rehearsal.
      4. Plan at least four ways that you will provide appropriate consequences for desired behavior throughout the project. At least three consequences must involve rewards. (Steps 1–4 are completed during the baseline observation period.)
      5. The initial contract is due. It should include a summary of your observation period, your specific goals and subgoals, specific methods and rules for obtaining each goal, recording methods, feedback, and escape clauses. The techniques used in Steps 1–4 may be incorporated into the contract, which should be signed and witnessed. The self-modification project begins immediately.

B. Implementation and self-modification
  1. At the end of the first week and for each remaining week of the self-modification project, students are required to share observations with the instructor and to complete a graph of their behavior.
  2. At the end of the second week and throughout the rest of the activity, students evaluate their progress weekly, rewriting their contracts as necessary. They must also prepare a specific program in advance for dealing with high-risk situations and lapses.
III. Termination
  1. One to 2 weeks before the end of the contract period, students build a program for termination. They must make use of the following: thinning of reinforcement, finding social or natural reinforcement, program for transfer, and plans for reinstatement.

Bringing in advisers to discuss the major topics has been popular. Select presentations on the basis of the students' own interests and have students incorporate material from them into their contracts. Typical presentation topics can include stress management, assertiveness training, relaxation techniques, nutrition, time management, and study skills. I have invited health educators and members of the university's Counseling Center and Center for Academic Excellence to make these presentations. Some of the guest lecturers may also be available to consult with individual students and groups. Students have often reported that these presentations were helpful in integrating two or more topics into one goal (e.g., including stress and time management into a nutrition program).

DISCUSSION   The groups formed at the beginning of the term should meet weekly to discuss their progress and to provide feedback about their projects as well as emotional support. Group meetings typically are focused on the most recent step that has been completed. Students also discuss their progress and difficulties, alternative behaviors, and future plans. This can be done within class or out of class. Previous research has indicated that students work better and learn more in cooperative settings (Johnson, Maruyama, Johnson, Nelson, & Skon, 1981), and that groups encourage cooperation among students (Bouton & Garth, 1983). Feedback from students confirms that groups have had a similar positive effect on the quality of their self-modification projects as well as their commitment to and enjoyment of the project. However, it is possible that a student will not want to work within a group setting. In that case, the student should be allowed to work independently.

Research indicated that about two thirds of students doing self-modification techniques are successful in improving their target behaviors (Dodd, 1986; Hamilton, 1980; Rakos & Grodek, 1984; Watson & Tharp, 2007). However, I do not base grades on the success of a given project. Instead, I consider the following in grading individual projects: the difficulty and complexity of the problem, the number and appropriateness of techniques used to change the behavior, comprehension of theory, willingness to modify project as appropriate, the insight used in combining techniques, the consistency of the effort, completion of required steps, daily detailed record keeping that was shared weekly, attendance and active participation within groups, and organization and presentation of final paper.

It is strongly advised that instructors have alternative assignments for this project. Students who do not want to change a behavior ethically should not be required to complete this intervention. Even once students start projects, some may withdraw voluntarily or be requested to withdraw if they have not been completing assignments, sharing observations, or meeting with their groups.

Barton, E. J. (1982). Facilitating student veracity: Instructor application of behavioral technology to self-modification projects. *Teaching of Psychology, 9,* 99–101

Berrera, M., & Glasgow, R. E. (1976). Design and evaluation of a personalized instruction course in behavioral self-control. *Teaching of Psychology, 3,* 81–84.

Bouton, C., & Garth, R. (Eds.). (1983). *Learning in groups.* San Francisco: Jossey-Bass.

Brigham, T. A., Moseley, S. A., Sneed, S., & Fisher, M. (1994). Excel: An intensive structured program of advising and academic support to assist minority freshmen to succeed at a large university. *Journal of Behavioral Education, 4,* 227–242.

Deffenbacher, J., & Shephard, J. (1994). Evaluating a seminar on stress management. *Teaching of Psychology, 16,* 79–81.

Dodd, D. K. (1986). Teaching behavioral self-change: A course model. *Teaching of Psychology, 13,* 82–85.

Epstein, R. (1997). Skinner as self-manager. *Journal of Applied Behavior Analysis, 30,* 545–568.

Hamilton, S. B. (1980). Instructionally based training in self-control: Behavior-specific and generalized outcomes resulting from student-implemented self-modification projects. *Teaching of Psychology, 7,* 140–145.

Johnson, D. W., Maruyama, G., Johnson, R., Nelson, D., & Skon, L. (1981). Effects of cooperative, competitive, and individualistic goal structure on achievement: A meta-analysis. *Psychological Bulletin, 89,* 47–62.

Menges, R. J., & Dobroski, B. J. (1977). Behavioral self-modification in instructional settings: A review. *Teaching of Psychology, 4,* 168–173.

Rakos, R., & Grodek, (1984). An empirical evaluation of a behavioral self-management course in a college setting. *Teaching of Psychology, 11,* 157–162.

Seligman, M. E. P. (1994). *What you can change and what you can't: The complete guide to successful self-improvement.* New York: Knopf.

Watson, L., & Tharp, R. G. (2007). *Self-directed behavior: Self-modification for personal adjustment* (9th ed.) Belmont, CA: Wadsworth.

Worthington, E. L. (1977). Honesty and success in self-modification projects for a college class. *Teaching of Psychology, 4,* 78–82.

53 Progressive Muscle Relaxation: One Component of Effective Stress Management

Paul Bracke

Stanford University

This in-class activity is appropriate for classes in introductory psychology, abnormal psychology, personal adjustment, motivation and emotion, or any class dealing with stress. It can be used in a class of any size but is most effective in classes where discussion can be held. This activity can be used to introduce students to the concepts of stress, stress management, and progressive muscle relaxation. You can purchase temperature-sensitive "biodots" to introduce a biofeedback element to this activity. No prior knowledge of psychology is necessary for this activity, and with the exception of purchasing the optional biodots, no extensive preparation is required.

CONCEPT

Chronic stress has been associated with a variety of psychological and physical disorders. A specific form of chronic stress, Type A Behavior Pattern (TABP), a lifestyle that generates chronic stress, has been linked to the development of coronary heart disease, as well as hypertension (Friedman & Rosenman, 1974). Because TABP has been identified in children and adolescents (Eagleston et al., 1986; Siegel, 1982), developing a personal stress management program is essential for young people as well as for adults. An effective stress management approach includes both changes in one's perspective, greater awareness of the events that trigger a stress response, and strategies to both avoid exposure to stress and strategies to reduce stress that has been absorbed. (Bracke & Thoresen, 1996; Bracke & Bugental, 1995; Thoresen & Bracke, 1993).

Formal relaxation strategies are very useful in reducing absorbed stress. Progressive muscle relaxation (PMR) has been shown to be an effective approach to reducing the psychological arousal and symptoms that characterize chronic stress (Davis, McKay, & Eshelman, 1982). This activity offers students (as well as teachers) an opportunity to become more aware of their unique symptoms of stress and to practice an important component of managing that stress. The basic activity can be modified to use other forms of relaxation strategies (e.g., abdominal breathing, autogenic training, or visualization), depending on the interest of students.

MATERIALS NEEDED

You will need a PMR script. Many are available but those provided by Davis et al. (1982) and Bernstein and Borkovec (1973) are especially good. Reading the PMR script in a slow, calm, and slightly monotonic manner will greatly enhance your effectiveness in doing this activity.

This is optional, but you may wish to purchase biodots—small, temperature-sensitive adhesive dots that change color as skin temperature changes. These enable participants to observe their level of relaxation as reflected in vasodilation and increased skin temperature and thus enhance the impact of the exercise. They may be obtained from

Biodots International (P.O. Box 2246, Indianapolis, IN 46206; [800] 272-2340). You may also be able to purchase biodots from other manufacturers of biofeedback devices. If you decide to use the biodots, it is useful to ask students to affix the dot to a fleshy area of the wrist but to *not* indicate how the dots will be used in the activity. This will help reduce the tendency to make the exercise a performance. Even an effective use of the PMR exercise may not result in any change in the biodots due to a variety of reasons (e.g., individual differences in skin reaction, poor adhesion).

INSTRUCTIONS   To reduce stress, it is essential that we become more aware of our individual physical and psychological experiences. To help students increase their awareness, ask them to monitor and record how often they experience the following sensations during the week prior to the PMR exercise: anxiety, depression, irritability or hostility, muscle tension, headaches, neck and backaches, indigestion, sleeping difficulties, chronic fatigue, cold hands or feet, and a general sense of being pressed for time. Your participation in this monitoring will provide you with an opportunity to share experiences and will also serve as an incentive for students.

The activity can be presented in either of two ways. First, the exercise can begin with a brief discussion of chronic stress, using the following questions.

1. **What is stress?** Elicit words and feelings that students associate with stress. Responses are often related to concepts such as tension or tightness. The word stress comes from *stringere* (Latin) meaning "to pull tight." There are several ways of defining stress, the most useful of which might be this: Stress occurs when we perceive an imbalance between the demands confronting us and the resources we possess to meet the demands. Physical, cognitive, and emotional symptoms may be indications of stress.

2. **Why is chronic stress a problem?** Fast-paced modern life is stressful. Some stress comes and goes, and we are able to handle it and live comfortable and productive lives. Often, however, stress becomes chronic; we are exposed to it too much of the time, and then it becomes a serious problem. Research indicates that chronic stress is associated with the development of many physical, cognitive, and emotional symptoms (Bracke & Thoresen, 1996; Bracke & Bugental, 1995). Most dramatic is the finding that Type A behavior, a specific form of chronic stress, increases the risk of coronary heart disease; in addition, studies clearly indicate that the disease that underlies it begins in the second decade of life.

3. **Self-observations.** Note that many of the sensations students monitored during the previous week may be symptoms of stress. Discuss.

4. **How can stress be managed?** Although an effective stress management program must consider one's attitudes and expectations, coping behavior, and physiology, learning to reduce the physical arousal that accompanies stress is one important component. An effective alternative approach is to begin the activity with the instructions needed to proceed to the PMR exercise, saving the previous questions for discussion after students have experienced the exercise. The advantage of this approach is that it allows students to have an experience with the PMR exercise that is relatively free of intellectual bias.

To prepare students for the PMR exercise, ask them to sit comfortably with enough space to stretch out legs and arms. It is important that students understand the basic strategy of tensing and releasing successive muscles. In addition, it is essential they understand that the goal of PMR is to gain awareness of the contrast between how tension and relaxation feel. Emphasize that relaxation is not a performance or a competition. PMR is most effective if the student is merely listening, following the simple instructions, and noticing his or her unique sensations. Finally, remind students to breathe during the exercise and to tense muscles only at 50% to 75% of their maximum.

You may present the PMR exercise in two ways. One approach that dramatically illustrates the difference between the students' "normal" tension and relaxation is to have them tense and relax muscles of the extremities on one side of the body (e.g., right arm, right shoulder, and so on) and then discuss how the relaxed side feels compared with the "normal" (unrelaxed) side. The other approach is to simply have students relax the entire body as you read the PMR script.

VARIATIONS AND MODIFICATIONS

The activity can be modified for use with larger groups in a variety of ways. For instance, one section of the group can be asked to simply sit quietly (control condition) while another section uses the PMR protocol (experimental section). These two groups can then be surveyed regarding their comparative physical and mental experiences.

The activity can also be modified through use of a different relaxation strategy. For instance, autogenic relaxation (Luthe & Schultz, 1969) is a strategy highly effective in relaxing the mind. This exercise can be very effectively modified by substituting autogenics or any of a number of visualization strategies that are available online. Instructions would be modified on the basis of the particular basics of the relaxation strategy that is used.

The value of considering using a different relaxation protocol is that doing so would highlight the different effects of a particular form of relaxation. One creative and useful variation would be to have students experience different forms of relaxation (e.g., PMR and autogenics) and discuss the differences in experience and effectiveness.

DISCUSSION

The goal of the exercise is to help students become aware of how they experience tension and relaxation. You may wish to ask students these questions to stimulate discussion: How would you describe the feeling of tension in your muscles (e.g., hard, stiff)? How did relaxation feel (e.g., warm, heavy)? Were there any muscles that felt particularly tense? (Note for students that these muscles may be useful as personal barometers of physical tension.) What other experiences did you have during the exercise (e.g., feeling peaceful)? If students used biodots, discuss any changes in color that indicated an increase in skin temperature, a sign of relaxation.

Direct the discussion toward how students can continue to practice some version of PMR (or any of the other potential relaxations strategies) as a way of becoming more generally relaxed, perhaps as part of a class experiment in reducing the stress symptoms students recorded prior to the PMR exercise. You can obtain additional exercises designed to develop the other habits and attitudes essential for effectively managing stress by consulting the literature in the References and Suggested Reading section.

REFERENCES AND SUGGESTED READING

Bernstein, D. A., & Borkovec, T. (1973). *Progressive relaxation training: A manual for the helping professions.* Champaign, IL: Research Press.

Bracke, P. E., & Bugental, J. F. T. (1995). Existential addiction: A new conceptual model for Type A behavior and workaholism. In T. Pauchant (Ed.), *In search of meaning* (pp. 65–97). San Francisco: Jossey-Bass

Bracke, P. E., & Thoresen, C. E. (1996). Reducing Type A behavior patterns: A structured-group approach. In R. Allan & S. Scheidt (Eds.), *Heart & mind* (pp. 255–290). Washington, DC: American Psychological Association.

Davis, M., McKay, M., & Eshelman, E. R. (1982). *The relaxation and stress reduction workbook.* Oakland, CA: New Harbinger Publications.

Eagleston, J. R., Kirmil-Gray, K., Thoresen, C. E., Wiedenfeld, S., Bracke, P. E., & Arnow, B. (1986). Physical health correlates of Type A behavior in children and adolescents. *Journal of Behavioral Medicine, 9,* 341–362.

Friedman, M., & Rosenman, R. (1974). *Type A behavior and your heart.* New York: Knopf.

Friedman, M., & Ulmer, D. (1984). *Treating Type A behavior and your heart.* New York: Fawcett Crest.

Jacobson, E. (1974). *Progressive relaxation.* Chicago: University of Chicago Press.

Luthe, W., & Schultz, J. H. (1969). *Autogenic methods.* London: Grune & Stratton.

Siegel, J. M. (1982). Type A behavior and self-reports of cardiovascular arousal in adolescents. *Psychosomatic Medicine, 43,* 311–321.

Thoresen, C. E., & Bracke, P. E. (1993). Reducing coronary recurrences and coronary prone behavior: A structured group approach. In J. Spira (Ed.), *Group therapy for the medically ill* (pp. 156–179). New York: Guilford Press.

54 Romeo, Juliet, and Conflict Resolution

Robert A. Goodale

Late of Westfield State College (MA)

This activity uses a role-playing and discussion exercise based on Shakespeare's tragedy, Romeo and Juliet, *to explore the process of conflict resolution, emphasizing productive rather than destructive solutions, such as the joint suicide of the star-crossed lovers. It is an in-class activity that can involve one or two class periods and is appropriate to classes in introductory psychology, social psychology, abnormal psychology, or any other course in which conflict resolution or suicide are subjects. It can be used in a class of any size but is best suited to a size that permits good discussion.*

CONCEPT

In the past 25 years, suicides in the United States have been declining, but for the age range of 15 to 24, they have increased threefold. Up to the age of 14 the number of young persons who commit suicide is only about 1 in 200,000, although many more attempt it. By age 19 the number of deaths due to suicide has increased tenfold. Suicide is the second- or third-leading cause of death among adolescents (depending on the survey), and, even at that, is thought to be seriously underreported. Investigation of successful suicides and suicide attempts shows a pattern of helplessness and hopelessness among participants and feelings of isolation, alienation, and failure at integration into the larger society.

A famous story of teenage suicide is that of William Shakespeare's *Romeo and Juliet.* Juliet and Romeo fall madly in love and secretly marry even though their respective families are engaged in a long-standing feud marked by hatred, bitterness, and death. At the same time, Juliet's parents plan her marriage to an older man, and later Romeo is banned to another land for slaying Juliet's cousin. Shakespeare works the dynamics of love and hate, parents and children, duty and impulse, and life and death into a heroic crisis that sends Juliet to the family priest for help in her most desperate hour. Faced with being pledged by her parents to marry a man she does not love, and having already defied her parents by secretly marrying the now-banned Romeo only the day before, Juliet concocts a bizarre plan with Friar Laurence to preserve her pure love for Romeo and protect herself from compromise. Before the play ends, Shakespeare skillfully interweaves additional contrasts between church and state and the individual versus society, and any resolution of the conflict dooms some member of the cast to moral compromise.

Modern psychology would characterize Juliet's plight as one of conflict resolution and crisis. Quite consciously Romeo and Juliet make several decisions that corrupt the trust they enjoy from several relationships, and any major change or disclosure at the point at which Juliet seeks out the friar will result in rejection, humiliation, family scandal, and perhaps even the loss of each other. From the perspective of psychologist Morton Deutsch, Romeo and Juliet are engaged in a competitive struggle with the people around them. Communication among all of the conflicting parties becomes impoverished and unreliable, solution of the problem takes on a win–lose rigidity, and the differences among parties are emphasized instead of their commonalities. The antagonistic forces at work expand and escalate until only a destructive outcome for any or all parties is imminent. Under Shakespeare's direction all of the parties do lose, of course, and though the conflicting dynamics eventually are made clear to all, the resolution for all is something none of them would have chosen.

The purpose of the present exercise is to draw attention to the dynamics of conflict and crisis and to consider methods of arriving at productive solutions rather than destructive ones. In Deutsch's (1973) view, productive solution finding is akin to creative problem solving—the task is to get as many interested parties as possible involved in looking for mutually rewarding trade-offs rather than Pyrrhic victories. According to Deutsch, a productive process requires (a) open communication, (b) mutual recognition and respect for the concerns of all parties involved, and (c) a trusting, friendly attitude that emphasizes common interests and minimizes differences among the parties. Substituting productive process for the competitive process that Shakespeare gave Romeo and Juliet, the class will consider alternative solutions for the star-crossed couple other than the one they chose—love through death.

PREPARATION OF CLASS

Depending on how much you prefer that students get their information directly, you can either assign or summarize for them the story of Romeo and Juliet. Films of the play are also available. Still, the best alternative may be to have students read the play, allowing them their own interpretation of Shakespeare's words. In class, go over the critical events and key elements that shape the crisis: the reigning social mores that decree that Juliet's parents will choose her bridegroom, the decision by the pair to keep their love a secret from their feuding parents, Romeo's decision to kill Tybalt to avenge the death of Mercutio, and so forth. Pick up the story at the point where Juliet goes to Friar Laurence with the news that Romeo has been banished for killing Tybalt and that she herself will be publicly pledged to marry Paris, her parents' choice, on the following day. At this point Juliet is in a state of panic because she must resolve her conflict before morning.

INSTRUCTIONS

Tell the class that this time when Juliet and the friar meet, they must work together to reach a realistic, productive resolution utilizing the three principles of productive process identified by Deutsch, rather than choosing the destructive process that Shakespeare gave them, which would have resulted in a variety of negative consequences for the lovers and their families even if the scheme had succeeded.

Have the class consider, for example, the benefits that could arise if Juliet and the friar went to all of the principal parties and revealed the entire story before morning (open communication). Have several students role-play the principal parties and express their perceptions of the problem (recognition and respect for the views and concerns of all). Consider whether Juliet, when imploring the friar for help, had a realistic understanding of how each of the parties would feel about her marriage to Romeo or if she was largely responding to what she imagined they would do if they knew (trust vs. mistrust).

The point is to explore alternative solutions for productive outcomes. Individuals in crisis are severely constrained in their thinking, and part of the service that good friends and therapists provide at such times is a discussion of alternatives, an examination of what is real and what is imagined, and a nonjudgmental reminder of their strengths in the past and of how apparent setbacks can often be a stimulus for growth. Recognize that in actual practice a person in crisis rejects all solutions as costing too much because if they did not, he or she would have picked one of them earlier and warded off the crisis. Discuss what it was in Romeo and Juliet that led them to box themselves in as badly as they did before the crisis came to a head.

DISCUSSION   Here are some ideas for further discussion.

1. Explore with your students the series of events that seem to lead people to presume that suicide is the most reasonable solution to a tough crisis.
2. How memorable would Shakespeare's classic be if he had led Romeo and Juliet into productive process right from the start? What does it mean that so many people over the years have identified with Romeo and Juliet and have seen them as victims of parental insensitivity?
3. If one party is searching for a productive solution and no one else involved seems to care, what should the one party do?
4. If the class is comfortable exploring such topics, examine present conflicts students report having with their parents or conflicts they have had in the past. You can gather such information anonymously in one class and then present it for discussion in another class. Regarding these conflicts, to what extent have students applied Deutsch's three steps to productive resolution to each conflict? To what extent have they characterized the problem as a personal defeat rather than an opportunity for self-growth? Examine how the same situations result in a problem for some students but not for others.
5. Evaluate the homily "You catch more flies with honey than vinegar."

REFERENCES AND SUGGESTED READING

Berman, A. L., Jobes, D. A., & Silverman, M. (2006). *Adolescent suicide: Assessment and intervention* (2nd ed.). Washington, DC: American Psychological Association.

Deutsch, M. (1973). *The resolution of conflict: Constructive and destructive processes.* New Haven, CT: Yale University Press.

Deutsch, M., & Coleman, P. T. (Eds.). (2000). *The handbook of conflict resolution: Theory and practice.* San Francisco: Jossey-Bass.

King, R. A. (Ed.). (2003). *Suicide in children and adolescents.* New York: Cambridge University Press.

Murphy, J. M. (1999). *Coping with teen suicide.* New York: Rosen Publishing.

Nelson, R. E., & Galas, J. C. (2006). *The power to prevent suicide: A guide for teens helping teens.* Minneapolis, MN: Free Spirit Publishing.

Roleff, T. L. (Ed.) (2000). *Teen suicide.* Chicago: Greenhaven Press.

55 THE INSANITY TRIAL OF HAMLET: A TEACHING ACTIVITY

Elizabeth V. Swenson

John Carroll University

This activity allows students to study the insanity defense and jury dynamics by viewing a C-SPAN DVD, "Insanity Trial of Hamlet," and then deliberating in jury groups. This activity is appropriate for classes in introductory psychology, social psychology, psychopathology, and psychology and law. The activity could also be used in an interdisciplinary humanities course or in an ethics course. It is an in-class activity that involves all the students and can be used in any size class.

CONCEPT

This activity deals with the question of whether Hamlet was insane when he killed Polonius. It demonstrates the relevant evidence needed to determine insanity, the role of the forensic mental health expert, and the need to view the evidence from different perspectives to come to a conclusion. Students also experience the dynamics of jury deliberation.

MATERIALS NEEDED

The materials needed are a DVD player; a copy of the DVD "Insanity Trial of Hamlet," produced by the Boston Bar Association in 1996 or the Washington Bar Association in 1994, and available from C-SPAN; a verdict form; pencils and paper; and space for groups of 6 to 12 students to deliberate together. The Boston DVD runs 3½ hours and the Washington DVD runs 2 hours, so you may want to edit out material that is not the actual mock trial, such as interviews and debriefing. The following materials are available in hand-out form: The American Law Institute (ALI) (1962) Model Penal Code test for insanity, the diagnostic criteria for depressive and manic episodes from the *Diagnostic and Statistical Manual of Mental Disorders* (4th ed.; DSM–IV–TR; American Psychiatric Association, 2000), a list of the experts and the attorneys for each side with space for taking notes, and a printed copy of the jury instructions from the DVD. (Copies of the handouts for this activity are available from the author at Department of Psychology, John Carroll University, University Heights, OH 44118 or at swenson@jcu.edu.)

INSTRUCTIONS

Prior to the beginning of this activity, students have studied the insanity defense in class. In addition, so that all of the students are familiar with the fact pattern of this case, they must all have read the play *Hamlet*. Ask them to try to read the play from a psychological, rather than a literary, point of view. Although it would also be acceptable for students to view one of the videos of Hamlet or see the play in live format, I prefer that they read the play so that they will not be biased by a particular actor's interpretation of the character.

Tell students that they should put themselves in Hamlet's place and try to understand his feelings and motivations. At the beginning of the class, give the students the following instructions:

You are serving on the jury to decide whether or not Hamlet was insane at the time he killed Polonius. The record in this case is the play *Hamlet*, which you have read. Pay attention to the arguments of the experts, but do not make up your mind until the end of the trial. Because the DVD of this trial will not be completed in one class period, you must not discuss this case with your classmates between this class and the next.

Then have students view the DVD of your selected parts of the mock "Insanity Trial of Hamlet." When the DVD is completed, divide the students into juries of 6 to 12 people, depending on the number in the class.

Give students a printed copy of the jury instructions read by the judge in the DVD. These instructions stress several points. It is a fundamental principle of our criminal law that a person is not criminally responsible for an act if the person was insane at the time of the act. It is the job of that person's defense to prove insanity by a preponderance of the evidence (i.e., it is more likely than not). The ALI (1962, § 4.01) Model Penal Code test for insanity will require the students to think through several steps in coming to their decision. It states the following: "A person is not responsible for criminal conduct if at the time of such conduct as a result of mental disease or defect he lacks substantial capacity either to appreciate the criminality [wrongfulness] of his conduct or to conform his conduct to the requirements of the law."

First the students must determine whether the defendant has a mental disorder. If the answer is yes, then they must decide whether this disorder resulted in the lack of a substantial capacity to either appreciate the criminality of the conduct (a cognitive consideration) or to conform the conduct to the law (a volitional consideration). Finally, the student jurors are told not to concern themselves with Hamlet's actual guilt or innocence in the crime of killing Polonius. If he is criminally responsible, then he will be tried on criminal charges at some other time and place.

I also give the students a copy of the manic and depressive diagnostic criteria from the *DSM–IV–TR* because the defendant's expert argues that Hamlet suffers from a bipolar disorder.

The juries then go to their deliberation rooms or spaces and are given 30 minutes to 1 hour to elect a foreperson and to come to a verdict. Those students who have been absent from class for the DVD are observers but do not participate in the deliberation. At the end of the time period the students reassemble and the verdicts are read. The verdict form asks the students whether, in the *Matter of Denmark v. Hamlet*, the members of the jury, find the defendant Hamlet criminally responsible or not criminally responsible (i.e., not guilty by reason of insanity). Then the foreperson states whether the jury verdict was unanimous or not unanimous, as well as how many jurors were in favor of and against this verdict. (The verdict does not have to be unanimous.) The foreperson then signs the form. This is followed by either a discussion or a written assignment in which students reflect on the evidence that was most persuasive and the process their jury went through to reach its decision.

Every time I have used this activity students have been excited, enthusiastic, and diligent in their deliberations. Juries have unanimously found Hamlet criminally responsible or have been unable to reach a unanimous verdict, but have never been unanimous for a verdict of not guilty by reason of insanity. The deliberations are usually heated and even the quieter students seem eager to talk about the evidence that was the most persuasive for them.

What I particularly like about this mock trial DVD is that the experts arguing for and against the criminal responsibility of Hamlet are Alan Stone, MD, and Thomas

Guttheil, MD, two eminent scholars in this field. The DVD is worth showing just to see the method of analysis used and the way the behavior of an individual can be interpreted from two different perspectives. It also illustrates the use of forensic mental health experts in the courtroom. An extra bonus is that the trial is presided over by Justice Anthony Kennedy of the United States Supreme Court. His judicial temperament is exemplary and worthy of comment in the class.

The earlier version of "The Insanity Trial of Hamlet" was produced by the Washington, DC, Bar Association (1994) with different attorneys but the same experts and presiding judge. It is somewhat shorter in length. After using both DVDs, I now combine the two so that my favorite attorneys do the questioning and opening and closing statements. One potential problem with doing this is that the burden of proof is on the government in the Washington, DC, DVD and on the defendant in the Boston DVD. I deal with this conflict by instructing the juries that the defendant must prove himself not guilty by reason of insanity by a preponderance of the evidence. This avoids the more difficult issue of having to prove the defendant sane and provides an interesting point of discussion by referring to the DC standard used in the case of John Hinckley (the man who shot President Ronald Reagan). In fact, I do not think that most students consider the burden of proof at all but rather focus on the question of sanity or insanity, whether or not the defendant was criminally responsible.

From start to finish this activity takes about 3 hours and could easily take another hour or 2 if you use the Boston DVD in its entirety and do not edit it. An activity that takes this much class time must be worthwhile. Although many course topics in the area of psychology and law use more class time for student-conducted mock trials (American Psychology–Law Society, 2007), this activity brings together more of the substantive content. It has a real courtroom atmosphere. It illustrates the role of forensic mental health experts. It allows the students to use their critical thinking skills to evaluate the evidence and then to come to a verdict on the mental state of the defendant. It gives the students an opportunity to analyze the jury process. And by using a Shakespeare play, it brings a humanities focus to the course.

REFERENCES AND SUGGESTED READING

American Law Institute. *Model penal code* (1962 official draft), § 4.01.

American Psychiatric Association. (2000). *Diagnostic and statistical manual of mental disorders* (4th ed.). Washington, DC: Author.

American Psychology–Law Society. (2007). Retrieved from http://www.apls.org/academics/downloadUndergrad.html

Boston Bar Association. (Producer). (1996, March 11). *Insanity trial of Hamlet*. [DVD]. Available from C-SPAN Video Library Web site, http://www.c-spanstore.org

Greene, E., Heilbrun, K., Fortune, W. H., & Nietzel, M. T. (2006). *Wrightsman's psychology and the legal system* (6th ed.). Pacific Grove, CA: Brooks/Cole.

Hermann, D. H. J. (1997) *Mental health and disability law*. St. Paul, MN: West.

Reisner, R., Slobogin, D. W., & Arti, R. (2004). *Law and the mental health system: Civil and criminal aspects*. St. Paul, MN: West.

Sales, B. D., & Shuman, D. W. (1996). *Law, mental health, and mental disorder*. Pacific Grove, CA: Brooks/Cole.

Shakespeare, W. (1947). *The tragedy of Hamlet, Prince of Denmark*. New Haven, CT: Yale University Press. (Original work published 1603)

Slobogin, C. (2006). *Proving the unprovable: The role of law, science, and speculation in adjudicating culpability and dangerousness*. New York: Oxford University Press.

Washington, DC, Bar Association. (Producer). (1994, March 17). *Trial of Hamlet* [DVD]. Available from C-SPAN Video Library Web site, http://www.c-spanstore.org?

CHAPTER 11
SOCIAL PSYCHOLOGY

This collection of social psychology activities reflects many of the principal areas of the field, including the nature of persuasion and attitude change, helping behavior, the nature of groups, and attribution theory, including an activity on the fundamental attribution error. You will also find some activities in other chapters that are appropriate for social psychology, especially in chapter 12, which includes activities on such topics as leadership, prejudice and discrimination, and stereotyping.

In Activity 56, students are asked to create their own theories of how romantic relationships emerge and develop. These theories are written outside of class and a subset of five of them, ideally diverse, is selected by the instructor for class discussion. Students are asked to comment on how realistic the theories are. Are they idealized or romanticized? What interpersonal qualities are present or absent in the theories? These and other questions allow the instructor to tie the student theories to theories of interpersonal relations.

The ability of television advertisements to generate attitude change is the subject of Activity 57. Working in small groups, students watch three different taped advertisements and evaluate their effectiveness using worksheets provided by the instructor. This activity is based on the message-learning approach to persuasion, also called the Yale model, which deals with the credibility and likeability of the communicator and various characteristics of the message. This activity not only familiarizes students with a principal model for understanding persuasion but also strengthens their critical thinking skills in evaluating advertisements.

Activity 58 is an experiment on helping behavior. Students are presented four scenarios of a "wrong number" phone call from a woman who is stranded on the side of a road because of her car's malfunction. Students are asked to predict the success of each scenario in getting an individual to help the stranded motorist. The discussion is centered on the relationship of the predictions to two social norms: the norm of social responsibility and the norm of self-sufficiency.

What is a group? Are the New York Yankees a group? What about the pedestrians standing on the corner of State and Monroe Streets? What about students attending a lecture? What about a construction crew building a house? Activity 59 explores the question of what constitutes a group. Students complete a brief questionnaire, the results of which are used for a discussion, including a discussion of how social psychologists define groups and whether those defining characteristics are part of the groups under discussion.

The author of Activity 60 describes it as "a simple, straightforward, and telling demonstration of the 'irrational' basis of person perception." It is a demonstration of the fundamental attribution error (FAE), in which students work in pairs in a quiz game. One student prepares the questions, and the others attempt to answer them. Both quizmaster and contestant also fill out a separate sheet estimating how well the other person will perform. Results typically strongly support a clear example of the FAE.

Activity 61 also concerns the topic of attribution. Specifically, this activity is designed to teach students about attribution theory in the context of learning about homelessness and about homelessness in the context of attribution theory. The exercise requires a great deal of class time—5–6 class periods—but the richness of the outcome and the value of the experience are considerable.

56 Romantic Relationships: Studying Theories of Personal Relationship Development

Elizabeth L. Paul

The College of New Jersey

The personal relationships field has developed over the past several decades into a thriving discipline. To introduce students to the subject matter, this activity requires each student to create her or his own theory of how romantic relationships develop. That is done outside of class. Then, students' theories are used as the basis for an in-class discussion about the psychological study of interpersonal relationships. This activity is useful for classes in introductory psychology, social psychology, and personal relationships. It involves all the students and can be used in any size class, although good discussion will be problematic for larger classes.

CONCEPT

This activity uses models of the development and progress of interpersonal relationships to introduce the personal relationships field. Social penetration, social exchange, attraction-based, individual developmental, and stage theory models of relationship development are demonstrated and discussed, as well as such interpersonal processes as communication, relationship cognition, conflict, relationship maintenance, and commitment. In addition, the functions of stereotypes, idealized or romanticized social scripts, and lay theories of relationship development are addressed.

To explore this activity, use the following scholarly models of relationship development:

1. *Social penetration theory* focuses on changes in communication (especially self-disclosure), starting with superficial or impersonal topics, broadening and deepening as uncertainty reduces to more intimate interactions (Altman & Taylor, 1973; Baxter, 1988).
2. *Social exchange theory* applies an economic model to relationship development in which individuals are motivated to maximize gains and minimize losses. Relationship development and satisfaction are based on rewards, costs, expectations, perceived alternatives, and investments (Levinger & Huesmann, 1980; Rusbult, 1983; Thibaut & Kelley, 1959).
3. *Attraction-based theories* focus primarily on the initial phases of interpersonal attraction, highlighting the importance of proximity, physical attractiveness, and similarity and complementarity in physical attractiveness and other personal characteristics (Berscheid, Dion, Walster, & Walster, 1971; Hatfield & Sprecher, 1986).
4. *Individual developmental models* build on such seminal developmental theories as those of Erikson (e.g., 1963) and Sullivan (1953) in which relationship development is an individual developmental milestone building on evolving psychological strengths and abilities (Franz & White, 1985; Paul & White, 1990).

5. *Stage theories* conceptualize relationship development as evolving through a specific set of stages in a particular order. These include the two-stage theory of Kerckhoff and Davis (1962), Reiss's (1960) four-stage theory, Lewis's (1972) multistage theory, and Murstein's (1976, 1987) stimulus–value–role theory.

MATERIALS NEEDED

You will need a chalkboard or white board and, of course, creative students.

INSTRUCTIONS

This activity must take place before students have been introduced to the personal relationships field in an introductory or social psychology course or at the beginning of a personal relationships course. In this way students are not biased by existing scholarly work in this area. One week prior to the introduction of this field, instruct students to create a theory of how romantic relationships develop and proceed. They may list and describe stages, draw a flow diagram, or identify general processes that occur. There is no limit to the creativity with which this assignment is completed (I have received collages, cartoons, and yard-long flow diagrams). Tell students that they must not consult their textbooks or any other scholarly materials for this assignment; however, encourage them to consult with friends. Students should bring their one- or two-page presentations of the theory to the next class period. (Alternatively, students may work in groups in class to develop theories. This is less effective than the take-home assignment but is still an effective discussion tool.)

Ask students to bring their theories to class in written form (if you want to collect them from all students) and/or in PowerPoint form on a USB flash drive or CD. Ask five students to volunteer to show their theories as PowerPoint presentations. Ask the volunteers to give a brief explanation of their theories to the class. Then encourage the students to discuss the theories as a class.

This exercise has been found to be very effective in seminar-style classes as well as large lecture classes. The following are suggestions for facilitating this exercise in a large lecture course: (a) have students hand in their theories ahead of time, which will allow you to select five diverse examples to share with the class as a whole, or (b) have students cluster in small groups to begin the discussion of their theories, assigning one student per group to be the recorder of issues raised by their group that can be used to facilitate contributions to the large group discussion to follow.

The following are two additional variations of the exercise suitable for any class format (e.g., seminar, lecture):

1. Have half of the students develop models of one type of relationship while other students develop models of another type. Possible relationship-type comparisons include (a) close platonic friendships with romantic relationships, (b) cross-sex friendships with cross-sex romantic relationships, (c) same-sex friendships with cross-sex friendships, (d) same-sex romantic relationships with cross-sex romantic relationships, and (e) same-sex friendships with same-sex romantic relationships. In the class discussion, examine relationship-type differences and similarities. Discuss possible causes of relationship-type differences.
2. As a follow-up to the relationship development theory exercise, review major scholarly theories of relationship development with students. Then divide the class into small work groups and assign a scholarly theory to each group. Select one student's relationship development theory and instruct each group to revise this personal theory, tailoring it to their specific assigned scholarly theoretical orientation (e.g., social penetration or social exchange theory). Have a member

of each group record the group's revision to share with the rest of the class. In the discussion that follows, compare and contrast the different theory revisions. Explore the strengths and weaknesses of each scholarly model. Looking across all the different scholarly theories, what is understood about relationship development and what questions are left unanswered?

DISCUSSION   Most students initially greet this assignment with excitement, thinking that it is easy. Once they start developing their own theories, they realize that this is quite a challenging task. They begin to recognize the many variables involved and the many variations such factors create. Use this new awareness of the complexity of interpersonal relating to expose students to the vast terrain of the personal relationships field.

The five volunteers usually present varied theories; there will be similarities, disagreements, and unique ideas. The following are suggestions for guiding the discussion:

1. Begin the discussion by asking the class to comment on the five theories. Compare and contrast the theories. What are the features with which students agree or disagree?

2. Are the theories realistic portrayals of how romantic relationships develop and proceed? Or are they idealized and romanticized? How do the idealized theories reflect societal myths or fantasies (i.e., social scripts) about romantic relating (emphasis on passionate love, "conflict phobia," living "happily ever after")? What is the function of such social scripts? How do social scripts affect interpersonal relationships?

3. What interpersonal processes or qualities are reflected in the theories (e.g., attraction, trust, honesty, commitment)? Are they described in any detail or are they simply listed as unreflective or automatic responses? What is the function of such glib responses? In what order do various interpersonal processes or qualities occur in theories? For example, when does sexual interaction (if noted) occur? When does commitment occur? Many theories reflect a very fast-paced sequence in which sexual interaction and commitment come directly after attraction and meeting the partner. Discuss such sequences in the context of the current social and sexual climate. How does such sequencing affect the later course of a relationship?

4. What interpersonal processes or qualities are absent from students' theories? Students often do not include communication (other than superficial chatting), conflict and the negotiation of conflict resolution strategies, relationship cognition (including active decision making about the course of the relationship or future planning), or relationship maintenance strategies (most theories end with engagement or marriage without thought to processes or qualities necessary for maintaining a long-term relationship). Many theories do not include sexual interaction. Discuss with students their hesitation about including sexual interaction, societal taboos about direct communication about sexual interaction, and how such factors affect romantic relationships. For example, could such reticence be the root of sexual conflict or unwanted sexual activities in relationships?

5. What is the function of a theory in a field such as personal relationships? For decades, scholars have tried to develop models of how relationships develop and proceed. Identify the scholarly models most closely represented by students' theories (social penetration, social exchange, attraction-based, and individual developmental). In what ways could such models be useful for research and

application? Should a relationship development model be an idealized model to which we should strive or a realistic model detailing the difficulties that often arise?

6. Explore individual differences in personal relationship development theories. For example, are there sex or race differences among students' theories? Is a universal model of romantic relationship development and progress possible? Is it useful? Should theories vary by age, cohort, gender, sexual orientation, ethnicity and race, health, socioeconomic status, geographic region within the United States, or nationality? How? Have scholarly theories considered such variation? How inclusive has personal relationships theory and research been?

7. Ask students to comment about how their ideas of relationship development changed as a result of the class discussion.

REFERENCES AND SUGGESTED READING

Altman, I., & Taylor, D. A. (1973). *Social penetration: The development of interpersonal relationships.* New York: Holt, Rinehart & Winston.

Baxter, L. A. (1988). A dialectical perspective on communication strategies in relationship development. In S. Duck (Ed.), *Handbook of personal relationships* (pp. 257–273). New York: Wiley.

Berscheid, E., Dion, K., Walster, E., & Walster, G. W. (1971). Physical attractiveness and dating choice: A test of the matching hypothesis. *Journal of Experimental Social Psychology, 7,* 173–189.

Erikson, E. (1963). *Childhood and society.* New York: Norton.

Franz, C., & White, K. M. (1985). Individuation and attachment in personality development: Extending Erikson's theory. In A. Stewart & B. Lykes (Eds.), *Gender and personality* (pp. 136–168). Durham, NC: Duke University Press.

Hatfield, E., & Rapson, R. (2005). *Love and sex: Cross-cultural perspectives.* Lanham, MD: University Press of America.

Hatfield, E., & Sprecher, S. (1986). *Mirror, mirror . . . The importance of looks in everyday life.* Albany: State University of New York Press.

Kerckhoff, A. C., & Davis, K. E. (1962). Value consensus and need complementarity in mate selection. *American Sociological Review, 27,* 295–303.

Levinger, G., & Huesmann, L. R. (1980). An "incremental exchange" perspective on the pair relationship: Interpersonal reward and level of involvement. In K. K. Gergen, M. S. Greenberg, & R. H. Willis (Eds.), *Social exchange: Advances in theory and research* (pp. 165–188). New York: Plenum Press.

Lewis, R. A. (1972). A developmental framework for the analysis of premarital dyadic formation. *Family Process, 11,* 17–48.

Miller, R., Perlman, D., & Brehm, S. (2007). *Intimate relationships* (4th ed.). Boston: McGraw-Hill.

Murstein, B. I. (1976). The stimulus-value-role theory of marital choice. In H. Grunebaum & J. Christ (Eds.), *Contemporary marriage: Structures, dynamics, and therapy* (pp. 165–168). Boston: Little, Brown.

Murstein, B. I. (1987). A clarification and extension of the SVR theory of dyadic pairing. *Journal of Marriage and the Family, 49,* 929–933.

Parks, M. R. (2006). *Personal relationships and personal networks.* Mahwah, NJ: Lawrence Erlbaum.

Paul, E. L., & White, K. M. (1990). The development of intimate relationships in late adolescence. *Adolescence, 25,* 375–400.

Reis, H. T., & Rusbult, C. E. (Eds.). (2004). *Close relationships: Key readings.* New York: Psychology Press.

Reiss, I. L. (1960). Toward a sociology of the heterosexual love relationship. *Marriage and Family Living, 22,* 139–145.

Rusbult, C. E. (1983). A longitudinal test of the investment model: The development (and deterioration) of satisfaction and commitment in heterosexual involvement. *Journal of Personality and Social Psychology, 45,* 101–117.

Sullivan, H. S. (1953). *The interpersonal theory of psychiatry.* New York: Norton.

Thibaut, J. W., & Kelley, H. H. (1959). *The social psychology of groups.* New York: Wiley.

Vangelisti, A. L., & Perlman, D. (Eds.). (2006). *The Cambridge handbook of personal relationships.* New York: Cambridge University Press.

57 ATTITUDE CHANGE FACTORS IN TELEVISION COMMERCIALS

Margaret A. Lloyd

Georgia Southern University

In this in-class activity, students identify various attitude change factors used in pretaped commercials and record their findings on a work sheet. The activity is appropriate for introductory and social psychology courses of any size. The activity employs small groups, so a classroom with moveable seats is helpful, but not essential. The instructor must record commercials (three are recommended) that illustrate various attitude change factors and prepare copies of a work sheet. The discussion of the message-learning approach to persuasion (Hovland's Yale model) in an introductory or social psychology text should provide sufficient coverage of the attitude change principles covered in the activity.

CONCEPT   The message-learning approach to persuasion (Yale model) is characterized by the question: "*Who* says *what* to *whom?*" (Hovland, Janis, & Kelley, 1953). In this model, *who* refers to the communicator or source of an appeal; *what* refers to the communication or persuasive message; and *whom* refers to the receiver of the persuasive appeal. Using this model, researchers have identified a host of source, message, and receiver variables that operate in persuasion attempts. This model assumes that a persuasion attempt is likely to be successful if the receiver understands the message and perceives its arguments to be compelling. The purpose of this activity is to increase students' awareness of some of the attitude change principles used in media advertising.

Some of the source and message factors that researchers have studied are listed below. (Some factors and subfactors have been excluded to limit the scope of the activity.)

I. The Source of the Communication (*Who*)
  A. Credibility
    1. Expertise
    2. Trustworthiness
  B. Likability
    1. Familiarity (celebrities, etc.)
    2. Physical attractiveness
    3. Similarity to receiver (gender, age, ethnicity, etc.)
II. The Nature of the Message (*What*)
  A. Repeated exposure to message (brand name)
  B. Association of message with a positive emotional state (upbeat music, humor, etc.)
  C. Negative emotional state (fear or threats)
  D. Rational appeals
  E. One-sided versus two-sided arguments

It is also good to remind students that current theorizing and research on attitude change focuses on the cognitive processes that underlie persuasion. A good example is

Petty and Cacioppo's (1986) elaboration likelihood model, which focuses on the cognitive effort involved in processing persuasive messages. This research has shed helpful light on the workings of the various source, message, and receiver factors.

MATERIALS NEEDED

To participate in this activity, students view prerecorded commercials. Thus, prior to class, the instructor must record commercials for replay in class. After recording a number of commercials, the instructor should select at least three that illustrate many of the attitude change factors the students are to look for. (Limiting the number of commercials to three will allow sufficient time to complete the activity in a 50-minute class period.) The instructor must also prepare a work sheet for each student that lists the attitude-change factors students are to look for (see those listed above).

INSTRUCTIONS

This activity works best when students work in small groups, so a classroom with moveable seats is helpful. (If your class is an auditorium, you can ask students to make groups by turning to face each other.)

Prior to presenting this activity, you will need to lecture on the message-learning approach to persuasion and the attitude change factors that will be used in the activity. (This information should be covered in any introductory or social psychology textbook.) Obviously, the instructor must be able to identify and discuss the factors operating in each of the commercials.

To begin the activity, hand out the work sheet and explain to students what they are to do and the relevance of the activity to the course material. Go over the factors on the work sheet and be sure that students understand the meaning of the various factors.

Then, split the students into small groups (3–6 students). (You will need at least four groups for the activity.) Once students are in their groups, assign each group the factors they are to monitor in the commercials: Group 1: source-credibility factors (expertise and trustworthiness); Group 2: source-likability factors (familiarity, physical attractiveness, similarity to receiver); Group 3: message factors (repeated exposure, positive emotional state); Group 4: message factors (negative emotional state and rational appeal). (Note: Assign at least one person in Group 3 to count the number of times they hear the product name mentioned and a second person to count the number of times they see a visual representation of the product.) There is no problem in having more than one group monitor the same factors, but because each group reports their results to the class, this lengthens the time the activity takes. To limit the number of groups, you can increase group size, but groups should not be so large that discussion is inhibited.

Once students are in their assigned groups, ask each group to select (quickly) a spokesperson who will report for the group at the end of each commercial. Check with the groups to be sure that they know what they are to do, and then show the first commercial. (Stop the tape immediately after the commercial ends to avoid distracting students with extraneous information and because you will have to rewind the commercial and play it again.) After showing the commercial, it is good to doublecheck that students are clear about their assignments. Respond to any questions. Remind students that not all factors will be operating in any given commercial.

Then, rewind the commercial and show it again, stopping the tape at end of the commercial. When the commercial stops, tell students to make notes on their work sheets and discuss with group members whether factors they identified were used in the commercial and how. When the groups are ready, ask a spokesperson from each group to report (in order of group number) on whether the group found factors they identified operating in the commercial and how. Troubleshoot and support as necessary.

Repeat this procedure for the second and third commercials. (It is important to show each commercial twice so students will be familiar enough with it to do their analysis.)

DISCUSSION If there is time after the last commercial has been analyzed, you can generate class discussion by asking students to mention some popular commercials and to identify the attitude-change factors operating in them.

REFERENCES AND SUGGESTED READING

Cialdini, R. B. (2001). *Influence: Science and practice* (4th ed.). Boston: Allyn & Bacon.

Crano, W. D., & Prislin, R. (2006). Attitudes and persuasion. *Annual Review of Psychology, 57,* 345–374.

DeBono, K. G. (2006). Self-monitoring and consumer psychology. *Journal of Personality, 74,* 715–737.

Hovland, C. I., Janis, I. L., & Kelley, H. H. (1953). *Communication and persuasion.* New Haven, CT: Yale University Press.

Petty, R. E., & Cacioppo, J. T. (1986). *Communication and persuasion: Central and peripheral routes to attitude change.* New York: Springer-Verlag.

Any social psychology textbook that covers in some depth the attitude-change factors in the message-learning approach (Yale model) and Petty and Cacioppo's elaboration likelihood model would be a useful reference.

For a review of contemporary attitude change theories and research, see P. S. Visser and J. Cooper. (2003). Attitude change. In M. A. Hogg & J. Cooper (Eds.), *The Sage handbook of social psychology* (pp. 211–231). Thousand Oaks, CA: Sage Publications.

58 Human Judgment Versus Empirical Evidence

Jane A. Jegerski
Elmhurst College

This activity, dealing with helping behavior, consistently demonstrates the value of research (as opposed to common sense) as a means of understanding behavior. It is appropriate for classes in introductory psychology, social psychology, or any course with a discussion of research methodology in field and lab settings. This in-class activity involves all of the students in classes of any size and requires about 15 minutes of class time.

CONCEPT

This exercise demonstrates the need to test common social beliefs scientifically using a research study. This is accomplished using counterintuitive results from a study on helping behavior. The exercise also highlights the phenomenon of discrepant findings from laboratory study and field study and introduces a discussion of the norms that govern helping.

MATERIALS NEEDED

A reading of the Gruder, Romer, and Korth (1978) study on dependency and fault as determinants of helping behavior may be helpful to the instructor.

INSTRUCTIONS

Present the design and procedure of the Gruder, Romer, and Korth (1978) study as follows:

> Randomly selected telephone subscribers received a "wrong number" phone call from a Mrs. Vernon, who was supposedly stranded on a nearby highway. She asked for Ralph's garage, and when she was told that she had the wrong number, she asked the subject to make the correct phone call for her in one of four randomly assigned ways:
>
> 1. Low dependency, fault. "... and I'm so upset. I was supposed to take the car into the shop last week to be repaired, but I forgot to do it. Now it's broken down."
> 2. Low dependency, no fault. "... and I'm so upset. The car was just repaired last week and it just broke down."
> 3. High dependency, fault. "... and I don't have any more change for the phone. Oh, I'm so upset. I was supposed to take the car into the shop last week to be repaired, but I forgot to do it. Now it's broken down."
> 4. High dependency, no fault. "... and I don't have any more change for the phone. Oh, I'm so upset. The car was just repaired last week and it just broke down."

The dependent measure was whether the subject helped by making the call.

After the class is familiar with the design of the study, have the students predict the results and tell why they made these judgments. My introductory and social psychology students invariably decide that the most help will be given to the target victim, Mrs. Vernon, in the high dependency, no fault condition and the least will be provided in the two fault conditions. Gruder, Romer, and Korth (1978) reported the following actual helping rates: high dependency, fault = 86%; low dependency, no fault = 69%; high dependency, no fault = 55%; and low dependency, fault = 52%.

Discuss the results in relation to the hypothesized operation of two norms: the norm of social responsibility and the norm of self-sufficiency. Social responsibility suggests that we help others in need, especially when the victim's need is high (and being negligent about getting a car fixed can indicate greater dependency needs). The norm of self-sufficiency (that people take responsibility for their own welfare) would predict less helping when the victim's immediate dependency is low. It appears that these norms may be activated only in a realistic helping situation because the authors could not duplicate these results in a laboratory study in which subjects were asked to judge the likelihood of their helping in the four conditions.

Conclude the exercise with a discussion of possible reasons for the differences in helping responses in the lab and in the field settings (e.g., empathy as a mediator in the field, being asked the likelihood of helping rather than actually being asked to help). The discussion should emphasize the variable that might make the data run counter to one's intuitions about behavior.

REFERENCES AND SUGGESTED READING

Giere, R. N. (1997). *Understanding scientific reasoning* (4th ed.). Fort Worth, TX: Harcourt Brace.

Goodwin, C. J. (2007). *Research in psychology: Methods and design.* (5th ed.). Hoboken, NJ: Wiley.

Gruder, C. L., Romer, D., & Korth, B. (1978). Dependency and fault as determinants of helping. *Journal of Experimental and Social Psychology, 14,* 227–235.

Pelham, B. W., & Blanton, H. (2007). *Conducting research in psychology: Measuring the weight of smoke* (3rd ed.). Belmont, CA: Wadsworth/Thomson Learning.

59 THE NATURE OF GROUPS: AN EXERCISE FOR CLASSROOM DISCUSSION

Robert P. Agans

University of North Carolina at Chapel Hill

The purpose of this activity is to generate a class discussion about the nature of groups. The activity is suited for both large and small classes in social psychology, group dynamics, and introductory psychology. It requires little preparatory work and can easily generate 30 minutes of classroom discussion.

CONCEPT
This activity is designed to generate class discussion about various aspects of group life and to sensitize students to the perplexities that psychologists face when attempting to describe group phenomena. Though social scientists do not agree on one precise group definition, four important characteristics distinguish groups from nongroups (Pavitt & Curtis, 1994). These essential characteristics are (a) interdependence (Cartwright & Zander, 1968), (b) structure or patterned behavior (Newcomb, 1951), (c) common goals (Mills, 1967), and (d) perceived groupness (Smith, 1945).

MATERIALS NEEDED
Make copies of the questionnaire given below and distribute.

WHAT CONSTITUTES A GROUP?
Check each statement that you believe represents a group.

1.____ patients in a physician's waiting room
2.____ a classroom full of students
3.____ sorority sisters attending a fraternity party together
4.____ an army platoon defending its borders
5.____ all people on planet earth
6.____ a mob of angry protesters marching on Capitol Hill
7.____ a family
8.____ Robert and Rani out on their first date
9.____ two strangers speaking over the telephone to resolve a billing mistake
10.____ newborns on the maternity ward
11.____ three gang members from rival gangs stranded on a desert island
12.____ colleagues assigned the task of writing a final report
13.____ friends standing in line to purchase concert tickets
14.____ members of Greenpeace
15.____ the Dallas Cowboys
16.____ natives entertaining a foreign visitor for the evening
17.____ people from the Republic of China
18.____ a construction crew building a house
19.____ pedestrians on the corner of Fifth and Main Streets
20.____ a tennis match

At the beginning of the class, give each student a copy of the questionnaire. Instruct the class to read each statement carefully and mark the items that depict a group. Have them leave nongroup items blank. Tell them to respond to items on the basis of their personal beliefs, not what they think others would say or what they think their instructor wants. Tell them the questionnaire will be collected, but that they should not put their names on it.

Allow students 5 minutes to finish the questionnaire. An easy way to tabulate the data is to collect the questionnaires and redistribute them in random order so that students get a copy other than their own. This precaution reduces the embarrassment students may feel about sharing their individual responses. Next, use a show of hands to record the data on the board. For each item, count the number of students who checked the item as representing a group. By subtracting this number from the total number of students, you can quickly calculate the number of students who did not believe the item represented a group (adopted from Benjamin, 1985). Students relate to the data most easily if you take the time to quickly convert these raw scores to percentages. Tabulating the data takes only about 5 minutes in a small class.

In large classes, consider administering and collecting the questionnaire the class period before you discuss this topic. This gives you plenty of time to tabulate the results in advance for the appropriate class period, thus allowing the majority of the class time to be spent on discussion.

DISCUSSION

Despite the lack of a unified definition of groups in the social sciences, most of the experimental work consists of groups whose members (a) are shown to be interdependent on one another to complete a specified task or goal, (b) have developed a unique structure or patterned behavior when interacting, (c) have identified common goals, and (d) have created an atmosphere of perceived groupness. This activity allows students to discover and explore these characteristics as they identify groups from nongroups.

Start class discussion by identifying items least likely to be identified as groups. For example, Items 1, 5, 10, and 19 should yield the lowest percentages of endorsement because they are generally considered nongroups. On the other hand, Items 4, 7, 12, 15, and 18 should have the highest percentages of endorsement. These items incorporate the four essential characteristics of groups: interdependence, structure or patterned behavior, common goals, and perceived groupness.

The remaining items reflect varying degrees of these four characteristics. They should be marked by only a portion of the students and should evoke the most controversy. Items 8, 9, 16, and 20 are based on the interdependence theme. Items 2, 3, 6, and 13 are chiefly structural or patterned. Items 11, 14, and 17 could be psychological groups if the people involved perceive a sense of groupness or common goals.

It may be useful to point out characteristics that are missing for certain items. For example, it should be evident that friends standing in line to purchase concert tickets (Item 13) do not constitute a group because there is no interdependence among these people. Even though norms guide individual behavior and create expectancies under such circumstances, one could just as easily buy concert tickets without such a crowd. On the other hand, two strangers speaking on the telephone (Item 9) are dependent on each other to hold the conversation and resolve the dispute, but would not be considered a group because no unique patterned behavior or structure has emerged that separates them from the society at large. People from China (Item 17) or members of Greenpeace (Item 14) may be perceived by outsiders to have a sense of groupness or perhaps even a common goal, but it's unlikely that such individuals would come to the same conclusion if, for example, they were suddenly thrown together in a room and forced to interact. These people, though loosely connected by country of origin or membership, are not interdependent in a psychological sense and have not spent enough time together to develop expectations and normative behavior.

In sum, authentic groups, as operationalized in the psychological literature, have the following characteristics: (a) they consist of individuals who come together with the sole purpose of accomplishing a task that no one member could complete on his or her own, (b) they have developed a unique structure or patterned behavior between or among its various members that is not mimicked elsewhere, (c) they can articulate a common goal that connects them, and (d) they have come to see themselves as unified. With these characteristics in mind, it becomes easier for students to distinguish groups from nongroups.

REFERENCES AND SUGGESTED READING

Benjamin, L. T., Jr. (1985). Defining aggression: An exercise for classroom discussion. *Teaching of Psychology, 12,* 40–42.

Cartwright, D., & Zander, A. (1968). *Group dynamics: Research and theory* (3rd ed.). New York: Harper & Row.

Levine, R. L., & Moreland, R. L. (2006). *Small groups: Key readings in social psychology.* New York: Psychology Press.

Mills, T. M. (1967). *The sociology of small groups,* Englewood Cliffs, NJ: Prentice-Hall.

Newcomb, T. M. (1951). Social psychological theory. In J. H. Rohrer & M. Sherif (Eds.), *Social psychology at the crossroads* (pp. 31–49). New York: Harper.

Pavitt, C., & Curtis, E. (1994). *Small group discussion: A theoretical approach.* Scottsdale, AZ: Gorsuch Scarisbrick.

Smith, M. (1945). Social situation, social behavior, social group. *Psychological Review, 52,* 224–229.

60 THE FUNDAMENTAL ATTRIBUTION ERROR

David L. Watson
University of Hawaii

This activity is a simple, straightforward, and telling demonstration of the "irrational" basis of person perception. You must reproduce handouts, but no prior knowledge of psychology is necessary. This in-class activity is best for classes of 20 or more and involves all students in the class. It requires about 15 to 20 minutes to complete. It is appropriate for classes in introductory psychology and social psychology.

CONCEPT

The *fundamental attribution error* is the idea that, in explaining a person's behavior, we tend to discount the effect of the situation on the behavior and overestimate the effect of personality factors (see Nisbett & Ross, 1980, and Ross, Amabile, & Steinmetz, 1977). When we try to explain someone's behavior, we make an attribution. These attributions can emphasize causes of behavior that lie within the person (in personal characteristics) or lie in the situation involved (in the environment). Actually, causes of behavior often lie in both, although sometimes one is more important than the other. But researchers in social cognition consistently find that when making attributions, people tend to ignore the effects of the situation and overemphasize the role of personality.

In this activity, a condition is created in which the situation is primarily the cause of what happens. This is even made clear to the participants. Yet many of them will attribute the cause of the event to personality factors, ignoring the role of the situation. This has been called the fundamental attribution error by Lee Ross and his colleagues.

MATERIALS NEEDED

Before the demonstration, make one photocopy of the question sheet (shown in Appendix 60.1) for each student who participates in the demonstration.

INSTRUCTIONS

The demonstration takes 10 to 15 minutes. You can use the whole class. First, form pairs of students who do *not* know each other well. (If they know each other, they may have formed an opinion about the other's store of general knowledge.) Ask each pair of students to sit together. It is best not to explain the nature of the experiment beforehand, because you will not get the effect if the students know what you expect.

When the students are seated, say to them, "We're going to play a quiz game in which one of you in each pair will be the contestant and the other the quizmaster. First, let's decide who will play each role. We want to assign the numbers 1 and 2 to each pair. So right now, decide in each pair who will be number 1 and who will be number 2." Pause for a few seconds until everyone has designated themselves as 1 or 2. Then say, "I'm going to flip this coin. If it is heads, then the number 1s will be the quizmaster; if it is tails, the number 2s will be the quizmaster." Flip the coin and then remind them who in each pair is the quizmaster and who is the contestant.

Now say to the quizmasters (but allow the contestants to hear you): "Please make up five questions along the lines of 'What is the capital of Maine? (or some far-away state).' The questions should be challenging but not impossible. Use questions like 'Who was President in 1950?' or 'What do the initials in the poet W. H. Auden's name stand for?' but not questions like 'What is my brother's middle name?' The questions should concern general knowledge but be challenging. Go ahead now and make up your five questions. Don't let the contestants see your questions yet. If you want to consult me, please do."

Say to the contestants: "All you have to do is wait while the questions are prepared. Please don't talk with anyone during this period." Give the quizmasters about 5 minutes to write the questions.

When the questions are ready, say to the pairs, "Now you can begin. The quizmaster should ask a question about every 30 seconds. The contestant just answers them aloud. The quizmaster should announce whether the answer is correct, and both members of each pair should keep a record of whether or not each question was answered correctly." The contestants usually will not know the answers to several of the questions posed to them. When the questions are finished, ask both students to fill out the question sheet. Remind the students that the other person will not see their answer and that they do not have to put their name on the sheet.

Once the sheet is filled out, the experiment is complete. Now you can explain the purpose of the demonstration to the students. Ask them why you could not have explained it before.

Next, collect the question sheets from the students and arrange your data on the chalkboard as shown below. If the class is too large to tally the data during class time, you can tabulate them outside of class and take the data to the next class meeting.

	Contestant	Quizmaster
Less	_____	_____
Slightly less	_____	_____
About the same	_____	_____
Slightly more	_____	_____
More	_____	_____

For each line, tally the number of students who gave that particular answer. For example, if one quizmaster chose "less," you would put a tally mark on that line. After all sheets are tallied, compute the average scale rating given by contestants and quizmasters. Assign 1 to "less," 2 to "slightly less," 3 to "about the same," 4 to "slightly more," and 5 to "more." Assuming that this scale constitutes interval measurement, compute the mean. For example, if one quizmaster rated the contestant at 2, four rated the contestant at 3, and one rated the contestant at 4, the mean is $2 + (3 \times 4) + 4$, divided by 6; in this case, the mean is 3.

There will be some overlap in ratings, of course, but I have always found that the average rating of the contestants is clearly different from that of the quizmasters. Typically, the difference between the average ratings is about 0.5, or one-half a scale point. Contestants tend to rate quizmasters as having greater general knowledge than they have.

DISCUSSION   Ask the students why contestants rate themselves lower. Aren't they ignoring the effect of the situation? In their presence, you encouraged the quizmasters to think of challenging questions, ones the contestants probably would get wrong. But when they were wrong, they attributed the cause of this to the greater general knowledge of the quizmaster. They made an attribution on the basis of personal characteristics, not on the situation.

You can also point out that not all students do this, and ask why not. Sometimes quizmasters, for example, will refrain from rating contestants lower than themselves out of politeness. Also, if the students know each other, they may know that the other is not much different from themselves. You can point out various controls in the study, such as using students who do not know each other well and randomly assigning one person to be a contestant and one to be a quizmaster.

REFERENCES AND SUGGESTED READING

Moskowitz, A. B., & Tesser, A. (Eds.). (2005). *Social cognition: Understanding self and others.* New York: Guilford Press.

Myers, D. G. (2008). *Social psychology.* New York: McGraw-Hill.

Nisbett, R., & Ross, L. (1980). *Human inference: Strategies and shortcomings of social judgment.* Englewood Cliffs, NJ: Prentice-Hall.

Ross, L. D., Amabile, T. M., & Steinmetz, J. L. (1977). Social roles, social control and biases in social-perception processes. *Journal of Personality and Social Psychology, 35,* 485–494.

Ross, L., & Nisbett, R. E. (1991). *The person and the situation: Perspectives of social psychology.* New York: McGraw-Hill.

Appendix 60.1

Question Sheet

Were you a contestant_____ or quiz master_____? (check one)
Please rate the general knowledge of the person you worked with by comparing that person with yourself. Please be truthful. The other person will not see your answer. Your answer will not be shown to anyone, and you do not have to put your name on this sheet.

Compared with myself, the other person seems to have (check one):

1. ____ less general knowledge than I have
2. ____ slightly less general knowledge than I have
3. ____ about the same level of general knowledge that I have
4. ____ slightly more general knowledge than I have
5. ____ more general knowledge than I have

61 APPLICATION OF ATTRIBUTION THEORY TO THE SOCIAL ISSUE OF HOMELESSNESS

Susan H. Franzblau
Fayetteville State University

The objective of this activity is to show students, by their own experience, the relevance of applying social psychological principles to the analysis of important social events. Students role-play opposing sides on the issue of homelessness, using various applications of attribution theory to support their positions. Their use of attribution theories, as well as emergent ethnocentrism as a result of establishing opposing groups, is addressed in both oral and written form. This is an in-class activity that requires approximately 5 to 6 class periods and involves all of the students. It can be demonstrated in a large class, but should be broken down into 10 students per group. It is appropriate for classes in social psychology and any course emphasizing diversity, social class, power dynamics, or multicultural issues.

CONCEPT

The objective of this activity is to show students that psychological principles can be used to analyze important social events. This exercise is designed to teach students about attribution theory in the context of learning about homelessness. It is also designed to teach students about homelessness, in the context of learning about attribution theory. It requires students to make a presentation in a hearing or courtroom form, taking one or the other side of an issue.

MATERIALS NEEDED

You will need two versions of the attribution exercise, each typed on a single sheet of paper and alternatively handed out to each student. In Version 1 (Appendix 61.1) the student is a member of a group of homeless people. In Version 2 (Appendix 61.2) the student is a representative of New York City government (or any other city around your university/college).

INSTRUCTIONS

Groups of not more than 10 students are preferable. Five periods should be allowed, or students could work with their groups outside of class. Although this is a long exercise, you could ostensibly use it for the entire social psychology unit because it covers so much social psychological material.

Set up the activity by requiring that students do preliminary reading on attribution theory in their introductory text. Then either lecture or hold a discussion on attribution theory that includes the following topics: naive tendencies to determine attributions of causality on the basis of consensus, distinctiveness, and consistency (Kelley, 1967); fundamental attribution errors (Ross, 1977); actor–observer effects (Jones & Nisbett, 1971); self-serving bias and self-defeating bias (Miller & Ross, 1975); impression formation (Asch, 1946); and creating a psychological perspective (Storms, 1973).

Have the students divide themselves into groups of not more than 10 students per group, forming circles in separate parts of the room. Each group will get either Version 1 or Version 2 of the exercise (see Appendixes 61.1 and 61.2).

Discuss the exercise with the entire class, advising them that each group's mission is to prepare themselves to testify on behalf of their group at a citywide hearing on homelessness, for which they must pull together all they have learned from attribution theory. Their job is to convince the officers at the hearing that (a) as representatives of New York City, the homeless are mentally ill, cannot be responsible for themselves, and should be evicted from the subways and placed in temporary shelters or (b) as members of a group of homeless people, homeless people have the right to sleep in the subways if they wish, they are not mentally ill, and the problem of homelessness will not be solved by building more shelters but by building more low-cost homes.

After approximately a week of group discussion and planning, the hearing/debate should take place. The judges should include the principal interrogator (the instructor) and one judge from each group, chosen by each group. Each group is to prepare a list of expert witnesses who will sit before the judges and plead their case (these witnesses can be role played by the students in each group). Each group's witnesses are presented alternatively with the other group's witnesses. The debate can be conducted formally or informally, according to the dynamics of the class and the instructor's preference. I have used a debate format in which each side was represented in alternating sequence. After flipping a coin to determine which side goes first, I ask them to consider the benefits of recency and primacy effects (Asch, 1946).

At the end of the debate you should initiate an open discussion that includes the following topics:

1. each student's feelings before, during, and after the exercise regarding the likeability of the group they are in and their feelings toward the out-group;
2. what factors drew them closer to their group;
3. the techniques they used to attribute causality of the problem of homelessness to the other group and to build a psychological perspective in their favor;
4. the disequilibrium caused by the other group;
5. the general effectiveness of the exercise; and
6. what they learned about themselves as persons in social situations.

DISCUSSION   At first the groups might be disorganized and uninvolved, but interest will increase as the groups continue to meet. To inspire involvement, it is critical to remind them of the hearing component. As the groups evolve, group leaders will emerge and people will take on different roles, depending on the dynamics of each group (Sherif, Harvey, White, Hood, & Sherif, 1961). In-group ethnocentrism (Sumner, 1906) will also develop as they create a psychological perspective favorable to their group (Storms, 1973). Each time you try this exercise you will find that group members are affected differently, depending on their perspectives on homelessness when they first enter the group. The work the groups do, including research on homelessness, will also depend on the dynamics of each group. In one situation, the city group chose to remain objective inasmuch as they entered this group with a bias toward homeless people; however, at the end of the exercise most indicated that they were unable to remain objective and were drawn into defending the arguments of their group. Some people became more involved than they initially believed they could, which surprised them. Although the activity was presented to the students as an exercise on use of attribution theories, they also came to an experiential understanding of group polarization, the role of social comparison and information, and ethnocentrism, which then enabled them to read about and discuss these processes from their own experience. During the hearing, the involvement of the students will increase as the hearing evolves.

Assign students to write an analysis of their use of attribution theory to prove their case at the citywide hearing. You could also have them discuss their experience of identifying with a new group and how it affected the group process and their feelings toward the other group. Appendix 61.3 presents the directions for students to use when completing the writing assignment.

This activity is very powerful and tends to influence students' beliefs about particular issues. It is possible to explore other socially useful topics in the context of teaching about attribution theory. For example, I have done this exercise to teach students about how attribution theory can be used to defend lesbians and gay men against discrimination. I tend to tread very carefully when organizing opposing groups on issues such as lesbian/gay rights or racism, given that students can be influenced by the group process to change or enhance their initial attributions. You can do this exercise without using the opposing-groups method. However, if you choose the opposing-sides method, depending on the circumstances, I suggest having students use the writing assignment to defend the alternative perspective.

REFERENCES AND SUGGESTED READING

Asch, S. E. (1946). Forming impressions of personality. *Journal of Personality and Social Psychology, 41,* 258–290.

Children's Defense Fund. (2005). *The state of America's children—Yearbook 2005.* Washington, DC: Author.

Jones, E. E., & Nisbett, R. E. (1971). The actor and the observer: Divergent perceptions of the causes of behavior. In E. E. Jones, D. E. Kanouse, H. H. Kelley, R. E. Nisbett, S. Valins, & B. Weiner (Eds.), *Attribution: Perceiving the causes of behavior* (pp. 79–94). Morristown, NJ: General Learning Press.

Jones, J. M., Levine, I. S., & Rosenberg, A. A. (Eds.). (1991). Homelessness [Special issue]. *American Psychologist, 46,* 1188–1207.

Kelley, H. H. (1967). Attribution theory in social psychology. In D. Levine (Ed.), *Nebraska Symposium on Motivation* (Vol. 15, pp. 192–240). Lincoln: University of Nebraska Press.

Miller, D. T, &. Ross, M. (1975). Self-serving biases in the attribution of causality: Fact or fiction? *Psychological Bulletin, 86,* 93–118.

Parker, E., & Spears, R. (Eds.). (1996). *Psychology and society: Radical theory and practice.* London: Pluto Press.

Ross, L. (1977). The intuitive psychologist and his shortcomings: Distortions in the attribution process. In L. Berkowitz (Ed.), *Advances in experimental social psychology,* (Vol. 10, pp. 173–220). New York: Academic Press.

Sherif, M., Harvey, O. J., White, B. J., Hood, W. R., & Sherif, C. W. (1961). *Inter-group conflict and cooperation: The Robbers Cave experiment.* Norman: University of Oklahoma Book Exchange.

Spurlock, J., & Robinowitz, C. B. (Eds.). (1990). *Women in context: Development and stresses.* New York: Plenum Press.

Storms, M. D. (1973). Videotape and the attribution process. Reversing actors' and observers' points of view. *Journal of Personality and Social Psychology, 27,* 165–175.

Sumner, W. G. (1906). *Folkways.* Boston: Ginn.

Appendix 61.1

Attribution Exercise, Version 1: Member of a Group of Homeless People

You are a group of homeless people who have just found out that the city of New York is planning to evict more than 5,000 of you from the subways during the winter, even during times of below-freezing weather. Because of the actions of other groups against this policy, a citywide hearing has been called during which both sides (the homeless people and their advocates and the city representatives and their advocates) will be called to testify. Your job is to show that the situation of homelessness needs remedy requiring building apartments and homes for homeless people, that the homeless are not just a bunch of crazy people who do not know better than to stay out of the cold, that homeless people are intelligent enough to speak for themselves and do not need others to speak for them, and that homelessness is a problem in many cities not because of a type of person called "homeless" but because of the severe economic crisis and resultant unemployment, gentrification (kicking out poor people to build high-income housing), and warehousing (keeping buildings empty when the market will not allow for high rents).

Use all that you have learned from attribution theory to make your case at this hearing, including (a) naive tendencies to look at consensus, distinctiveness, and consistency to determine attributions of causation, (b) fundamental attribution errors, (c) actor–observer effects, (d) self-serving bias and self-defeating bias, (e) impression formation for creating salience, (f) the power of creating a psychological perspective, and (g) the effects of power and status in creating attributions.

Appendix 61.2

Attribution Exercise, Version 2: Representative of New York City

You are representatives of New York City. Your administration has just enacted a policy of evicting the estimated 5,000 homeless people from the subways during the winter, including times when the weather is below freezing. Because of the actions of other groups against this policy, a citywide hearing has been called during which both sides (the homeless people and their advocates and the city representatives and their advocates) will be called to testify. Your job is to show that homeless people are mentally ill and that their occupation of the subways is creating problems for citizens of the city who want to go to work unoffended by the presence of people who beg, evade fares, and sleep in the subways. You advocate putting homeless people in shelters and have advanced a strategy of busing them systematically from the subways to the shelters during the winter months. You are to convince people at the hearing that homelessness results from a desire of people who do not want to sleep in shelters and who have voluntarily opted to sleep in the streets or subway stations, despite attempts to give them shelter. You are to advocate that the homeless create problems for businesses that want to attract customers to their stores, which is the more critical problem during this time of economic recession. Business must be picked up and the homeless are getting in the way.

Use all that you have learned from attribution theory to make your case at this hearing, including (a) naive tendencies to look at consensus, distinctiveness, and consistency to determine attributions of causation; (b) fundamental attribution errors; (c) actor–observer effects; (d) self-serving bias and self-defeating bias; (e) impression formation for creating salience; (f) the power of creating a psychological perspective; and (g) the effects of power and status in creating attributions.

Appendix 61.3

Directions for Writing Assignment

Your assignment is to write up your in-class exercise on the application of attribution theory to the issue of homelessness. The following is a general outline you might adopt:

> First state the problem; then describe how you went about solving it, beginning with an investigation of the literature on how attributions are made, including theories on our naive tendencies to determine causation on the basis of consensus, distinctiveness, and consistency. Then discuss the fundamental attribution errors we make that result in actor–observer effects and self-serving biases. Next go into the work on impression formation and other information from perception to show how salience is created, including the work showing how to create a psychological perspective. All of this research is to be put together to show how you influenced the citywide hearings to see the perspective of either homeless people or representatives of New York City regarding the evictions of homeless people from the subways.

Your essay is to be 3–4 pages in length, typed and double-spaced, and should follow APA style. Assume the naive reader, define your terms, and support your opinions and assertions with research.

CHAPTER 12
RACE, GENDER, AND MULTICULTURALISM

The activities in this chapter include explorations of prejudice and discrimination, sex-role stereotyping, and multicultural issues focusing on cultural differences. Whereas these activities are especially appropriate for units on ethnicity, gender, or culture, they also are well suited to units on social psychology, personality, developmental psychology, and abnormal psychology.

Activity 62 is a catalog of suggestions for places to teach about prejudice and discrimination throughout the introductory psychology course. It includes suggestions for lectures, discussion, and activities, all intended to integrate this important material more broadly in the course.

How are leaders selected for small groups? That's the question answered in Activity 63, which asks groups of four students (ideally two males and two females) to select a leader from their group prior to playing a game. The instructions given for the game indicates one of two kinds of games. In one game the goal is hard-fought competition; for the other the goal is cooperation and agreeing with one another. Can you guess the outcome of the leader selection?

Activities 64 and 65 could be considered companion pieces because both are on the subject of gender role socialization. In Activity 64, students are asked to visit a toy store or toy department of a store and write a report detailing their observations about gender messages in children's toys. Those reports are the basis for an interesting class discussion. Activity 65 asks students to visit the children's book section of a school library or public library, where they are to select 10 books at random. Information about those books is recorded according to instructions given to the students, and their data reports are brought to class for class discussion.

Multiculturalism is the theme for Activity 66, which exposes students to a variety of developmental experiences via reciprocal, cross-cultural interviews. The interviews focus on the concept of the social clock, a "culturally set timetable [that] establishes when various events and endeavors in life are appropriate" (Berger, 2001, p. 531). Conditions are described, based on the contact hypothesis, that ensure meaningful interviews. The results described by the authors detail several positive outcomes for the students who participate in what amounts to a real growth experience.

Activity 67 also explores multicultural issues using a role playing exercise of a family of three aliens whose spacecraft has landed in the United States and who are doing their best to assimilate into their new culture. Two students play the role of reporters who have been assigned to interview this novel family. This exercise often leads to discussions of discrimination, prejudice, acculturation, and communication styles. Further, the activity showcases some of the benefits and difficulties with naturalistic observation.

62 Teaching About Prejudice and Discrimination in the Introductory Psychology Course

Joseph I. Lamas
Cambridge Global Studies Academy
Miami Dade County Public Schools

This activity offers a variety of teaching suggestions to help students learn about the causes and effects of prejudice (attitudes and beliefs) and discrimination (behavior) based on those attitudes and beliefs at different points of the introductory psychology course. This material is of key importance in the course, and it can be taught with a minimum of class time or extra preparation, using topics that are included in most introductory psychology textbooks.

CONCEPT

Prejudice and discrimination are at the core of innumerable issues, problems, and interactions in everyday human behavior and as such should be an intrinsic part of the introductory psychology course. The desired pedagogical objective is the student's own analysis and internalization of what scientific psychology has to say about prejudice and discrimination. This understanding is a basic need in a multicultural, multiethnic society and in an increasingly global community.

MATERIALS NEEDED

No special materials are needed to implement any of the following teaching suggestions. Although more elaborate activities and demonstrations could be developed from the ideas provided, I have attempted to make the coverage of prejudice and discrimination as smooth and instructor friendly as possible.

INSTRUCTIONS

The following material is not really an activity, but a list of questions and statements grounded in psychological research that the instructor can use to help students achieve a greater understanding of prejudice and discrimination. There are many ways to apply the diverse suggestions offered. Whereas you may wish to devote 10 to 15 minutes to some questions, you may be content with 1 to 2 minutes for others. It is also possible, even desirable, to raise a question in the context of a lecture without providing an immediate answer. Discussion of possible answers may be assigned for a future class meeting, or it may become part of the writing component of the course. A written discussion of a question raised in lecture may be a most effective manner to proceed in many cases. Such assignments may be short but powerful learning experiences for most students.

In some cases, ideas are presented just for the use of the instructor, possibly to be included in a lecture. Often the points to be made are so simple and self-evident that they do not merit discussion or further analysis.

For most of the suggestions included, the core of the learning experience is asking the student to engage in critical thinking about the relationship between the topic under study and prejudice–discrimination. Your role as the instructor is to challenge the student with the relevance or implications of the topic under study as it relates to prejudice/discrimination and provide minimal assistance to the student as he or she attempts to develop the necessary relationships or implications.

Prejudice and discrimination are obviously sensitive and value-laden topics. When you want your class to discuss an issue, create an environment in which respect and acceptance prevail. Instruction devoid of values is a mirage. We do hold significant scientific, pedagogical, and human values that are part of our teaching persona. However, students should be made to understand that almost nobody willingly chooses to become prejudiced. Most of our attitudes and their consequent behaviors are given to us by influences and conditioning prior to our ability to analyze, decline, or reject particular information or learning experiences. Therefore, acceptance and understanding are necessary, particularly toward those students who may appear to be prejudiced.

Introductory Chapter

Education and training of a psychologist: Psychology as a profession is not keeping pace with the changing demographics of American society with regard to race and ethnicity. The introductory psychology course may be key in motivating students of all ethnic backgrounds to pursue psychology as a career. Ask students why an ethnically diverse profession of psychology is desirable. What might happen to psychology if its ethnic make up does not closely mirror that of the general population?

Research methods in psychology: Most theory building and research have focused on male nonminority Americans. To what extent are the results of this theory building and research applicable to other segments of the population? What about to other cultures? Note the Freud–Horney and Kohlberg–Gilligan controversies.

Biological Bases of Behavior

Dendritic branching: Laboratory research with rats has shown that dendrites develop more complex and intricate branching when subjects are exposed to enriched and variable external stimulation. What could this mean for many infants and children reared in deprived or limited socioeconomic environments? (An appreciation of the need to enrich every child's environment may be one of the most powerful outcomes of any introductory psychology course.)

Perception

Effect of organismic variables on perception: Human perceptions are not an accurate representation of stimulus variables. Rather, they represent the interplay of stimulus variables with such organismic variables as motivation, set, attitudes, interests, and memories. Learning plays a key role in this process. To what extent are perceptions of minority individuals and groups realistic? To what extent are our perceptions distorted by organismic variables?

Selective attention: How could selective attention affect the social perceptions of a Klan member? Of a misogynist?

Perceptual processes: How can perceptual processes such as perceptual constancy and perceptual organization affect prejudice?

Top-down processing: Explain the following in terms of the acquisition and maintenance of prejudice and give appropriate examples related to prejudice or discrimination. (a) Perceptual set: The perceiver has some kind of perceptual readiness, or expectancy—that is, the observer is *set* to perceive something. (b) Schemas: All information is processed and fit into the individual's schema, distorting the input when necessary to make it fit. (c) A Chinese proverb states, "We see what is behind our eyes" (i.e., what is already in our minds); today, we call it the effect of expectation on perception. What does a racist, sexist, or homophobe perceive that may be different from someone else's perception?

Learning

Classical conditioning: How can prejudice be learned through the contiguity or contingency models of classical conditioning? Ask students to think of examples.

Instrumental learning: How can prejudice be learned through instrumental or operant conditioning? Ask students to think of examples.

Schedules of reinforcement: Variable ratio and variable interval schedules of reinforcement are particularly resistant to extinction. What does this mean when applied to the attitudes or behavior of a prejudiced individual?

Learned helplessness: Can we better understand the behavior of certain individuals who are members of oppressed groups by applying the concept of learned helplessness?

Reinforcement-induced stereotypy: Can society at large better understand (not necessarily accept) the aggressive behavior of minority gang members by applying the concept of reinforcement-induced stereotypy (the tendency to follow a previous pattern of responses that has produced consistent rewards)?

Observational learning: In what settings are we most likely to learn prejudice and discrimination through the process of observational learning? Ask students to think of examples.

Memory

Episodic memory: Would a negative personal experience have a disproportionate effect on the creation of prejudice?

Reconstructive memory: As nonminority members remember past events regarding minority individuals or groups, are they likely to retrieve only the factual details from long-term memory or are they likely to combine the factual memories with items that seem to fit the occasion?

Thought and Language

Defining attribute: In a prejudiced individual, what could be the defining attributes for a Black, Hispanic, Asian, Native American, or woman? Once these defining attributes are developed, what effect will they have on our perception of reality?

Basic-level categories: Is Black or African American, as applied to race, a basic level or a subordinate category? Categories at the basic level are easy to differentiate and members of a basic-level category are easily classified even with only visual information.

Basic-level categories appear to be the first categories learned in life. If *Blackness* is a basic-level category, what impact does this have on the possible formation of prejudice?

Misuse of availability heuristics: Are more crimes committed by Blacks or Whites? Do Blacks commit more crimes of aggression than crimes that involve no aggression? Do Whites commit more or fewer white-collar crimes? The mere availability of partial information and not of other, complementary information could lead us to wrong answers.

Language development: Universal adaptability refers to the capacity of all human babies to make the same sounds and acquire the phonemes of any language. They begin to lose this plasticity after 1 year of age. What does this mean regarding the nature versus nurture controversy as it relates to language behavior of different national, cultural, or social groups? What does this mean regarding the oneness of the human species?

Sexism and language: What effects does male-oriented, gender-biased language have on the development of the self-concept of females? Could gender-biased language contribute to perpetuating stereotypical expectations of behavior for both sexes?

Human Development

Piaget's cognitive theory: According to Piaget, prior to the formal-operations stage (adolescence and adulthood), humans are not able to engage in abstract, hypothetical, or deductive thinking. Does this mean that up to that point we are more at the mercy of family and societal conditioning with respect to the development of prejudicial attitudes?

Peer interactions: What situations affecting prejudice and discrimination may develop as a result of the increased importance of peer pressure during adolescence?

Kohlberg's stages of moral judgment: What racial, ethnic, or sexist attitudes are individuals likely to internalize as part of their moral schemas prior to the development of Level III (the postconventional, or principled, level)? If Kohlberg is correct in indicating that not many people reach Level III, what does this mean in terms of dealing with the problems of prejudice and discrimination in our society?

Sex differences in moral judgment: Did Kohlberg (or Freud, Erikson, or Piaget) persistently misrepresent women by using male filters to interpret information and build theory? Carol Gilligan, Karen Horney, and others would say yes.

Erikson's psychosocial theory: What special problems might members of oppressed minority groups have when reaching the industry versus inferiority stage (age 6 to puberty) and the identity versus role-confusion stage (adolescence).

Motivation and Emotion

Cognitive dissonance theory: When an individual experiences thoughts, attitudes, or beliefs that are dissonant (inconsistent) with the individual's behavior, a stressful, psychologically uncomfortable state predominates. This motivates the individual to try to reconcile the existing discrepancies, achieve consonance, and diminish stress. How can this phenomenon facilitate or hinder the development and maintenance of prejudicial attitudes or discriminatory behavior?

Achievement motivation: What effect could perceived prejudice against yourself have on the interplay between the tendencies to achieve success and avoid failure?

Affiliation motivation: In a school in which 90% of the students are White, what effect could the environment have on the affiliation motive of minority students?

Universality of emotional facial expression: What does this mean regarding the sameness or differentiation of human beings around the world?

Development of fear and anxiety: What effect could lack of familiarity with someone from a different ethnic or cultural group have on the development of fear or anxiety toward that group?

Personality

Freud's psychosexual theory: To what extent are Freudian stages of development applicable to women? What criticism does Karen Horney have of Freudian theory?

Personality differences: Are some personality types more likely to become prejudiced than others? How can we help students who possess a so-called authoritarian or prejudiced personality deal with the extra risks they bear? (See Allport, 1954.)

Psychological Assessment

Test construction and standardization: Most psychological tests are normed on a White, middle-class standardization sample. To what extent can those tests be applied validly to members of a population that was not included in the standardization sample?

Examiner effects: What does the research show about the effects of male versus female examiners on test performance of males and females? Ask the same question for examiners who are White versus those from various ethnic minorities.

Race and IQ testing: Can we fully separate nature from nurture factors as we try to compare Black and White IQ scores? "To attribute racial differences to genetic factors granted the overwhelming cultural–environmental differences between races is to compound folly with malice" (Kamin, 1974, p. 7).

Culture and psychological testing: Some psychological tests are described as "culture-free" or "culture-fair." Are they? How are such tests constructed?

Health, Stress, and Coping

Addictive behaviors and health: To what extent does the socioeconomic environment of the inner city affect substance abuse and substance dependence?

Sources of stress: If we compare the average upper-class suburbanite with the average inner-city resident on Holmes and Rahe's (1967) list of life change events, what differences would we be likely to find? How valid would that list be in assessing the sources of stress for high school or college students?

Coping with stress: To what extent are the usual avenues to cope with stress (e.g., support groups, relaxation training, meditation, biofeedback, etc.) available to low-socioeconomic-level minorities?

Abnormal Psychology and Treatment

The sociological model of abnormality: Some conditions, such as depression, are "more common among people in lower socioeconomic groups and among women, perhaps because they have fewer options for dealing with the stress of daily living" (Benjamin, Hopkins, & Nation, 1994, p. 639).

Availability of treatment: Given that approximately one third of all persons in the United States will suffer some type of acute mental illness in their lifetime, what is the likelihood of a poor male or female finding adequate mental health treatment if he or she cannot pay for it and has no health insurance?

Deinstitutionalization: What is the relationship between deinstitutionalization and homelessness in America? Does racial prejudice play a role in our society's ability to deal effectively with this problem?

Therapist variables in treatment: Is the field of psychology recruiting and maintaining sufficient numbers of Blacks, Hispanics, Asians, and other minorities to supply much-needed services to these groups and to their expected growth in America in the twenty-first century? According to the American Psychological Association (APA), psychology as a profession is not doing well in recruiting minorities into the discipline (APA, 1997).

Social Psychology

Attitude formation: People are not born with a set of attitudes; those attitudes are learned via the principles of learning.

Attitude change and persuasion: Attitude change is possible when the communicator is perceived as a credible expert who is likable and the message is not very different from the listener's own position.

Fundamental attribution error: People are more likely to make personal attributions than situational attributions when evaluating other people's unacceptable behavior. (If he's poor and has no job, it's because he's lazy.) Does the society at large often think in this manner about members of minority groups?

The self-fulfilling prophecy in education: Teacher's expectations for their students' performance can have a very strong effect on what students do in the classroom, as well as on the ways teachers evaluate student performance. Do we relate in the same manner and expect as much from Blacks, Hispanics, and other ethnic groups as we do from Whites? Elementary students tend to perform better when they are expected to. This Pygmalion effect is reached by teachers creating a warmer verbal and nonverbal climate, teaching more material, interacting more, giving more differentiated feedback, and not accepting low-quality responses (see the movie *Stand and Deliver,* based on the true story of a high school math teacher, Jaime Escalante, who set high expectations for his students and helped them reach those lofty goals).

Deindividuation: "An individual in a group may become so caught up that he or she loses a sense of individual responsibility, and a kind of mob psychology takes over" (Benjamin et al., 1994, p. 564). Can this help us understand behavior during riot situations?

Conformity: How much of a student's prejudice and discrimination is an attempt to adopt the social norms or attitudes of a reference group or of the society at large?

Stereotypes: Are we aware of our own stereotypes? Why do we use stereotypes, that is, what functions do they serve? What stereotypes do others have of us? Are they valid? Are the stereotypes we hold of others any more valid? If we allow ourselves to maintain stereotypes of others, do we in fact give permission to others to hold stereotypes of us?

Development of racial prejudice: Children appear not to be sensitive to racial differences until they reach 4 or 5 years of age. Why are children not sensitive to racial differences before that age?

How easy is it to develop prejudice? Jane Elliot's third-grade class at Ricefield Community Elementary School in Iowa made "blue eyes" smarter and superior to "brown eyes," creating differentiation and segregation. The students placed in the role of superiors changed their behavior more, and the others developed instant hate against the teacher for being assigned to an inferior group. "Those who are seen as inferior and those who are seen as superior feel and act accordingly" (Zimbardo, 1990). What do we learn from this demonstration? Discuss why it would be considered unethical to repeat this demonstration today.

Reducing prejudice and discrimination: Contact alone is not enough. Ask students to discuss conditions that might achieve productive integration in American society.

Superordinate goals: The introduction of goals that are important to both groups but that could only be attained if they cooperated can lead to reduced intergroup conflict. Can we structure this into our teaching by using cooperative learning groups?

Ethnocentrism: Ethnocentrism is the belief that one's own group—especially racial, ethnic, or national group—is superior. How does ethnocentrism affect self-esteem?

Industrial–Organizational Psychology

The following observations and comments are derived from the author's 15 years of experience in major American corporations and in different industrial sectors (transportation, heavy industry, food distribution, and financial services), prior to moving into education:

Discrimination in hiring: Stereotypical views of women's ability and corporate roles are still alive and well. "Good ol' boys" in charge of most major corporations have internalized the values and expectations of their predecessors. The perspective that "We will hire as many Blacks and minorities as it takes to stay out of trouble with the government or the media" still exists. Can students find evidence in the media of how prejudice or stereotyping affects employment?

Discrimination in promotions: Women, Blacks, Hispanics, and other minorities are often accepted in the corporate structure up to the middle-management level; beyond that, they are suspect in ability and style. Women are often expected to masculinize in the process, and yet are often criticized for being "too masculine." What is seen as competitiveness in men is seen as aggression in women. Ask students about the concept of the "glass ceiling."

Plight of ethnic minority managers: Ethnic minority managers know that it is probable that superiors as well as subordinates have racist attitudes. Hence they tend to distrust subordinates and superiors until proven trustworthy, and are extra careful and conservative in most organizational climates. This distrust interferes with everyday management functions such as delegating, motivating, and monitoring progress. The cut-throat climate of many corporations adds to the insecurity and sense of alienation. How does a concept such as self-fulfilling prophecy work in such environments?

Some Final Thoughts

> The teaching of psychology implies a special social responsibility. The understanding of human learning, cognitive and moral development, attitude formation, etc. . . . can have a profound effect on the creation of a world where understanding replaces prejudice, acceptance takes the place of discrimination, and social justice prevails over oppression. Because knowledge of psychology has an especially powerful potential to bring about a better future, teachers must embrace this special responsibility and commit to the teaching of these critically important goals (from the mission statement of the Committee on Ethnic and Minority Affairs of Teachers of Psychology in Secondary School, an APA affiliate).

If you now have a feeling that it is impossible to do justice to all the possibilities for teaching about prejudice and discrimination in the introductory course, remember that it is not necessary to hammer the message home too often. We know what our students can take before their attitudes turn negative toward the message. Pick and choose those areas that you are comfortable with, add your own, and join an increasing group of teachers who are making the teaching of psychology not only scientifically solid but humanly and socially valuable.

REFERENCES AND SUGGESTED READING

Adorno, T. W. (1993). *The authoritarian personality.* New York: Norton.

Allport, G. W. (1954). *The nature of prejudice.* Reading, MA: Addison Wesley.

American Psychological Association. (1997). *Visions and transformation—The final report.* Washington, DC: Author.

Baird, R. M., & Rosenbarum, S. E. (Eds.). (1992). *Bigotry, prejudice and hatred: Definitions, causes, and solutions.* Buffalo, NY: Prometheus.

Benjamin, L. T., Jr., Hopkins, J. R., &. Nation, J. R. (1994). *Psychology* (3rd ed.). New York: Macmillan.

Bronstein, P., & Quina, K. (Eds.). (2003). *Teaching gender and multicultural awareness.* Washington, DC: American Psychological Association.

Clark, K. B. (1963). *Prejudice and your child* (2nd ed.). Boston: Beacon Press.

Dovido, J. R., &. Gaertner, S. L. (Eds.). (1986). *Prejudice, discrimination, and racism.* Orlando, FL: Academic Press.

Gilligan, C. (1982). *In a different voice: Psychological theory and women's development.* Cambridge, MA: Harvard University Press.

Gioseffi, D. (1993). *On prejudice: A global perspective.* New York: Anchor Books.

Herek, G. M. (Ed.). (1998). *Stigma and sexual orientation: Understanding prejudice against lesbians, gay men and bisexuals.* Thousand Oaks, CA: Sage.

Holland, J. (2006). *Misogyny: The world's oldest prejudice.* New York: Carroll and Graf.

Holmes, T. H., & Rahe, R. H. (1967). The Social Readjustment Rating Scale. *Journal of Psychosomatic Research, 11,* 213–218.

Jones, J. M. (1997). *Prejudice and racism* (2nd ed.). New York: McGraw-Hill.

Joshi, S. T. (Ed.). (2006). *In her place: A documentary history of prejudice against women.* Amherst, NY: Prometheus.

Kamin, L. J. (1974). *The science and politics of I.Q.* Hillsdale, NJ: Lawrence Erlbaum.

Lerner, R. M. (1992). *Final solutions: Biology, prejudice and genocide.* University Park, Pennsylvania State University Press.

Matsumoto, D., & Juang, L. (2003). *Culture and psychology* (3rd ed.). Belmont, CA: Thomson Wadsworth.

Nagayama Hall, G. C., & Barongan, C. (2001). *Multicultural psychology.* Upper Saddle River, NJ: Prentice Hall.

Sachs, M. (2006). *First impressions.* New Milford, CT: Roaring Brook Press.

Stem-La Rosa, C. (2000). *The Anti-Defamation League's hate hurts: How children learn and unlearn prejudice.* New York: Scholastic.

Waller, J. (2000). *Prejudice across America.* Jackson: University of Mississippi Press.

Zanna, M. P., & Olson, J. M. (Eds.). (1993). *The psychology of prejudice: The Ontario Symposium* (Vol. 7). Hillsdale, NJ: Erlbaum.

Zimbardo, P. (1990). *Discovering psychology.* [Video series]. Burlington, VT: The Annenberg/CPB Project.

63 GENDER BIAS IN LEADER SELECTION
Michelle R. Hebl
Rice University

This activity, which requires minimal preparation, illustrates how stereotypes can result in biased leader selection. It is appropriate for classes in introductory psychology, psychology of gender/women, industrial/ organizational psychology, and social psychology. It is an easy in-class activity to conduct that requires approximately 20 minutes of class time, involves all students, and is best demonstrated in larger size classes that include both male and female students.

CONCEPT

This demonstration illustrates the potential behavioral ramifications of gender stereotyping and the notion that gender stereotyping may have a differential impact on leader selection when type of leadership is manipulated. Specifically, students are placed in initially leaderless mixed gender groups and asked to select leaders for a competitive or cooperative group activity. Overall, a disproportionate number of men are selected as leaders, substantiating the idea that gender stereotypes guide individuals in selecting leaders. The bias is strong in competitive groups, but weak in socially cooperative groups. Provocative discussion questions that address these findings are included.

MATERIALS NEEDED

You will need two sets of written instructions, one describing the task-oriented competitive task and the other describing the social cooperative task. Each student in the class will get a written copy of one set of the instructions, so you will need to make as many copies as there are students.

INSTRUCTIONS

Divide students into groups of four or six, each composed of an equal number of men and women. If your class is lopsided with more women than men, ensure that at least one man is in every group and do this in a way that does not seem obvious—if there are groups that contain only one gender, these groups should be discarded in the analysis. If possible, students should not know other members of their group because previous direct experience may override the heuristics of gender stereotyping and weaken the effects of the demonstration. Thus it might be best to use this activity at the beginning of a course.

The demonstration should be used before students read about gender stereotypes and group dynamics. The activity can be introduced as a "psychology game." Distribute written instructions describing the group task to each member of each group, otherwise the person receiving or reading the instructions might be chosen or accepted as the leader. Each group receives multiple copies of **one** of two sets of instructions.

Task-Oriented Competitive

Give students the following instructions:

> You will be playing a board game with your group. The board game involves competition against another group and you will focus on specific tasks. Try your hardest to win the game. To do this, focus on the game's objectives as

much as possible. To start, your group should first select a person who will be in charge of the group. After this leader is selected, I will give you specific instructions about the game and you will start playing.

Social-Oriented Cooperative

Give students the following instructions:

> You will be playing a board game with your group. The board game does not involve winning but instead involves agreeing with each other, supporting one another, and setting aside differences to get along maximally with each other. To start, your group should first select a person who will be in charge of the group. After this leader is selected, I will give you specific instructions about the game and you will start playing.

Playing the Game

Students take 2 minutes to read their instructions and select group leaders. Groups are not specifically instructed about how to select leaders. Any method of nomination and selection is acceptable as long as all group members ultimately agree on the leader.

After verifying that leaders for each group have been chosen, inform the groups that they will not play a game after all. Instead, the actual purpose of the activity was to examine leader selection and processes. Compile a list that specifies the gender of those students chosen as task-oriented and social leaders. Then you or a student volunteer can record both the gender of the leader selected as well as the technique each group used in selecting its leader.

DISCUSSION This activity was derived from past research, which shows that men are significantly more likely to be chosen as leaders than women in initially leaderless, mixed-gender groups (Eagly & Karau, 1991, 2002; see also Kellerman & Rhode, 2007). Gender stereotypes about leadership likely play a large role in influencing these findings. For example, men are more likely than women to be perceived as able to "separate feelings from ideas," "act as leaders," and "make decisions" (Broverman, Vogel, Broverman, Clarkson, & Rosenkrantz, 1972). These and other stereotypically masculine items have been positively correlated with college students' perceptions of leaders (Lord, De Vader, & Alliger, 1986). Eagly and Mladinic (1989) proposed that gender stereotypes also are composed of beliefs that men occupy advantaged social positions of power and status relative to women. Such views lead us to perceive men as more in control and powerful than women, even when they are not. Indeed, research by Porter, Geis, and Jennings (1983) has revealed that given an ambiguous setting involving both men and women, independent raters perceive men to be in charge much more often than women.

Stereotypes about women may also enhance biases in leader selection (Geis, Brown, Jennings, & Corrado-Taylor, 1984; Nye & Forsyth, 1991). Geis, Brown, Jennings, and Porter (1984) suggested that the most general stereotype about women is that they are not autonomous and are unqualified to assume achievement-oriented responsibilities in the world. However, women, relative to men, are believed to be more "talkative," "tactful," and "aware of others' feelings" (Broverman et al., 1972) and more expressive and communal (Eagly & Mladinic, 1989).

Gender stereotyping has a differential impact on leader selection when type of leadership is manipulated (Eagly & Karau, 1991). Whereas task-oriented competitive leaders focus on task contributions and productivity, social cooperative leaders focus on social contributions, prosocial behavior, and social climate. Male group members make more task-oriented contributions than do females (Wood, 1987), so males may be chosen as leaders in task-oriented competitive situations more often than they are chosen as social leaders. By contrast, social leaders may focus on prosocial behaviors, and therefore females may be selected as social leaders more often than they are selected as task-oriented competitive leaders.

The results obtained from this demonstration can be compared with Hebl's (1994) results indicating that, overall, leadership positions were most likely to be filled by men, especially under task-oriented (competitive) conditions in which the ratio of male to female leaders was nearly 4 to 1. Eagly and Karau (1991) suggested that as leadership goals change from a position that requires task-oriented behaviors to one requiring socially complex tasks or the maintenance of good interpersonal relations and group harmony, slightly more women than men emerge as leaders, a trend also visible in Hebl's study (1994; see Table 63.1).

In sum, this classroom activity produces reliable and provocative effects that should make students more cognizant of gender stereotypes and their effects on leader selection. Class discussion after the activity could be stimulated by the following questions:

1. How was the selection procedure determined? Did men or women more commonly nominate themselves? Which gender was more commonly nominated by other group members? What were the common procedures used in selecting leaders? In Hebl's (1994) study, students' descriptions of their selection process included "He was chosen because he was the tallest . . . he looked like he should be in charge," "I knew from the beginning he would be the leader—he just looked the part," and "The two women in our group asked him to be the leader."
2. What stereotypes were used in selecting leaders? When and why are stereotypes about men and women likely to influence leader selection? Are these stereotypes used when the groups meet for longer periods of time?
3. What were the possible causes for the bias against female leaders? In everyday life, we witness more men than women as leaders; how might that affect leader selection? Do women avoid leadership positions? When women become leaders, how are they typically viewed in comparison with men?
4. What gender differences result when the task becomes one in which a social leader is required? Does the gender bias disappear? If so, why?

Table 63.1.   *Number of Leaders Selected by Gender and Instructions*

	Gender		
	Men	Women	Total
Type of instruction	Observed/expected		
Task-oriented	40/32.2	11/18.8	51
Social	25/32.8	27/19.2	52
Total	65	38	103

Note. Results from M. R. Hebl (1994).

One possible variation of the current demonstration is to assign groups to either feminine or masculine gender-typed activities. For instance, one group might be told to choose a leader for a discussion of the use of cloth versus disposable diapers for babies. The other group's discussion topic could be the choice of repairing cars at home with the guidance of manuals and friends versus taking the car to a repair shop. The visibility of stereotypes should be demonstrated as women are selected more often when the task is feminine gender-typed and men when the task is masculine gender-typed. In both cases, gender stereotypes guide individuals in their selection of leaders.

REFERENCES AND SUGGESTED READING

Broverman, I. K., Vogel, S. R., Broverman, D. M., Clarkson, F. E., & Rosenkrantz, P. S. (1972). Sex-role stereotypes: A current appraisal. *Journal of Social Issues, 28,* 59–78.

Eagly, A. H., & Karau, S. J. (1991). Gender and the emergence of leaders. *Journal of Personality and Social Psychology, 60,* 685–710.

Eagly, A. H., & Karau, S. J. (2002). Role congruity theory of prejudice toward female leaders. *Psychological Review, 109,* 573–598.

Eagly, A. H., & Mladinic, A. (1989). Gender stereotypes and attitudes toward women and men. *Personality and Social Psychology Bulletin, 15,* 543–558.

Geis, F. L., Brown, V., Jennings, J., & Corrado-Taylor, D. (1984). Sex versus status in sex-associated stereotypes. *Sex Roles, 11,* 771–785.

Geis, F. L., Brown, V., Jennings, J., & Porter, N. (1984). TV commercials as achievement scripts for women. *Sex Roles, 10,* 513–524.

Hebl, M. R. (1994). Gender bias in leader selection. *Teaching of Psychology, 22,* 186–188.

Kellerman, B., & Rhode, D. L. (2007). *Women and leadership: The state of play and strategies for change.* San Francisco: Jossey Bass.

Lord, R. G., De Vader, D. I., & Alliger, G. M. (1986). A meta-analysis of the relation between personality traits and leadership perceptions: An application of validity generalization procedures. *Journal of Applied Psychology, 71,* 402–410.

Nye, J. L., & Forsyth, D. R. (1991). The effects of prototype-based biases on leadership appraisals: A test of leadership categorization theory. *Small Group Research, 22,* 360–379.

Porter, N., Geis, F. L., & Jennings, J. W. (1983). Are women invisible as leaders? *Sex Roles, 9,* 1035–1049.

Wood, W. (1987). Meta-analytic review of sex differences in group performance. *Psychological Bulletin, 102,* 53–71.

64 GENDER MESSAGES IN TOYS: AN OUT-OF-CLASS PROJECT

Margaret A. Lloyd
Georgia Southern University

This activity requires students to visit a toy department and write a report summarizing their observations regarding gender messages in children's toys. The activity is appropriate for any course level, from high school through undergraduate, and any size class can participate, depending on how many papers you want to read. The only materials needed for the project are an instruction sheet outlining the assignment. After students have submitted their papers, you can generate an interesting discussion by asking students to share their observations and their perspectives on gender messages in children's toys. This exercise can be used in courses in introductory psychology, developmental psychology, and the psychology of sex and gender.

CONCEPT

The purpose of this project is to make students aware of an important aspect of gender-role socialization, namely, the presence of gender-role stereotypes in children's toys. Children's play constitutes an important arena in which beliefs are developed at a very young age about the appropriateness of certain behaviors for the two sexes (Miller, Trautner, & Ruble, 2006).

MATERIALS NEEDED

Students will need a handout to complete this out-of-class activity. You can easily construct one by combining relevant portions of the Concept and Instructions sections.

INSTRUCTIONS

Ask students to visit a toy store (or the toy section in a department store) that has a relatively wide range of toys. Once in the store, they are to survey the toys and make general observations that will permit them to respond to the questions listed below under "Results—General Observations."

After students have completed their general observations, they should select three toys that they believe exemplify *each* of the following categories: girls' toys, boys' toys, and gender-neutral toys (nine toys altogether).

As each of the nine toys is selected, students should note the specific features of the toys that caught their eye and motivated them to list the toy in one of the three categories.

Students should be instructed to pay particular attention to toys in packages because they are likely to have pictures, labels, or advertising messages that can be analyzed for gender stereotypes. For example, does a chemistry set or doctor kit have a picture of a boy on the front and either no girl or a girl in the background?

Students should summarize their observations in writing in the following format:

Introduction. Briefly explain the purpose of the project (¼ page).

Method. Briefly describe the steps you used in conducting the project. Also include the location of the toy store and a brief description of the toy department (number and length of display shelves and whether the toys were organized by gender and/or age) (½ page).

Results—General Observations. Respond to the following questions, based on all of your observations: (a) Did gender stereotyping occur more often in toys for a particular age range? (b) Was it common that boys' and girls' toys were related to adult roles (and, therefore, serve as vehicles of gender stereotyping)? (c) Were there many gender-neutral toys relative to the number of boys' and girls' toys? (d) What were the two most common themes (e.g., aggression) among boys' toys? (e) What were the two most common themes (e.g., housekeeping) among girls' toys (1–2 pages)?

Results—Specific Observations. Describe your findings on the nine toys you selected. Organize the toys into the categories of girls' toys, boys' toys, and gender-neutral toys and use the following page format. Use three columns. In the left-hand column, list three girls', three boys', and three gender-neutral toys. In the middle column, briefly describe the advertising features of each toy. In the right-hand column, state the explicit and implicit gender messages for the prospective buyers/users (see example below; 2–3 pages).

Girls' Toys	Description of Package and Advertising Features	Gender Messages
1. Doll	Girl (only) on package with doll; pastel colors	This toy is only for girls; only girls are interested in babies

Discussion. (a) Did you find what you expected to find or were you surprised? (b) Select any "girls' toy" and any "boys' toy" and suggest how they could be made gender-neutral.

DISCUSSION

After students have turned in their papers, it is easy to generate a lively discussion about the similarities and differences in their observations and on their views of the implications of their observations.

REFERENCES AND SUGGESTED READING

Miller, C. F., Trautner, H. M., & Ruble, D. N. (2006). The role of gender stereotypes in children's preferences and behavior. In L. Balter & C. S. Tamis-LeMonda (Eds.), *Child psychology: A handbook of contemporary issues* (2nd ed., pp. 293–323). New York: Psychology Press.

Raag, T. (1999). Influences of social expectations of gender, gender stereotypes, and situational constraints on children's toy choices. *Sex Roles, 41,* 809–831

Wood, E., Desmarais, S., & Gugula, S. (2002). The impact of parenting experience on gender stereotyped play of children. *Sex Roles, 47,* 39–49.

65 Sex Role Stereotyping in Children's Books

Lita Linzer Schwartz
Pennsylvania State University

This activity focuses on how young children acquire gender stereotypes from books. It is appropriate for courses in introductory psychology, and also for courses in developmental psychology, educational psychology, and psychology of women. Students will need to spend perhaps an hour outside of class doing research in a school or public library, and, with the aid of a simple form, should be able to discuss, in class, gender stereotyping and also apply the format to other forms of stereotyping. This activity is appropriate for any size class, although the discussion component would make it difficult to accomplish in very large classes.

CONCEPT Stereotypes are oversimplified generalizations about people in a particular category, whether race, country of origin, ethnicity, age, religion, or gender. This activity focuses on stereotyping by gender. Different cultures define femininity and masculinity in different ways, ascribing (and sometimes *prescribing*) roles and behaviors to each. These presumably gender-appropriate roles are taught to children in varied ways, from direct instruction to modeling. If females are constantly taught that they have fewer skills than males, or that they are limited to certain adult roles, then girls will grow up with lowered self-esteem and aspirations. If boys are constantly taught that they need to be aggressive and competitive to prove their masculinity, or that they must not show emotional reactions, or both, they are likely to grow up with lowered sensitivity to others. If children are shown, through parental modeling, children's books, or television stories, that adventure and curiosity are the exclusive province of boys and passivity is the role for girls, the potential negative effects will be seen in their personalities, academic performance, adult behaviors, and other areas as they mature. Conflict is also created when either a boy or girl prefers behavior or roles ascribed to the other gender. Does the individual try to impress others as being an "ideal" or "typical" male or female regardless of his or her personal traits or preferences?

MATERIALS NEEDED Students should have access to a local library that has a children's book section. They might also find it useful to have a simple form that indicates decade of publication and allows the student to check off whether the leading characters are male or female, the nature of characters' activities, whether these are stereotypical of boys or of girls, and whether adults shown are engaged in stereotypical roles.

INSTRUCTIONS Ask students to choose 10 books at random from the picture book section of the library (e.g., the Golden Books series). Have them look at both the illustrations and the text in each book and answer the following questions: (a) Who are the leading characters in the story? (b) How do you know? (c) What are the leading characters doing in the story? (d) Are the characters doing things that are more typical of one gender or the other? (i.e., Are boys being active in sports or girls seen playing with dolls, in the kitchen, etc.)

If women are shown, are they in stereotypical roles (e.g., housewife, teacher, nurse, secretary)? (e) Are there examples of characters portrayed in roles opposite to those typically assigned to that gender? Students may wish to look for books published in different decades, such as in the 1960s, 1980s, and in the current decade, to see whether any change is apparent. They should note author, title, and copyright/publication date (original, and latest if the book is a reprint).

DISCUSSION

Several questions can be raised during the discussion, such as the following: (a) What messages do the characters and story line convey to girls and boys about gender roles in American society? (b) Do these reflect contemporary reality or traditional stereotyping? (c) Are there differences between the earlier and the more recently published books with regard to gender stereotypes?

Supplementary activities: A similar survey may be made of history texts used in elementary and secondary schools, allowing students to compare the apparent versus the actual role of women in history.

Students could also survey Saturday morning children's cartoons or after-school features, sitcoms, and magazine advertising for indications of gender-role stereotyping. If the TV option is chosen, refer students to articles in the *Journal of Broadcasting* (now the *Journal of Broadcasting & Electronic Media*), beginning about 1978, as well as articles in various APA journals.

If students compare books from different decades, they are likely to find that there was some move away from rigid stereotyping beginning in the mid-1970s, although some continues to exist. If they survey history texts, they are likely to find that there are still limited references to women or to women's contributions. If they work with the television activity, they will probably find a wide variety of perspectives, although the sitcoms appear to derive at least some of their "humor" from stereotyping and from inept (if any) attempts to overcome it.

At the very least, students should come away from these activities with a greater awareness of and sensitivity to gender stereotyping. Some students may perceive the general injustice of stereotyping. Others may become more aware of alternative behaviors and goals that they had previously thought closed to them because of their gender. Still others may become alert to the effects of modeling and other forms of socialization on the personal, social, and intellectual development of children.

REFERENCES
AND
SUGGESTED
READING

Barner, M. R. (1999). Sex-role stereotyping in FCC-mandated children's educational television. *Journal of Broadcasting & Electronic Media, 43,* 551–564.

Diekman, A. B., & Murnen, S. K. (2004). Learning to be little women and little men: The inequitable gender equality of nonsexist children's literature. *Sex Roles, 50,* 73–385.

Gooden, A. M., & Gooden, M. A. (2001). Gender representation in notable children's picture books: 1995–1999. *Sex Roles, 45,* 89–101.

Hamilton, M. C., Anderson, D., Broaddus, M., & Young, K. (2006). Gender stereotyping and under-representation of female characters in 200 popular children's picture books: A twenty-first century update. *Sex Roles, 55,* 757–765.

Roberts, L. C., & Hill, H. T. (2003). Come and listen to a story about a girl named Rex: Using children's literature to debunk gender stereotypes. *Young Children, 58*(2), 39–42.

Taylor, F. (2003). Content analysis and gender stereotypes in children's books. *Teaching Sociology, 31,* 300–311.

66 THE CONTACT HYPOTHESIS: INTERVIEWING ACROSS CULTURES

Pat A. Bradway
Siena College

Sarah Atchley
Berkshire Community College

This multicultural classroom activity, based on the model of the contact hypothesis, demonstrates the concept of the social clock and promotes the exchange of information among psychology students and students of different cultural backgrounds. It is appropriate for classes in developmental psychology, social psychology, or to demonstrate developmental or social psychology topics in introductory psychology classes. The activity is intended as an in-class activity involving all students for classes of approximately 20 students. For larger classes see suggested adaptations of the exercise. Students develop an understanding of the diversity of human experience through the investigation of culturally determined social clocks, a developmental concept, and of the contact hypothesis as a model of optimal conditions for intergroup contact. The activity consists of reciprocal interviews and culminates in a brief writing exercise.

CONCEPT

Western psychology is often confused with universal experience. The activity described is designed to expose students to the variety of experiences in development through cross-cultural interviews. This application bases the interviews on the concept of the social clock, a "culturally set timetable [that] establishes when various events and endeavors in life are appropriate" (Berger, 2005, p. 531). To ensure successful interviews, the guidelines of the contact hypothesis as described by Amir (1976) and Norvell and Worchel (1981) are followed: equal status and participation, an intimate setting, and support.

MATERIALS NEEDED

You will need handouts of previously developed interview questions, a large enough classroom to accommodate many small groups, moveable furniture, a world map, and refreshments. The participation of an organized group of culturally diverse students, such as an English as a second language (ESL) class, an international students' organization, or an intercultural club is also necessary.

INSTRUCTIONS

This activity requires prior collaboration between the psychology instructor and the instructor/advisor/leader of the international students. In preparation, students in both the psychology class and the multicultural group develop a set of questions about social clocks to elicit information about the timing of life events for adults in different cultures. Typical questions developed by students include the following:

- At what age is it considered acceptable to begin dating in your country?
- Is that age the same for both men and women?
- When are young people expected to be self-supporting and to live on their own?
- At what age do people marry?

Ten questions is a manageable number. The question sets are exchanged before the groups meet, allowing preparation time for students less proficient in English or less knowledgeable about psychological concepts.

The international students and the psychology class combine for a single class meeting. After brief introductions and refreshments, assign students to small groups—ideally made up of two international students and two psychology students. Cultural background, language proficiency, and gender are other important factors to attend to in the composition of groups. Once in small groups, students interview each other using the questions they previously developed but allowing for related digressions. Encourage the students to take notes. At this stage faculty intervention is minimal, although the presence of instructors in the classroom keeps the interviews focused and ensures everyone's participation.

The classroom is typically somewhat quiet at first; however, the volume quickly increases. Although changing the makeup of groups would increase exposure to more cultural variations, it is not advisable unless the class period is especially lengthy. In our experience, students are still on task and content in their original groups after 50 minutes of discussion. It takes time to establish a level of comfort that allows for an exchange of information.

Four conditions based on the contact hypothesis help to ensure effective interaction among group members (Amir, 1976; Norvell & Worchel, 1981):

1. Group members must have the same status in the contact situation or the status of the minority group must be the higher of the two. The psychology students and the international students are all students and in this sense equals. Both groups have information the other needs; members of each group spend time asking and answering questions.
2. Authority figures in the situation must promote contact. Scheduling class time for this exercise affirms the importance of the activity. Teachers circulate among the groups; however, most of the group facilitation occurs preparing for the class meeting and developing and interpreting the interview questions.
3. The contact should be pleasant and intimate. Small groups concentrating on interview questions of an often personal nature promote intimacy; sharing food helps to make the contact pleasant, easing initial awkwardness.
4. The success of the activity depends on the contributions and cooperation of both groups. Each student needs information from other students. To gather information for their papers, the psychology students are dependent on the responses of the international students. Objectives of the international students may be to gather information for a paper on multicultural experiences or to practice their English-speaking skills.

The four conditions of the contact hypothesis are equally important in establishing an effective reciprocal exchange (Pettigrew & Tropp, 2006).

The final minutes of the class period are spent in a large group discussion in which students are encouraged to share their impressions. This exposes students to the experiences of other groups and gives them the opportunity to reflect on the process while it is still fresh. A successful opening question to get discussion started is, "What did you learn today that surprised you?"

This exercise might be adapted in larger classes in which there are teaching assistants by dividing into smaller groups, each facilitated by a teaching assistant or the professor. The entire class would reconvene, either that day or the next class day, for discussion. Note that the professor should participate by facilitating one of the groups and not turn the exercise over to teaching assistants. The professor's presence and participation affirms the importance of the activity through endorsement by the "authority figure" (the second condition of the contact hypothesis). If the combined number of students is too large for the classroom, an alternative space should be prearranged.

The classroom exchange can serve as a basis for a wide variety of topics in subsequent class sessions. Psychology students might be encouraged to think critically about the lack of diversity in populations commonly researched in psychology. The values and drawbacks of the interview method of gathering information could be discussed. Another focus might be the importance of the conditions established by the contact hypothesis to the success of the classroom interaction and the application of this concept to more encompassing issues such as breaking down stereotypes and overcoming prejudice. Students might also be asked to consider which of the conditions of the contact hypothesis might be present in everyday interactions between groups (Dixon, Durrheim, & Tredoux, 2005).

Finally, psychology students might write a two- or three-page paper in which they address some of the following questions: How does the information gathered in the interviews illustrate the concept of social clock? What are the limitations and benefits of the interview as a research method? What problems did you encounter when conducting the cross-cultural interview? How does information about other cultures expand our knowledge of psychology and of human development?

Students respond well to the writing component of this exercise: Writing about a real experience is immediate and therefore easier for some students than reacting to the research of others. Analyzing the process they themselves have designed encourages critical thinking.

DISCUSSION   This activity generates enthusiasm because an interview is an interactive experience. Students have control of the class; they have designed the interviews, and their participation reflects their involvement. The idea of multiculturalism is no longer an abstract concept. When students realize how difficult it is to speak for their culture as a whole, they are more reluctant to generalize about the cultures of others.

For students who have never interacted with people from another culture, the experience can expand their interpersonal comfort zones. One student who works as a police officer in a small rural town wrote: "This interview was the most interesting task I have ever experienced. . . . I have never had an opportunity to talk with international students before. I almost stayed home because of fear I guess. . . . I have never talked to anyone out of this state let alone the country." After this formal introduction to people from other cultures, informal contacts on campus become less threatening and more frequent.

International students gain confidence in their language skills and in themselves. As a result of the experience, they too feel more comfortable seeking out new friends. The fact that their cultures are of interest to others is empowering; however, in our experience, at times the psychology students overwhelm the international students with their questions, making them feel, as one student said, "like guinea pigs." This underscores the importance of keeping the interaction equal. During the class, we intervene when we sense that the exchange is becoming one-sided.

In our experience, students have been eager to meet again to continue their multicultural exploration. Although this activity limits the discussion to the social clock, other successful topics for the interviews have included cultural comparisons of dating practices, marriage and divorce, gender roles, parent–child relationships, views of abnormal behavior, and treatment of older persons. We have used this interview technique in a number of courses: introduction to psychology, developmental psychology, psychology of women, and, of course, ESL. The approach works; it can be used to explore psychological concepts in a number of courses. Most important, we believe, this activity promotes not only college community but global community.

REFERENCES AND SUGGESTED READING

Amir, Y. (1976). The role of intergroup contact in change of prejudice and ethnic relations. In P. A. Katz (Ed.), *Towards the elimination of racism* (pp. 245–308). Elmsford, NY: Pergamon Press.

Amir, Y. (1994). The contact hypothesis in intergroup relations. In W. J. Lonner & R. Malpass (Eds.), *Psychology and culture* (pp. 231–238). Needham Heights, MA: Allyn & Bacon.

Berger, K. S. (2005). *The developing person through the life span* (6th ed.). New York: Worth.

Dixon, J., Durrheim, K., & Tredoux, C. (2005). Beyond the optimal contact strategy: A reality check for the contact hypothesis. *American Psychologist, 60,* 697–711.

Norvell, N., & Worchel, S. (1981). A reexamination of the relation between equal status contact and intergroup interaction. *Journal of Personality and Social Psychology, 41,* 902–908.

Pettigrew, T. F., & Tropp, L. R. (2006). A meta-analytic test of intergroup contact theory. *Journal of Personality and Social Psychology, 901,* 751–783.

Stephan, W. G., & Brigham, J. C. (1985). Intergroup contact: Introduction. *Journal of Social Issues, 41*(3), 1–8.

67 CROSS-CULTURAL SENSITIVITY IN PSYCHOLOGY

Lani C. Fujitsubo
Southern Oregon University

This activity requires a minimum of preparation while demonstrating the importance of cross-cultural understanding and communication. It can be used for introductory psychology, cross-cultural psychology, counseling psychology, and graduate-level courses on related topics. It uses a role-play exercise to display the challenges and difficulties inherent in cross-cultural interactions. This exercise can be used as a classroom demonstration or can involve the entire class with the use of small groups. It should take between 15 and 20 minutes.

CONCEPT

As our world becomes more global in emphasis, cross-cultural sensitivity and communication are becoming more and more important. This activity illustrates the difficulties and challenges involved in cross-cultural sensitivity as different cultural rules, standards, mores, and traditions come into play. Students should also be encouraged to write or discuss what the impact of these misunderstandings can have on relationships and interactions.

MATERIALS NEEDED

You will need written vignettes for the role-play (an example appears later). The "reporters" in the role-play will need paper and a pen.

INSTRUCTIONS

Five volunteers are needed for a class demonstration. Three of the volunteers will role-play a family, and two volunteers will be role-playing newspaper reporters who will be interviewing the family for the local paper. The volunteers who are acting as family members are given a written vignette describing the rules for their communication and their interactions.

The following is an example of a vignette:

> You are a family (mother, father, and child) from outer space whose spacecraft recently landed in the United States. You are doing your best to assimilate into this society, but have had limited interactions with earthlings. You are being interviewed by two local newspaper reporters because your child won the local spelling bee. On your planet there is no such thing as competition, so winning is a very foreign concept. Respect on your planet is shown by laughing out loud before answering a question. Men do not speak directly to people outside the immediate family, but whisper their requests and answers to females who then communicate directly. It is traditional to offer a gift or compliment to someone before making a request or asking for anything. If offended, you use nonverbal communication to express your hurt feelings, the most common form of which is to briefly (for 2 to 3 seconds) turn your back to the person. Eye contact with males is considered offensive. No one on your planet is considered more important or of higher status than anyone else, so

that is why competition is unheard of. A question is usually never answered directly, because this implies that someone is an expert and causes others to lose face.

If you are doing this exercise as a classroom demonstration, ask the volunteer family to step outside for a few minutes to discuss and rehearse their roles. At this time explain to the volunteers who are acting as reporters that their job is to interview this family in a way that would be of interest to the local readers of their paper. At the end of the interview, they should have a working idea of what they would write about this family in their article. Ask all the volunteers to sit in front of the class. The interview should last 5 to 7 minutes.

You may choose from several alternatives when conducting this activity. You might read the vignette to the class while the volunteer reporters are out of the room. This alternative allows the class to watch the dynamics and the impact of the cross-cultural variables during the role-play. After the interview the reporters should share their interpretation and understanding of this family. You may choose to have the class watch the interview without prior knowledge of the family and have the entire class offer interpretations of the family and their behaviors after the interview.

This activity can also be used as a whole class activity by breaking up the class into groups of five. Three people in each group would be the family and two people would be the reporters. The exercise is then run the same way. At the end of the interview the reporters share with the class their interpretation and understanding of the family. The family members share their feelings concerning the interview.

DISCUSSION

This activity demonstrates the impact and importance of cross-cultural variables in everyday life. Students role-playing the reporters often express frustration, confusion, feelings of being misunderstood, anger, or helplessness in trying to interview this family. Students role-playing as family members might find themselves feeling offended, disrespected, minimized, angry, frustrated, sad, and misunderstood. These feelings lead to a powerful discussion focusing on the impact of cross-cultural variables in communication, understanding, respect, and future interactions.

In introductory psychology classes this exercise could lead to meaningful discussions of discrimination, prejudice, problems and benefits of naturalistic observation, attribution theory, acculturation, and communication styles. Students usually contribute their own experiences of prejudice or racism and speculate on how these experiences are rooted in misunderstandings and ignorance.

In counseling or family therapy courses this exercise can be used to demonstrate possible effects of transference and countertransference. It is also useful as an introduction to the importance of counselor self-awareness, particularly their own personal cross-cultural variables.

If you want to add a writing component, have students write several rules, traditions, standards, and rituals that would be important for others to know about their own culture. The possibilities include various ways of celebrating or acknowledging important events, ways of interacting or communicating, rules involving sex or gender roles, or rites of passage.

Students could be asked to write a one-page reaction paper on several possible topics. Some topics might be times when cross-cultural factors affected them, how cross-cultural factors might be impacting what is happening globally, or how to address the impact of cross-cultural dynamics.

REFERENCES AND SUGGESTED READING Guadalupe, K., & Lum, D. (2005). *Multidimensional contextual practice: Diversity and transcendence.* Belmont, CA: Thomson.

Matsumoto, D., & Juang, L. (2004). *Culture and psychology.* Belmont, CA: Thomson.

Okun, B., Fried, J., & Okun, M. (1999). *Understanding diversity: A learning-as-practice primer.* Pacific Grove, CA: Brooks/Cole.

Shiraev, E., & Levy, D. (2004). *Cross-cultural psychology: Critical thinking and contemporary applications* (2nd ed). Boston: Pearson.

Sue, D. W., & Sue, D. (2003). *Counseling the culturally diverse: Theory and practice* (4th ed). New York: Wiley.

INDEX

ABOUT THE EDITOR

Ludy T. Benjamin, Jr., is a professor of psychology and Presidential Professor of Teaching Excellence at Texas A&M University, where he teaches graduate and undergraduate courses in the history of psychology, introductory psychology, and a graduate course on the teaching of psychology. His published works include 22 books and more than 150 journal articles and book chapters, divided between the history of psychology and the teaching of psychology. On teaching, his published works have emphasized the importance of active learning.

Benjamin was elected a fellow of the American Psychological Association (APA) in 1981 and has served as president of two of APA's divisions—the Division on the History of Psychology and the Division on the Teaching of Psychology. He received the prestigious Distinguished Teaching Award from the American Psychological Foundation in 1986, and in 2001 he was awarded the Distinguished Contributions to Education and Training Award from APA. At Texas A&M University he has held the Fasken Chair and the Glasscock Professorship, both awarded for teaching excellence.

Benjamin began his academic career in 1970 at Nebraska Wesleyan University, a small liberal arts college. From 1978 to 1980 he served as director of education for APA before moving to Texas A&M University. When not engaged as a professor of psychology he enjoys traveling, baseball, theater, and fishing.